FAITH SEEKING FREEDOM
LIBERTARIAN CHRISTIAN ANSWERS TO TOUGH QUESTIONS
UPDATED & EXPANDED

AUTHORS

DR. NORMAN HORN

DOUG STUART

KERRY BALDWIN

DICK CLARK

CODY COOK

JACOB WINOGRAD

In a country and a time when people are increasingly wary of government and religion, *Faith Seeking Freedom* pulls off two miracles at once: It lays out the most compelling argument for principled libertarianism I've read in years while also underscoring that Christianity properly understood is a means of defending and expanding individual rights in all aspects of life.

Despite being a self-described apatheist—I just don't care that much about religion—I was knocked out by the Libertarian Christian Institute's vision of both libertarianism and Christianity. This book is essential reading for believers in Christ who are serious about a theologically sound governance. It's equally compelling for small-government types who are serious about understanding how believers can be indispensable allies in reducing the size, scope, and spending of government at all levels.

In the 17th century, the great religious freedom fighter Roger Williams argued for a total separation of Church and State because "forced worship stinks in God's nostrils" and politics would corrupt religion in America like it had done in England and Europe. *Faith Seeking Freedom* updates Williams' insights and warnings for a 21st century where secularists are trying to limit freedom of conscience and religionists are seeking to impose their views on society. The Libertarian Christian Institute has provided a serious, comprehensive, and deeply thoughtful book that is needed now more than ever.

Faith Seeking Freedom deeply increased my understanding of both Christianity and libertarianism. Especially in these times of increasingly unhinged secular and religious apocalypticism, it deserves as wide an audience as possible.

Nick Gillespie—Editor at Large, Reason

Christians affirm that every person is made in God's image, entrusted with stewardship, and called to meaningful work. *Faith Seeking Freedom* makes a compelling case that these convictions align with a vision of free people and free markets, offering a clear and thoughtful defense of libertarian principles.

Jacqueline Isaacs—President and Chief Content Officer of Bellwether Communications, contributor to *Called to Freedom: Why You Can Be Christian and Libertarian*

We've lost vision for freedom. As the state has become the great responder and the choice of help for many when crises arise, we have slowly but surely surrendered many of our natural liberties. Once soundly rejected, too many now turn to centralized power for answers rather than each other

Endorsements for the 2026 Edition

LCI hits it out of the ballpark once again! This new, expanded edition of *Faith Seeking Freedom* covers so much ground and answers so many important questions that it will quickly become an indispensable addition to every truth-seeker's library. Readers of every faith and political persuasion will find it immensely informative.

Lawrence W. Reed—President Emeritus,
Foundation for Economic Education

The updated and expanded version of *Faith Seeking Freedom* answers just about every question that a Christian might have about the libertarian ideal. It uses many Old and New Testament references to make the case for political freedom. Indeed, it would be difficult to walk away from reading this book without recognizing that liberty is the political expression of loving our neighbors as ourselves.

Mary Ruwart—Chair, Liberty International;
Author of *Short Answers to the Tough Questions*

Faith Seeking Freedom offers a thoughtful and well-organized exploration of the relationship between Christianity and libertarianism. Through careful scriptural engagement and clear argumentation, my brothers and sisters in Christ at Libertarian Christian Institute give you their perspective on what the Bible tells us about government, immigration, healthcare, abortion, and many other pressing subjects. Whether you agree with their conclusions or not, this book provides a serious contribution to the current (and perpetual) debate over faith and politics. I pray that God gives you wisdom and discernment as you read it.

Spike Cohen—2020 Vice Presidential Bronze Medalist

The task taken on in *Faith Seeking Freedom* is especially important in a time of significant government overreach. It serves as an effective tool for increasing understanding of the harmony between faith and libertarianism, presented in a clear, digestible, and engaging way.

Kara Smith—Founder, Christian Caucus of the Libertarian Party and community when in need. Yet, because faith and freedom are foundational to a flourishing society, we should ask anew, "What does a free society look like?" Rather than a utopian response, the authors of *Faith Seeking Freedom* have answered that in great detail. This book brings a realistic and hopeful tangibility to the dream of freedom. It's doable...and Faith Seeking Freedom proves it.

James Whitford—Co-founder, CEO, True Charity

If you ran out of conversation-starters with the 2020 edition, the new edition contains even more. *Faith Seeking Freedom* is a handy guide to the sometimes-surprising conclusions many Christians draw from their faith.

Art Carden—Margaret Gage Bush Distinguished Professor of Economics, Samford University

Faith Seeking Freedom is an intellectually stimulating page turner that every Christian (and non-Christian) should read and examine! You might not agree with everything in it (I don't), but it is extremely elucidating and necessary, nonetheless, because a believer who does not care about "politics" will soon realize that "politics" cares about him intensely. The history of the Church is a history of State usurpation of prerogatives, and each Christian's ultimate choice is whether his loyalty rests with Christ the King or the rulers and authorities of this World (Eph 6:12). This book sharpens believers' discernment vis a vis the State and encourages us to stand firm against the yoke of slavery imposed by Government, because "Christ has set us free" (Gal 5:1).

Albert Veldhuyzen—Colonel, U.S. Army (retired); Executive Director, Project Paraguay Foundation & Libertyprolife.org; Secretary, Pro-Life Libertarian Caucus

Achieving liberty will require enlightening our fellow men about its eternal truths. Building on the success of the first edition, this updated and expanded second edition of *Faith Seeking Freedom* features additional authors and new insights from Christians who are also principled and articulate libertarians. They argue for a more libertarian interpretation of Christian teachings, explaining to fellow Christians and other people of faith the glory and morality of liberty in relatable terms. While remaining accessible and not overburdened with scholarly jargon, it still manages to show that libertarian principles are supported by biblical teachings—such as the explanation, in Chapters 12, 14, and 15, of the connection between the libertarian principles of non-aggression, self-ownership, homesteading, and production, on the one hand, and the biblical teachings about treatment of neighbors, stewardship of the gifts God has bestowed, and the admonition to be productive—to "be fruitful and multiply"—on the other. These insights and principles support and complement each other.

Liberty is ultimately about peace, love, and cooperation—a message that can appeal to the billions of Christians worldwide. This remains a big potential audience, and this enhanced book is an even more important undertaking. In addition, while the book is aimed at Christians, its linkage of principles of freedom to deeper moral truths is valuable to nonreligious libertarians as well. Liberty is not an isolated value; connecting related but different areas of thought is important. I am delighted that this book exists.

Stephan Kinsella—Attorney, Director,
Center for the Study of Innovative Freedom

People like to say you should never talk about religion and politics in the same breath. This book rejects that false choice and does so unapologetically.

It approaches both subjects from a liberty-first perspective that will resonate with Christian libertarians and, frankly, anyone serious about examining principles. For Christians, it applies Scripture to political philosophy in a way that challenges complacency and forces a deeper look at what the Bible actually says about authority, responsibility, coercion, and freedom. It moves beyond clichés and asks whether our political assumptions truly align with Christ's teachings.

For readers of other faiths, or for those who hold no religious belief at all, it provides clarity. It explains how a Christian, operating in good faith, can consistently arrive at libertarian conclusions about limited government, individual sovereignty, and moral agency. You do not have to share the theology to understand the framework.

At its core, this book is about liberty, spiritual, and civil. It makes the case that Christ's principles, rightly understood, call people out of bondage: bondage to sin, bondage to coercive power, and bondage to systems that substitute force for conscience. Whether you ultimately agree or disagree, it is worth reading if you are willing to examine the relationship between faith, freedom, and the proper role of power in a fallen world.

Paul Darr—Vice Chair, Libertarian National Committee

If you're drawn to Christianity but wary of how easily religion gets recruited into power games, *Faith Seeking Freedom* is a breath of fresh air. The authors affirm historic Christianity while offering brief, substantive responses to tough questions about government authority, the non-aggression principle, economics, and culture—designed for real conversations rather than ideological posturing. You don't have to accept every conclusion to benefit from the clarity: it's a strong toolkit for anyone trying to integrate faith, freedom, and responsibility without baptizing either the state or the market.

Alexander McCobin—Founder & CEO, Liberty Ventures

Faith Seeking Freedom is a compelling exploration of the harmony between Christianity and libertarianism, boldly arguing that the non-aggression principle flows naturally from the moral teachings of Christ. With clarity and conviction, the easily navigable Q&A style text demonstrates that a deep commitment to individual liberty is not a departure from Christian faith, but a profound expression of it. This book challenges believers and liberty-minded readers alike to recognize that culture and free-market solutions, rather than the state, most adequately protect the dignity of all human life.

Amity Dolby—Catholic libertarian activist dedicated to promoting the Consistent Ethic of Life from the womb to the tomb

Although Scripture doesn't teach any detailed political theory, Christians rightly seek the welfare of their political communities. For Christians weary of expansive state action, endless entanglement in foreign conflicts, burgeoning government indebtedness, lawfare, and the like, which no major political party seems interested in stopping, *Faith Seeking Freedom* provides a refreshing and clear alternative. Even Christians who don't embrace everything here will be challenged in all sorts of good ways to consider what they believe about political life and why.

David VanDrunen—Robert B. Strimple Professor of Systematic Theology and Christian Ethics, Westminster Seminary California

Some critics of libertarianism dismiss it as anti-Christian. Some critics of Christianity think of it as irredeemably collectivist and statist. This very fine primer, helpfully organized in Q&A form, makes clear why critics of both sorts are mistaken. If you've ever wondered how it might make sense to think about the drug war, immigration, or public safety from a standpoint that is simultaneously Christian and libertarian, you've come to the right place. *Faith Seeking Freedom* is a gem because it meets challenging questions with authentically libertarian and Christian responses that are crisp and readily digestible but also informed by careful scholarship and by theological, moral, and social-scientific insight. This book doesn't offer the final word, nor does it pretend to do so; and of course every reader will doubtless find something here with which to argue. But every reader will also find in Faith Seeking Freedom a thoughtful guide through the thicket of contemporary politics; I commend it with confidence and appreciation.

Gary Chartier—Distinguished Professor of Law and Business Ethics, La Sierra University

This is a very serviceable manual on how Christian libertarians can, do, and ought to think about a whole range of modern social and political questions and challenges. Not every Christian libertarian will agree with every proposal in this book (would they be libertarians if they did?), but everyone—Christian, libertarian, or otherwise—will find here a serious attempt at applying a consistent and objective ethic of the use of coercion and a rational approach to distinguishing between the moral and the merely legal.

Jonathan McIntosh—The George Buchanan Forum

Endorsements for the 2020 Edition

Faith Seeking Freedom is a basic primer on serious libertarianism seen through the informed intellects of serious Christians. Its Q&A format is easy to read, utterly faithful to Christian doctrine and libertarian beliefs, and leaves you fulfilled yet asking for more. I strongly recommend it.

Hon. Andrew P. Napolitano—

Senior Judicial Analyst, Fox News Channel

"As a Christian libertarian, you get questions. A lot of questions. A lot of the same questions. Instead of stumbling for responses, why reinvent the wheel? Faith Seeking Freedom gives you the substantive and convincing answers you need in order to understand your own position more deeply and convey it to others."

Thomas E. Woods

Nothing true or worthwhile comes without skeptical inquiry, but a tough question doesn't always require a long-winded response. This latest contribution from the Libertarian Christian Institute proves that the best answers are often the concise ones, those that strike at the root of the matter while drawing from unassailable facts and the ripest wisdom.

Lawrence W. Reed—president emeritus of the Foundation for Economic Education and author of Was Jesus a Socialist?

In Faith Seeking Freedom, the authors draw on Judeo-Christian principles to provide a helpful and accessible guide to the ideas and public policies of a free society. For both modern Christians and secularists alike, this book offers insights into how to steer through the cultural seductions and dangers of tyranny to reach the greater human well-being only made possible through liberty.

David J. Theroux—Founder and President, Independent Institute;

Founder and President, C.S. Lewis Society of California

"It's tough to imagine any Christian reading this book and not embracing the non-aggression principle of libertarianism."

Mary Ruwart—Chair, Liberty International

We all have an almost endless number of questions, especially when it comes to an issue as complex as the relationship between government and our Christian faith. Answers—now those are much harder to come by. Faith Seeking Freedom is a good place to start. It offers some solid answers to those questions—over 100 of them! The Q&A format makes for easy reading but don't let the brevity of the answers fool you. They pack an intellectual punch presented with sound reason and plenty of scriptural support. And the authors put "tough questions" in the title for a reason. They don't skirt the most difficult issues. In fact, they take them head-on. Whether you're a long-time libertarian Christian seeking to better defend your position or a curious bystander trying to figure it all out, this book is a must-read.

Mike Maharrey—Host of the GodArchy Podcast

A very useful contribution that strikes a good balance between comprehensive answers and a wide variety of issues. The questions are indeed the tough ones that would come from Christians who do not embrace libertarianism; honest readers will appreciate the sincere attempts to meet these objections.

Robert P. Murphy—Senior Fellow, Mises Institute

Faith Seeking Freedom is wonderfully clear, concise, and kind to the reader. This book will help non-libertarian Christians to better understand, respect, and maybe even adopt libertarianism as their favored approach to political philosophy.

Kevin Vallier—Associate Professor of
Philosophy, Bowling Green State University

Faith Seeking Freedom is an excellent and useful collection of handy answers to important questions. Is it filled with conversation-enders? No—it's filled with conversation starters, and that's what makes it important.

Art Carden—Professor of Economics and Medical Properties
Trust Fellow, Brock School of Business, Samford University

You can find a fair amount of Christian libertarian theory online today, and in no small contribution from the authors that have collaborated here, but there are few options for comprehensive reading. Narrowing our options even further, would be the expressed desire for something thoroughly covering the breadth of Christian libertarian philosophy, while remaining accessible for the beginner and worthwhile for the familiar. Faith Seeking Freedom is an achieving apologetic. This catechism quickly surveys the vast subject, while responsibly addressing necessary distinctions in existing political theories that reside under the often umbrella terms of "Christian," and "libertarian." I am thankful for the authoring and editing efforts that went into the creation of this book. It can easily serve to clarify terms, and offer consistency, to formed or forming convictions, where our faith dictates our politics.

Stephen Rose—AnarchoChristian.com

I must confess that I am not fond of the term "libertarianism" for the same reason I find "capitalism" misleading. In almost any debate over libertarianism, one must spend half the time explaining what it is not before moving on to what it might be. If libertarianism means libertinism, count me out. As pointed out in this text however, libertarianism is not a full-fledged philosophy, much less a theology, as much as it is an argument that maintains (in Lord Acton's words) that "liberty is the political end of man,"—not, of course, his entire telos.

This book is not the final word on the argument between the Christian revelation and human liberty, but it nonetheless asks many of the right questions, questions that are rarely raised among Christians.

Rev. Robert A. Sirico—Acton Institute

Achieving liberty will require enlightening our fellow men about its eternal truths. The contributors to this volume, Christians who are also principled and articulate libertarians, argue for a more libertarian interpretation of Christian teachings, and seek to explain to fellow Christians and other people of faith the glory and morality of liberty in terms they will already relate to. Liberty is ultimately about peace, love, and cooperation, which is a message that can appeal to the 2.4 billion Christians on the planet. This is a big potential audience. This is an important book and undertaking.

Stephan Kinsella—Attorney, Director,
Center for the Study of Innovative Freedom

I am delighted, exhilarated, and deliriously pleased with the publication of this book. It is an excellent attempt to convince Christians, the co-creators of Western Civilization, to adopt libertarian principles. I can attest that the authors are well-steeped in libertarian theory. If anyone can make the case for the freedom philosophy to Christians, it is this team from the Libertarian Christian Institute.

Walter Block—Senior Fellow, Mises Institute

"As a Jewish agnostic who is also a libertarian, I found this book to be absorbing and persuasive. I can recommend it wholeheartedly to other Jewish agnostics, whether or not they're libertarian. On that basis, it looks like a must-read for folks of the Christian faith!"

Gene Epstein—Director of The Soho Forum

Other Books From Christians for Liberty Press

The Anarchist Anabaptist
Cody Cook

A House Divided
Benjamin D. Giffone

Strangers with Candy
Art Carden

Politics, Economics, and New Testament Interpretation (Sept 2026)
Alex Bernardo

More publications by CFL Press can be found at cflpress.com.

Christians for Liberty Press is a project of The Libertarian Christian Institute. Publications by CFL Press can be found at cflpress.com.

Typesetting by Nicole Sturk, nicolejonessturk.com

ISBN 979-8-9955169-1-0

To our friends who weren't afraid
to ask us tough questions on important issues.
And to the author of liberty, Soli Deo Gloria.

Contents

16 The American Revolution and the U.S. Constitution 174

17 Healthcare 183

20 Family and Education 219

21 Christian Nationalism 234

22 How Do We Get to a Free(r) Society? 243

FAITH SEEKING FREEDOM

LIBERTARIAN CHRISTIAN ANSWERS TO TOUGH QUESTIONS

UPDATED & EXPANDED

2026 Foreword

How should religion and politics relate? It is an eternal question. Throughout recorded human history politicians and clerics have used one another for their own advantage. Sometimes they have cooperated. Other times they have battled. All too often the result has been tyranny over most everyone else.

Common to both religion and politics was the role of faith. People believed that adopting a set of beliefs, responding to a group of leaders, and creating a new kind of person and form of society would create a better reality, though some focused on this world and others on the next. Commitment to both religious and political realms, which often effectively melded into one, remained strong entering the 20th century.

Even in the United States, where the Constitution famously separates the institutions of church and state, the onetime seemingly irreligious Abraham Lincoln sounded like an Old Testament prophet when he assessed America's terrible Civil War in his second inaugural address: If God "gives to both North and South this terrible war as the woe due to those by whom the offense came, shall we discern therein any departure from those divine attributes which the believers in a living God always ascribe to him?"

Yet as the European powers followed by the United States plunged into an even deadlier, more destructive conflagration early in the next century, faith in God waned, at least throughout the broadly constituted West, to be replaced by belief in the efficacy and morality of government, a process brilliantly described by historian Paul Johnson in *Modern Times: A History of the World from the 1920s to the 1980s*. Great leaders made ever more grandiose plans, both promising and spending lavishly. However, that wasn't all. It turned out politicians, in contrast to most clerics, usually controlled, and all too often misused, the vast powers to coerce, destroy, and kill reserved to governments. Unfortunately, hundreds of millions of people were oppressed, imprisoned, tortured, starved, and murdered, often with industrial efficiency. Eventually the political age crashed even more convincingly than the clerical era.

More recently liberal societies around the globe have been dealing with a loss of faith in traditional political ideologies, institutions, parties, and assumptions. At the same time, religious faith has also generally declined in the West, while burgeoning in some other lands. In cases around the world, increasingly polarized populations are disputing and contesting the role of faith, any faith, in politics. These fissures are evident in America as well, with differences exacerbated by the polarizing personality of Donald Trump. Particularly sharp has been criticism of evangelical leaders who have seemingly acted as if the president was auditioning for the first vacancy in the Trinity.

How should Christians apply their faith to the world of politics? In particular, how should those believing in orthodox Christianity, and adapting their behavior to biblical standards, assess classical liberal principles—featuring expansive individual liberty and limited constitutional government? The issues are many and complex, ranging from historic controversies over poverty alleviation, for instance, to modern questions such as environmental protection. What also of policies addressing drugs, sex, taxation, budgets, wars, and more?

Almost four decades ago I offered my own thoughts through the book *Beyond Good Intentions: A Biblical View of Politics*, published by Crossway, a small evangelical publisher. Much has changed in the world since then. The go-to volume today addressing the toughest challenges to Christian freedom advocates is *Faith Seeking Freedom*.

This volume, authored by a half dozen thoughtful analysts, is most obviously written for those who generally ascribe to a classical liberal philosophy. However, it also offers an important assist to anyone else who wonders if economic, political, and social liberty are consistent with Christian scripture and church teachings. *Faith Seeking Freedom* doesn't claim to provide the "correct" answer to any question. After all, the Bible primarily addresses our responsibilities to God and each other. Almost completely absent is any blueprint for the proper political order or even acceptable variants, for the community of faith, let alone modern secular societies. Rather, Scripture appears to set boundaries within which progressives, conservatives, and populists of most varieties reside. Falling outside are totalitarian ideologies. As the infamous Nazi Judge Roland Freisler explained: "Christianity and National Socialism have only one thing in common. They both demand the whole man." Of course, no politician of any ideological stripe can properly do so.

Beyond that limit God appears to leave most political decisions to people, religious and irreligious alike. In that they must, in practice, cooperate, using the wisdom that James, the brother of Jesus, instructed us to request: "If any of you lacks wisdom, you should ask God, who gives generously to all without finding fault, and it will be given to you" (Jas 1:5, NIV). Perhaps equally important in managing decisions that often are complex, uncertain, and emotional are charity and good will, which also should attend the Christian walk. It is in helping believers assess arguments, develop solutions, and convince others that *Faith Seeking Freedom* is directed. It helps Christians of all variants today by reaching back to the experiences and arguments of Christians yesterday, who had to confront similar, sometimes even more divisive, challenges.

Of course, libertarian Christians do not claim that God prescribes any political order, including classical liberalism. Rather, they generally believe that a commitment to human liberty is consistent with a biblical order. Moreover, they believe that in practice it is the best system, one that should be adopted by prudential and wise policymakers. Libertarians recognize that today's earthly residents will not develop paradise in this world. They can only do their best until the Eschaton, when God fulfills history as he sees fit. Until then, *Faith Seeking Freedom* will be a valuable resource for believers of all perspectives seeking to create a better society today.

Doug Bandow
Senior Fellow, Cato Institute
May 2026

2020 Foreword

"I would have written a shorter letter," the French theologian Blaise Pascal once declared, "but I didn't have the time."

Pascal's meaning was profound. To make a point, we have two length-related options. We can write on and on, tossing in every thought big or small, and hope readers will read it. Or we can be pithy and concise enough that no reader will have a good reason not to, a talent that poor writers envy. It's that course for which the authors of Faith Seeking Freedom have opted. The result is a one-stop shop of powerful and penetrating responses to more than a hundred excellent questions.

This is a book that addresses both Christianity and libertarianism, the political philosophy of liberty. In my teen years more than half a century ago, I was increasingly drawn to both but puzzled that they sometimes seemed at odds. However, the more I learned about Christianity and libertarianism, the more I came to understand their indissoluble compatibility. I even wrote a book titled Was Jesus a Socialist? that presented that case. Now, with this volume from the Libertarian Christian Institute, no one hereafter can ever make a convincing argument that the teachings of Christ and the principles of liberty are incongruous.

Liberty is an environment in which everyone makes choices about their life without fearing the initiation of force against them. In other words, liberty means you get to be the unique individual God intended you to be, so long as you do not threaten others. The Creator did not make us mindless robots to be programmed by some privileged central planner. The better we understand what liberty is, especially its insistence on strong moral character, the more it is obvious that it comports perfectly with the ethics of Christianity. Both libertarianism and the teachings of Christ demand that we respect one another, do no harm to each other, assist our fellows in distress, celebrate free will and diversity, and interact in peace.

It is a good thing to wonder and to raise questions. Even the Apostle Thomas had his doubts. There was a time, for example, when I was stumped over the matter of Jesus driving the so-called moneychangers from the Temple. A college professor told us it was an indication that Jesus had a problem with people who were trying to make money, that he was anti-market or anti-wealth. Why else would he do such a thing, I asked myself?

Later upon reflection, I realized that Jesus never drove a moneychanger from a bank or a marketplace. What seemed like a tough issue for a libertarian could be answered in a sentence or two. God's house simply was a uniquely holy and inappropriate place for what the moneychangers were doing.

The story of Jesus feeding some 5,000 people, as told in the books of Matthew and John, is well known throughout the world. It goes like this:

> As a large and hungry crowd gathers to hear Jesus, his disciples nervously ask him how so many people can be fed. The only food in their midst consists of five loaves of bread and two fishes. Jesus informs his associates of some rich people who live nearby. "Go and take what they have and give it to these who want it" he commands.
>
> So armed with swords and clubs the disciples raid the homes of the rich, as well as a grocery store and a bank, and redistribute the proceeds to the grateful multitude. After the event is over, Jesus lobbies Roman authorities to raise taxes on the rich and fork over the loot so that next time the disciples will not have to go steal it themselves.

Of course, that is not the real story at all. Jesus never commanded anyone to swipe somebody else's property, not even for a "good cause." In this instance, he solved the problem not by pilfering other people's pockets, but by the power of the Holy Spirit to create new wealth. However, I know there are many Christians out there who believe that this story of feeding the multitude shows that Jesus was sympathetic to a generous welfare state. They are usually the same folks who think the generous traveler in the Good Samaritan story was a socialist, even though he solved the stricken man's problem with private charity, not public handouts.

Reasonable questions, brief but pointed answers. That is the formula that makes this book work. And the authors never suggest that their responses are everything that can be said about an issue. Great recommendations for Additional Resources are provided in several places.

If you are already a libertarian Christian, you will still find this book to be of great value and loaded with insights you may not have previously considered. If you are new to either Christianity or to libertarianism, you will find gems on every page. This is a keeper, a book you will want to keep handy on your most prominent bookshelf and one that you will recommend to others repeatedly.

I could go on and on, but not without proving Pascal's wisdom at my own expense. Read this book with an open mind and you will be amazed at the extent to which its authors will fill it.

Lawrence W. Reed
President Emeritus and Humphreys Family Senior Fellow
Foundation for Economic Education
Atlanta, Georgia
September 2020

Introduction

The human heart has a natural orientation toward liberty. We are built this way, regardless of our religion or ethnicity; indeed, all men are endowed with liberty and a deep desire for it.

– Rev. Robert A. Sirico

Despite the accelerating rate of innovation and progress humans have made in recent centuries, we have yet to defeat our inner desire to conquer and dominate one another. Read the latest newspaper headline, watch half a news segment, or scroll for five seconds through a social media feed, and you will find ample evidence of the human yearning to control the lives of others. From your acquaintances on social media to the highest offices in the country, this yearning for power is evident. Lawmakers enact policies that manipulate the economic playing field to favor themselves or their friends. Law enforcement agents zealously use overwhelming force to stop minor infractions. Governors promise citizens that if they would just obey orders, their problems will soon be healed. To see these emerging social patterns takes stepping back and critically assessing what's happening, but it is visible to all who care to see it.

To make matters even more complicated, the corporate press and competing institutions exacerbate our social conflicts by weaving narratives that leave us tangled in confusion. We are inundated with demands to take a side and stake our claim to power, or else be shamed, canceled, or doxxed for not standing up for what the other side says is right. Standing up for truth has become all about rising up to grasp power.

Christians in America have also fallen prey to this phenomenon, seeking status, privilege, and power from an institution that the Church has historically viewed with suspicion. It is as though we have forgotten Jesus' words to his disciples in Matthew 20: "You know that the rulers of the Gentiles lord it over them, and their great ones are tyrants over them. It will not be so among you; but whoever wishes to be great among you must be your servant, and whoever wishes to be first among you must be your slave."

Even those who admire the American Founders' inherent distrust of the state have abandoned that ethos in pursuit of absolute power and dominance. Both Christians and non-Christians have become re-enchanted by the allure of empire. The days when it was patriotic to question your government seem like a bygone era. Worse yet, many Christians have lost the ability to think straightforwardly about the world without importing an agenda driven by the desire for political power. As Brian Zahnd says repeatedly, the world is "addicted to solving its problems through violence," but the cross "demands that we renounce violence as a means of achieving just ends." A truly Christian political philosophy includes embracing just means toward just ends, and violence is never the answer.

This lost habit of thinking about politics in a Christian way must be recovered. The biblical prophets preached against the evils of empire, and the Messiah declared his supremacy over the kingdoms of this world. Today, Christians need to model those examples and herald the good news that speaks truth to power.

This prophetic voice against empire should incline us, as Christians, toward promoting individual liberty, free markets, and non-aggression. Empire wants to subsume our human agency, robbing each of us of our dignity as image-bearers of God. We wrote this book because we believe the growing threat of empire is a battle worth fighting, and we fight against it by arming ourselves with clear, compelling, and (when possible) concise answers to tough questions.

To be clear, we wage battle not by wielding any kind of physical violence or threats of violence, but with words. As the Apostle Paul wrote, our struggle "is not against enemies of blood and flesh, but against the rulers, against the authorities, against the cosmic powers of this present darkness, against the spiritual forces of evil in the heavenly places" (Eph 6:12). Our fight is not with people but with ideas, and so we must endeavor to "destroy arguments and every proud obstacle raised up against the knowledge of God, and we take every thought captive to obey Christ" (2 Cor 10:4–5).

In any battle, a strong defense is necessary to win. We take seriously what Peter wrote in 1 Peter 3:15: "Always be ready to make your defense to anyone who demands from you an accounting for the hope that is in you." It is in Jesus Christ (not worldly powers such as the state) we find our hope. It is to Christ, not Caesar, we pledge our allegiance.

In the past decade or so, many Christians have affirmed what we believe about libertarianism: it is the modern political philosophy most consistent with the Christian faith. If you count yourself among us libertarian Christians (or close to it), we hope that this book will arm you with strong answers to questions. This is not a light endeavor. Convincing others that your political beliefs are the best way to think about the world is always challenging. Very rarely are people convinced by the mere articulation of a viewpoint. Objections must be dealt with and questions must be answered. Sometimes those answers are not wholly satisfying, but are enough to keep one searching and seeking. And if you are the one who is asked the questions, you want to be equipped with clear, concise answers that are convincing enough to move the conversation forward.

A word of caution is necessary, as well. While the battle of ideas rages on, we must always remember we are conversing with human beings whose minds can be changed. Being equipped with solid answers will help, but answers alone are not the solution. Our approach must always be seasoned with empathy, love, and respect for those who ask us questions. We must learn from their questions, both to understand their side better and to sharpen our answers for them. So while we wrote this book to help readers deal with an important aspect of the conversation, it is up to them to listen and respond in grace and with respect.

The purpose of this book is two-fold. If you are a libertarian Christian, we hope this book equips you with solid responses to the common objections so you can be better equipped to make the Christian case for a free society. If you are a non-libertarian seeking answers to the tough questions about politics, we hope this book will get you started on a journey that leads you to a greater understanding of the libertarian Christian perspective, and perhaps even convinces you to join us!

We want this book to be as clear and concise as possible while also being conversational in tone. The questions are grouped together into chapters topically, and those topics have been organized to represent a basic flow of a conversation. We recommend reading from beginning to end, but readers who choose to jump around will not lose much, if anything.

Each chapter ends with "Additional Resources," a curated list of books, articles, and other resources to learn more about the topics within that chapter. Of course, we do not endorse everything said by every author, but they provide a solid range of libertarian and Christian works, some of which have been highly regarded for many decades. You can also view the full reading list by visiting faithseekingfreedom.com, where we will add more resources even after the printing of this book.

Each contributor to this book has their own set of beliefs and opinions about politics and theology while also adhering to the historic Christian faith as proclaimed since the first century. Libertarian thought exists on a continuum, and so the authors will answer these questions from varying places along it. However, we all agree on the fundamental aspects of the libertarian creed and the broad outlines of what a free society looks like. Of course, like most libertarians, we enjoy arguing together over the particulars. What is important for the purposes of this book is that we all advocate for consistent application of individual liberty in every possible circumstance.

Lastly, we must note that, while we spend a great deal of energy defending a free society from a Christian perspective, none of these authors believe that libertarianism is the ultimate hope for our world. We firmly believe a free society with peaceful exchange is the best path to human flourishing, but the ultimate hope for humanity comes only from God through the saving work of Jesus Christ. Let us never forget that, "Salvation belongs to our God who is seated on the throne, and to the Lamb" (Rev 7:10). To God be the glory, as we seek to honor him even in our political ideas.

Doug Stuart
Lancaster, PA
Sept 2020 (updated April 2026)

1

Why Should I Care About Politics?

"The fact that the problem of Church and State is of such central importance is a corollary of the [end times] attitude of Christianity. Because the Gospel presents itself as the 'politeuma,' the community of the coming age, it must accordingly see as its most intrinsic concern its disposition toward the present 'polis,' the secular State, and therefore not [uncritically accept it]—as if the State itself were something final, definitive."

—*Oscar Cullmann*

1. Politics isn't a gospel issue, so why should I be concerned about politics?

Most people think of politics as electoral politics: elections, politicians, and voting. A more robust understanding is that politics is more like a subset of the ways in which human beings choose to relate, specifically with regard to the appropriate use of physical force and power.

Culture is another means of how we relate to each other, and while part of that is political, much of it is not. In this sense, the saying "politics is life" is true. When we advocate anything that affects the lives of others, we are doing politics in this very broad sense. Most Christians believe that the gospel has implications for the real world, which makes the gospel relevant to politics. This also means that Christians are political, whether they realize it or not.

Libertarian Christians care about how people in the world relate to one another in ways that align with the ethic and message of the Kingdom of God. We do not say that all Christians should vote for a particular type of candidate, or even vote at all. Not only do we want Christians to be aware of the human relationships that are part of what it means to be human, but also at the forefront of pushing human relationships toward mutual benefit and interacting peacefully (see Chapters 4–5).

2. Jesus said his Kingdom was "not of this world." Isn't political engagement being concerned with "this world"?

As Jesus announced the coming of God's Kingdom, throughout the Gospels we see that his Kingdom did not operate upon the principles of worldly kingdoms (John 18:36). This doesn't mean that the Kingdom of God is not for this world. The very word *kingdom* is inherently political, meaning "the king's domain."

Modern Christians often miss the explicitly political language of the New Testament. The titles "Jesus is Lord" and "Son of God" were, in Jesus' day, an affront to Caesar. It was Caesar who rode into cities on a war horse demanding people's allegiance, promising an age of peace won by violence, and demanding submission. In contrast, Jesus came promising the life of the age to come ("eternal life") through faith in him, a peace that was not won through violence, but through the forgiveness of sins and allegiance to him.

To give allegiance to Jesus Christ is to declare the power and authority of Rome is illegitimate. This is how the gospel is a direct challenge to the state and to its power. In part, when Christians invite others to believe the gospel, they are inviting them to declare allegiance to God, not the state.

3. Isn't political engagement a distraction from the real mission of the Church?

When a person gives their life to Jesus Christ, they are also giving their allegiance to a new king. Today this often does not amount to defying the current political regimes, but it does mean a new way of thinking, practicing, and evangelizing. Instead of allegiance to mammon, we preach allegiance to God. Instead of pursuit of pleasure for its own sake, we seek to enjoy all things to the glory of God. We honor the one true king when we promote the good news that Jesus is the messiah and through him we can have eternal life (which, by definition, begins before death).

To repent and believe the good news entails far more than what happens to us personally. It is not simply for us to have a private religious experience. Jesus inaugurated a Kingdom over which his rule would be established through what would become his followers: the body of Christ, or the Church. Kingdom people are his royal subjects, working to bring the whole creation to bear witness to the good news that Jesus is Lord, and Caesar is not.

To be engaged in spreading the gospel is to announce the arrival of God's Kingdom, followed by an invitation to repent and participate in this Kingdom. Participation happens in a variety of ways, some of which look more "political" than others. But every one of our efforts are political in the sense that we are engaging the world around us in ways that bring about more flourishing, even if these efforts are not directly engaged in electoral politics.

4. So what does God have to say about government?

God does speak about governance in scripture, and there has been much debate about the implications of what he says. Often, the question raised is whether a particular political philosophy is prescribed by God. In other words, would Jesus have been a socialist? A Republican? Alternatively, there is a popular view that Christians must submit to the government regardless of the lawlessness of its edicts. We disagree.

Scripture speaks to the fact of civil governance and its necessity (Rom 13:1–7; 1 Pet 2:13–14; Titus 3:1), but it does not explicate a precise way of administering civil governance. In other words, God doesn't give us an operations manual for providing the service of civil justice. What God provides are norms of civil justice that are evident in creation and are therefore comprehensible by all human beings. However, the systems by which humanity has administered (or attempted to administer) civil justice are human inventions known as political philosophies.

Political philosophies are attempts to articulate the best way of achieving a just system of governance. Libertarianism is one such philosophy, and we believe it's the best expression of Christian political thought because it most aligns with God-given norms expressed in scripture and evidenced in nature.

One important distinction we make is between "the state" and "civil governance," and in our view the state is inherently bad and tends to corrupt good civil governance. As Christians, we can take our cue from historic Christian orthodoxy and the historic confessions of faith. These only oblige Christian submission to civil authorities on matters that are lawful ordinances of God. But they don't obligate abject submission to all edicts and don't oppose resistance to unlawful or unrestrained sword power. Because of this, we hold the distinction between "the state" and "civil governance" to be legitimate and necessary.

5. Doesn't the Bible say that governments are established by God?

Paul does tell the church in Rome that the authorities that exist are "established by God" (Rom 13:1, NIV), but Romans 13 is definitely not a prooftext for justifying state power.

True, Paul proceeds to caution against rebellion and to encourage doing "what is right" in the eyes of the ruler to protect oneself. But these words were written to Christians in Rome who were constantly at risk of persecution, even unto death, from the Roman Empire. Paul's encouragement to them, and likewise to us, is that our interactions with state power are on a prudential basis. Our greater priorities are to live out the gospel and support our family and community, and we should not put ourselves into a compromising position against the state unless it is specifically for the cause of Christ and his message.

Therefore, we pay our taxes not because the government has a divine right to tax us, but rather because if we don't, we might end up in prison and unable to fulfill our true calling to protect our families and spread the gospel. Ultimately, we should also turn to other scriptures to get a full view of what the Bible has to say about the state instead of only reading Romans 13 and thinking that we fully understand God's intention for government.

Some libertarian Christians take different interpretive approaches to Romans 13 (provided in Additional Resources below), but the common thread is that the passage does not give special permission to governments to commit aggression against others.

6. What scriptural support is there that the state is inherently bad?

Amazingly enough, it all begins in the book of Genesis. The Tower of Babel narrative (Gen 11) is the "origin story" of the state. In the passage, we learn that the people of Babel aspire to build for themselves a tower that would "reach the heavens" so that they could "make for themselves a name." They do this as they "journey eastward," which parallels the language of separation from God being "east of Eden."

Many commentators as far back as the first-century Jewish historian Josephus have noted that these things together mean they are either literally or symbolically rebelling against God by trying to take over heaven itself. They are responding to their separation not by turning to God in repentance but by turning against God entirely.

In Jewish antiquities writing, it was Nimrod, the "mighty rebel" before the Lord (some versions read "hunter," but this is not the best translation) and the first king of Babel/Babylon, who incited them to do so. God disrupts their plan and scatters them about both in their location and in their languages. We can see this story as the theological beginning of all states, which are ultimately founded in rebellion against God and trying to take the place of God on the earth.

7. But didn't the Israelites have kings? Doesn't that mean having a state is okay?

It is true that the Israelites had kings, but do not forget that God brought them out of Egypt so that he alone could be their king. Their request for a human king as recorded in 1 Samuel 8 is granted, but not without a stern and prescient warning for what the government they asked for would ultimately do to them:

"These will be the ways of the king who will reign over you: he will take your sons and appoint them to his chariots and to be his horsemen, and to run before his chariots… He will take your daughters… He will take the best of your fields and vineyards… and you shall be his slaves. And on that day you will cry out because of your king, whom you have chosen for yourselves; but the LORD will not answer you on that day" (1 Sam 8:11–18).

This is an incredible statement! God says that because they are choosing a human king rather than God as their king, they will be set upon by the human government they have chosen. Their sons will be sent to war (conscription), the human king will take their land and possessions (taxation), and they will literally be made to be his slaves.

So much for the supposed virtue of the democratic process! Though God worked through Israelite kings to accomplish his ultimate plan, that was never God's preference from the beginning.

8. If the Old Testament is not favorable toward government, what about the New Testament?

A major theme of the New Testament is the contrast between the Kingdom of God and the kingdoms of this world. Jesus says one seeks to dominate and the other to serve (Matt 20:25–26). Which do you think Jesus wants us aligned with?

More importantly, Jesus' temptations in the desert give us a special insight into the nature and allure of state power. We read in Matthew 4 that Satan offered Jesus the Kingdoms of the world if only Jesus would bow down and worship Satan. Did Jesus respond with "What do you mean? They don't belong to you; you couldn't give them to me if you tried!" Nope. If that were the case, it wouldn't have been a temptation at all. Instead, Jesus gives tacit recognition that Satan could do what he offered, and retorts with "worship the Lord your God and serve only him" (Matt 4:10). The message to us, evidently, is that the state is inherently on board with Satan, not God.

Interestingly, Paul says in Ephesians 6:12 that our struggle is "not against flesh and blood" but against "the rulers, against the authorities, against the cosmic powers of this present darkness, against the spiritual forces of evil in the heavenly places." Even if we take that list as being primarily spiritual, we must still try to understand how Paul could say this while knowing that the Roman government was oppressing so many, especially Christians. We then realize that Christians can show godly love toward those in government positions while still seeing their power as evil.

9. Government rule, then, might not be the right way to go. What hope do we have against powerful states?

Glad you asked, because God has a plan for the state and its machinations, and we get to join into his plan through Jesus and his church. Of course, we have hope in the gospel message itself that brings salvation both right now and in the future. We have the Holy Spirit that indwells us right now and sanctifies us throughout our life. We have the ability to make a difference right now, and we have the great hope of final victory in the end. After all, as the book of Revelation shows us, we know that the final destination of these "powers that be" is destruction.

Remember all that weird language around "Babylon" in Revelation? We hear about the fall of it as a city, and it is even personified in three ways in the book: as the dragon, as the "beast out of the sea," and even as the "Mother of Prostitutes and Abominations." (Gross!) Theologians have debated how to interpret the Revelation to John for centuries, but the attentive reader can see in "Babylon" both the Roman Empire of John's day and the symbolic connection to Babel from Genesis. The symbol is a culmination and representation of statism—of violent, aggressive power—for all time.

God assures us that no matter what, Jesus has won the victory against all sin, all death, and all competing powers. Even the first time Babylon is specifically mentioned in Revelation, it is when an angel declares, "Fallen, fallen is Babylon the Great!" (Rev 14:8) In the end, God wins.

10. Does being a libertarian mean joining a political party?

Plato and Aristotle described the existence of political factions in classical Athens, and this dynamic is still characteristic of politics today. Modern political parties as we know them first began emerging in the 18th and 19th centuries. These parties sprang from political ideologies and existing—often pragmatic—political coalitions. In some countries, third parties play a substantial role in government. However, in the United States, there are two dominant political parties, and third parties are limited by ballot access rules, debate participation, and other constraints that drastically limit both their success in electoral politics and their ability to effect change in government.

Libertarianism is not really about party affiliation at all. Rather, it is first and foremost a theory of justice: a philosophical framework of rights and responsibilities. Some libertarians choose to become active in the Libertarian Party or another political party in order to try to influence elections or to have the opportunity to share libertarian ideas in a public forum. Other libertarians prefer to avoid electoral politics altogether. The formation of the Libertarian Party of the United States in 1971 was opposed by some prominent libertarians. The Libertarian Party remains controversial among libertarians today. Christians should be led by their convictions and prayerful reflection on the best ways to help build God's Kingdom and regenerate goodness into society's structure.

Additional Resources

Bible and Government: Public Policy from a Christian Perspective by John Cobin (Alertness Books, 2003).

Christian Theology of Public Policy: Highlighting the American Experience by John Cobin (Alertness Books, 2006).

"Jesus Wasn't a Libertarian (but He's Glad I Am!)" by Doug Stuart. *Libertarian Christian Institute*, 2018. https://libertarianchristians.com/2018/03/07/jesus-wasnt-a-libertarian/.

Kingdom Conspiracy: Returning to the Radical Mission of the Local Church by Scot McKnight (Brazos Press, 2014).

"New Testament Theology of the State" by Norman Horn. *Libertarian Christian Institute*, 2008. https://libertarianchristians.com/2008/11/25/give-to-caesar-bible-verses-government/.

Resisting Babel: Allegiance to God and the Problem of Government, ed. John Mark Hicks (Abilene Christian University Press, 2020).

The State in the New Testament by Oscar Cullmann (Charles Scribner's Sons, 1956).

2

Libertarian Basics

"Consider the roads blocked up by robbers, the seas beset with pirates, wars scattered all over the earth with the bloody horror of camps. The whole world is wet with mutual blood; and murder, which in the case of an individual is admitted to be a crime, is called a virtue when it is committed wholesale. Impunity is claimed for the wicked deeds, not on the plea that they are guiltless, but because the cruelty is perpetrated on a grand scale."

—St. Cyprian, 250 AD

11. What makes somebody a libertarian?

A libertarian is a person who opposes aggression against peaceful people. Aggression is defined as the initiation of physical force, coercion, or fraud against person or property, including credible threats thereof. The central, defining tenet of libertarianism is often referred to as the "non-aggression principle" (NAP). According to the NAP, actions such as murder, assault, rape, theft, kidnapping, slavery, or the like all constitute aggression, and are never justified.

Libertarians desire peaceful, voluntary cooperation with others. Libertarians categorically reject actions that violate the rights of others to their own lives, liberty, and property. A right is a legitimate, enforceable claim upon one's person or property. Libertarians believe that peace is both ethically preferable to violence and better for making society prosperous. However, the NAP differs from radical pacifism in an important way: it allows for the use of proportional force in retaliation against an aggressor (a person who violates the rights of another person). NAP also differs from the Harm Principle (see Question 174) in that the focus is on the action initiated, rather than the harm caused.

Libertarians do not believe in using physical force to prevent people from indulging in vices or to punish them for their bad habits. This is because libertarians do not believe the use of force is justified when a person's action does not violate the rights of others. Most libertarians still regard harmful vices as wasteful, undesirable, and even immoral. Libertarian Christians generally maintain the traditional, biblical view on being wise and fleeing from sinful indulgence (2 Tim 2:22). We deny that force and compulsion are the best means for addressing such sinful behavior and its earthly and eternal consequences.

12. How is the non-aggression principle (NAP) consistent with a Christian worldview?

The NAP is premised on the idea that people have individual rights, including the right to their own bodies and the right to their physical property. As Christians, we believe that God made man in his image. Living peaceably with other people (Rom 12:18; Mark 9:50) and treating them as we want to be treated is a thoroughly Christian idea that is specifically and repeatedly commanded in the Bible (Luke 6:31, Gal 5:14).

Refraining from murder (Gen 4:10–11), kidnapping (Exod 21:16), assault (Exod 21:18), theft (Matt 19:18), fraud (Prov 20:23), and other offenses against others is, of course, all in accord with the counsel of scripture. The legal principles set out by God for Israel included detailed protection for property rights and prescriptions for legal remedies (e.g., Exod 22:1–9).

Christians are called to be respectful to everyone, including those who temporarily occupy positions of social authority (1 Pet 2:17). But we should not be swayed by popularity and worldly rank when we are analyzing questions of right and wrong (Rom 2:11–12). A Christian theory of justice must apply equally to all people, including elected officials and people employed by government bureaucracies (see Question 35).

The NAP is not a comprehensive guide to righteous living. It is merely a principle of justice—a rule about when force may be employed as a solution. Its answer is clear: violence is justified only in response to aggression against people and their property.

13. How do libertarian Christians account for people who violate the non-aggression principle (NAP)?

Violations of the NAP constitute crimes. More precisely, they are rights violations. The proper role of civil governance is to administer justice when rights violations occur. Libertarians know these violations are just a fact of life. Christians know these violations occur as a result of the sinful nature of man. So what do we do when these violations occur?

Holding people accountable for rights violations is in many ways not too different from the system we have. The problem with the current system is its propensity to corruption, malfeasance, and an inability of the state to be impartial in its own case. But many of the principles we're already familiar with, such as presumption of innocence, proof beyond a reasonable doubt, and a fair and speedy trial, would still be present in a libertarian system. The punitive system would likely differ; restitution for rights violations would be preferable to prison sentences in many cases. Things such as mandatory minimums, solitary confinement, and special interests jockeying for preferential treatment from the state, wouldn't likely exist.

A libertarian minarchist society would be a decentralized version of what we have now, while a libertarian anarchist society would be some polycentric iteration which employs these principles. The colloquial use of the term "anarchy" implies a sense of chaos and lawlessness, and Christians are indeed morally obligated to reject chaos and lawlessness. However, this common usage isn't accurate. The etymology of the term simply means without rulers. The colloquial use implies that, without rulers we would have chaos and lawlessness.

Libertarian anarchists don't agree. Rather, they hold that chaos and lawlessness is produced through a monopoly on civil governance, since the state's very existence depends on violations of the NAP, namely theft (through taxation) and violence (through a monopoly use of legal force). In either a libertarian minarchist or anarchist society violations of the NAP can be handled in a just manner.

14. Why are property rights so important to libertarians?

Christians believe that all things are ultimately owned by God in Christ (Col 1:15–17). Humans, as image bearers of God, are given stewardship over themselves and their property. By property, we specifically mean the resources that a person owns in exclusion to others. Good stewardship not only involves fulfilling our responsibility to God, but also respecting the property rights of our fellow humans.

Human rights are foundational in a libertarian society due to their normativity. In the words of Frederic Bastiat, "[rights] do not exist because men have made laws. On the contrary, it was the fact that [rights] existed beforehand that caused men to make laws in the first place." But how do we identify or articulate them? This has been the problem philosophers have faced for centuries, even back to ancient times. Property rights, however, are a useful way to clearly identify human rights. Christians may claim property rights (in their person and of their things) vis-à-vis Christ's teaching in Matthew 20 (see especially verse 15) and Luke's reference in Acts 5:4.

In fact, property rights are so useful that Murray Rothbard said they're axiomatic; that is, self-evidently true. Christians can agree stating this is a God-given norm through creation, which is why they are self-evident. Because property rights are evidenced by nature, human beings (whether believers or not) may operate on the same rules, and we don't need to teach every individual a contrived political-economic theory.

Property rights are useful because everyone recognizes them regardless of their personal political proclivities. Even socialists believe in property rights; they simply believe the government has the right to a given property. So libertarians operate from a principle of property rights because they are universally understood and self-evident. And Christians may operate from this same principle because it's supported by scripture.

15. How do property rights relate to human rights? I thought humans weren't property.

It may sound odd that we would speak about human rights in terms of property rights. Isn't the argument against slavery, for example, that human beings are not property? We completely agree that slavery—owning another human—is both a sin and a rights violation. However, the reason why this is the case is because each individual already owns themself, and therefore no one else has a legitimate claim to own them. We call this self-ownership. You are your own property.

We then come to own things outside of ourselves through the just acquisition of ownership of scarce resources. This is an extension of our self-ownership. Humans have been called by God to "be fruitful and multiply" (Gen 1:28; 9:1; 9:7; 35:11; Jer 23:3). Though the immediate sense of these verses are most obviously about human procreation, we also fulfill this call through our own creative work. Biblical theologian, Dr. Meredith G. Kline in Kingdom Prologue notes,

"The procreation mandate was accompanied by the command to work. [Humankind] must labor to secure from [their] environment its life supporting stores for [the] multiplying race... [Humans were] to subdue the earth and rule its creatures. Human labor was to be an exercise of [humanity's] dominion and a march of royal conquest.... Appropriation of earth's riches for the cultivation of [humankind] was to be achieved through [humans'] cultivation of the earth."

We acquire things found in nature and mix them with our labor to create new things. This very concept, articulated by libertarian philosophers and Austrian economists, is illustrated for us in Deuteronomy 8:10–18. This passage references the wealth God gave his people as land, food, homes they build, and herds and flocks. It references part of that wealth is the multiplying of these things, the fact that human action has played a role in the production of these things, and that God is responsible for giving us the ability to produce it all. Add to this the prohibition in the 10 Commandments not to steal and murder, and we can see that we have a God-given right to our property, including that of ourselves.

These new things are our property by virtue of our own self-ownership. And as Matthew 20:15 and Acts 5:4 point out, it is lawful for us to do what we want with our own property, including selling and buying. So the foundations of human rights are very clearly indicated by what God gives us: our life, our ability to produce, the products of our labor, and the multiplicity of those things. We are stewards of these things in our relation to God, but owners of these things in relation to others.

So no one can claim to own you, nor lawfully sell you. Who owns you? Well, you do! And no one may make claims against the products of your labor; those are rightfully given to you by God because you produced them. The ultimate human right and the ultimate property right are one in the same: self-ownership.

16. If Christians believe that God owns all things, isn't it inaccurate to say humans can own something that really belongs to God?

The world and everything in it are God's to do with as he pleases (Ps 24:1, Deut 10:14). There is no claim against God that would have any merit; he rightly owns it all (Job 41:11). Indeed, it was by an act of divine sovereignty that God entrusted this physical world to humanity's stewardship (Gen 2:15). That includes our own bodies, which we are to use to honor God (1 Cor 6:19–20).

In relation to God, we are stewards who are ultimately responsible to our master for what he has seen fit to entrust to us. However, in relation to each other, we are self-owners and owners of our own property.

This arrangement is not arbitrary, but rather it reveals the very wisdom of God. God has entrusted creation to humanity, and scripture affirms the institution of property ownership for managing that creation. Property rights reduce conflict over scarce resources. In this fallen world, we live in a state of scarcity and decay. It takes work to get the natural world to yield up the things we need to survive (Gen 3:19). When property rights are reliably respected, that struggle for survival is made less burdensome. Property rights incentivize hard work and enable responsible planning for future needs (Prov 6:6–11; 13:22). Biblical commandments against stealing and punishments for theft prohibiting theft logically affirm the legitimacy and necessity of personal property rights.

17. But if humans are stewards, how are we held accountable in our stewardship?

Human beings have often squandered the blessings that God has given us. Social institutions should reward productive activities and punish wasteful ones. The best institution for the maintenance of those favorable incentives is called the market. The market—when allowed to function freely—works to reallocate scarce resources to their best and highest uses for the satisfaction of human wants and needs, away from wasteful or inefficient uses.

In state institutions, resources are budgeted based on the subjective or ideological predilections of elected officials and bureaucrats. Government agencies distribute resources based on political rather than economic concerns. No matter how brilliant and well-intended the bureaucrats are, they simply cannot successfully aggregate and analyze all of the market information necessary to rationally plan the economy. Government planning is not necessarily malicious, but it is fundamentally clumsier than market-based planning.

Far from being a promoter of good stewardship, government social policy incentivizes poor decision-making and too often rewards and reinforces destructive behavior. This is not limited to one type of government; central planners of every political flavor fall short of the mark. On the global scale, governments are also the worst polluters in the world, and experiments in compulsory communism and collective ownership of natural resources have been environmental and humanitarian disasters (see Chapter 15).

18. The book of Acts says the early church shared things in common. Doesn't this go against the idea of property rights?

Some progressive Christian groups argue that because the early church "held all things in common" (Acts 2:42–47; 4:32, NET), property rights are not a Christian ideal and that, therefore, libertarianism is incompatible with Christianity. But this biblical example is insufficient proof of such a claim. Acts 2 might indicate that the early church was a small communal collective who made choices toward their collective good, but the conclusion that it is intended for the church more broadly ignores several key points:

The community was voluntary. We read in Acts 2:46 that they did this "with glad and generous hearts." The phrase "held all things in common" doesn't indicate whether they had some sort of intra-communal stewardship arrangements.

Ownership is implied in the phrase "sold their possessions and property" (Acts 2:45, NIV) You can't sell what you don't own. While we don't get the full picture of all they did in this short passage, we do get the impression that they had property to begin with; otherwise they wouldn't be able to sell what they had.

It is also important to recognize that when the Bible discusses communal sharing, such as Acts 4:32, it is not indicative or suggestive of a legal arrangement, but a newly formed community centered around a common purpose. There is no reason to believe we are meant to apply this model to a nation-state, especially one made up of people who are not committed to the same gospel.

Additionally, it's notable that in Acts 5, Ananias and Sapphira's sin was not a lack of sharing, but in their lie. This is at least a small nod toward some semblance of stewardship required by those within the community itself.

For more on why this scenario isn't a model for a national or global economy, see Question 102.

19. Libertarianism just seems like a selfish philosophy to me.

Libertarianism is a philosophy that promotes self-interest, so it's easy to confuse this with selfishness. Selfishness implies a disregard for others. So the question then is, does libertarianism promote a general disregard for others? The short answer is, no.

Self-interested acts that disregard others by violating the NAP are considered criminal. There may be self-interested actions, which do not violate the NAP, that others would not choose for themselves and yet influence how they have to choose differently. This is simply the way life works. In our view, the individual and the community are of equal importance; we are individuals living in communities with one another, yet one is not more important than the other. Some people are inclined to believe that any self-interest is inherently selfish and therefore immoral. So let's consider what a completely altruistic world looks like.

Imagine a society where you could never say, "no." Where everyone belongs to everyone else and is meant to serve others. Any form of self-interest is considered selfish—a disregard for others in the community who have a right to your good will. Aldous Huxley's 1932 novel, *Brave New World*, depicts this utopian-dystopian world where all forms of self-interest are considered selfish. The implications of this sort of society turn out to be very anti-Christian with no monogamy, no family, no church, no love, and no privacy. Christianity is not opposed to self-interest. It is opposed to the general disregard of others. But the world Huxley predicted shows us what happens when we disregard self-interest and the individual right to choose. We are in fact acting selfishly, with disregard for others, when we don't acknowledge others' right to choose according to their self-interest. So we must consider self-interest as distinct from selfishness.

When two individuals voluntarily trade with one another, they do so from self-interest and the results are mutually beneficial. If it wasn't beneficial to both parties, they would voluntarily choose not to trade. As individuals within a community voluntarily trade, communities then voluntarily interact with one another. This too is for mutually beneficial ends as a result of individual self-interest. Libertarianism promotes regard for others through the principles of self-ownership, the NAP, and voluntary (mutually-beneficial) exchanges and associations.

20. Libertarianism feels too individualistic to be compatible with Christianity.

Libertarianism is neither individualist nor collectivist, though it's understandable that one might see it as individualistic, given that we begin with self-ownership and place such importance on individual human action. In fact, Murray Rothbard rightly pointed out that no libertarian thinker ever claimed an "atomistic" view of the individual. But libertarianism doesn't stop there. When we pan out from the individual to see multiple individuals acting and interacting with each other, then we see communities form. Communities are voluntary associations of individuals. So individuals can interact with individuals, individuals can choose to work together in communities, communities of individuals can interact with other communities, and so on. Neither individuals nor communities are more basic than, or have their origin in, the other. The beautiful part of this process is that it is spontaneous—that is, there is no mastermind centrally planning this process.

So is this compatible with Christianity?

Well, it certainly seems that Christianity was formed this way. Christianity started with a single individual: Jesus Christ. His interactions with other individuals (especially the Twelve) formed communities who then formed more communities called churches. The individuals of these communities interacted with other communities, such as other churches, synagogues, and the pagan communities around them. These individuals were encouraged to live peaceably with others (Rom 12:18) and to love their enemies (Matt 5:43–48). And we carry on (or should carry on) this pattern today. There are no human masterminds centrally planning these communities. There's certainly room for theological explanations of God's providential work behind it all.

Libertarianism doesn't artificially bind Christians morally where Christ has left them free (Gal 5). So not only do we think libertarianism is compatible with Christianity, but it actually affirms and works with what appears to be God's design for societal order.

Additional Resources

Called to Freedom: Why You Can be Christian and Libertarian, ed. Elise Daniel (Wipf & Stock, 2017).

The Ethics of Liberty by Murray Rothbard (Mises Institute, 1982).

For a New Liberty: The Libertarian Manifesto by Murray Rothbard (Mises Institute, 1973).

Free is Beautiful: Why Catholics Should Be Libertarian by Randy England (2019).

Free to Choose by Milton Friedman (Mariner Books Classics, 1990).

Healing Our World: In an Age of Aggression by Mary Ruwart (Sunstar Press, 2003).

"How We Come to Own Ourselves" by Stephen Kinsella. *Mises Institute*, 2006. https://mises.org/mises-daily/how-we-come-own-ourselves.

The Individualists: Radicals, Reactionaries, and the Struggle for the Soul of Libertarianism by Matt Zwolinski and John Tomasi (Princeton University Press, 2023).

The Law by Frederic Bastiat (1850)

The Libertarian Mind by David Boaz (Simon & Schuster, 2025).

Libertarianism: What Everyone Needs to Know by Jason Brennan (Oxford University Press, 2012).

Liberty Defined by Ron Paul (Grand Central Publishing, 2012).

The Market for Liberty by Morris and Linda Tannehill (Mises Institute, 1970).

The Most Dangerous Superstition by Larken Rose (2015).

The Revolution: A Manifesto by Ron Paul (Grand Central Publishing, 2008).

Turn Neither to the Right nor to the Left by D. Eric Schansberg (Alertness Ltd., 2003).

3

Christian Misconceptions of Libertarianism

"The one who first states a case seems right, until the other comes and cross-examines."

—Proverbs 18:17

21. Don't libertarians think greed and selfishness are virtues?

Certainly some libertarians are greedy and selfish—just like some political conservatives and progressives. But there is nothing about libertarian political theory that lauds such behaviors as good and right. On the contrary, libertarianism suggests that the nature of the aggressive political process is to attract those corrupt individuals who are indeed greedy and selfish to positions of power, where instead of having to satisfy others' needs to gain anything (as in the marketplace), they can use that power to steal what they want from others. While the marketplace rewards those who serve the needs of others through mutual exchange, politics incentivizes direct greed with its very structure.

However, you might also have heard of the "virtue of selfishness" as explained by Ayn Rand, whom many libertarians respect. Some of Rand's teachings are antithetical to Christian values, but it's notable that Rand's use of such language is meant to combat the oft-proclaimed mantra that the state is inherently altruistic and is "better" than the marketplace where everyone is always and only "greedy." Instead, Rand says that it is good to aspire, to achieve, to create, to act in one's self-interest. As Christians, we even believe it is in our own self-interest to seek after God because it is the end of man to glorify God and enjoy him forever! So, self-interest in the right perspective is a good thing (see Question 19).

22. Aren't libertarians hedonists who just want to live however they want to?

Libertarians don't promote libertinism (the total disregard of any form of authority or social convention); we're just about promoting liberty.

Libertarianism is not a full moral or aesthetic theory, but only a political theory, which is a subset of moral theory dealing with the proper role of violence in public life. Libertarianism suggests what the proper role of civil government is and how it should behave (if at all), since it claims for itself the power to coerce others with physical force. Ultimately, libertarians say that everyone should be free to do as they will so long as they do not initiate aggression against others. That may make it possible for people to live as a certain kind of hedonist (again, so long as they don't commit aggression), but libertarianism doesn't make a claim about every activity surrounding human life, much less condone hedonism.

With liberty, though, one is free to act upon their deeply held moral principles without fear of violent reprisal, and that includes the religious freedom that Christians have sought since the beginning of our shared faith.

23. Why do libertarians seem to think all people are good and don't need a state to control them?

On the contrary, libertarians don't assume people are good at all. James Madison wrote in the Federalist Papers, "If Men were angels, no government would be necessary." The libertarian takes this even further by saying that it is precisely because humans are not angels that a government founded on aggression should not exist. Humanity cannot be trusted with the reins of power as such, even if it is purportedly given "checks and balances."

Madison believed a state must first be "enable[d] to control the governed," and then "oblige it to control itself." But how is this to occur but for the same non-angelic people that we said could not govern themselves to begin with? The libertarian suggests that institutionalizing aggression in government is nonsensical because humanity is not inherently good enough to hold that power without corruption. No coercive government can be structurally set up to get around this; such is the nature of aggression and power.

24. Why do libertarians seem to reject the sinful nature of humanity?

Perhaps one can argue that because not all libertarians are Christians, these libertarians don't believe in the sinful nature of humanity in the first place, but it is the same for political conservatives and progressives as well.

As should be evident from the libertarian arguments against political power throughout this book, libertarians have a keen sense for the evil people can perpetrate against one another when social institutions are set up with aggression at their forefront. Libertarian historians take great pains to understand the depth of human depravity that takes place through states and their activities, especially wars and their effects on more common people. Libertarians don't reject the sinful nature of humanity, but rather pinpoint just how awful the sinful nature of people can come out when political power corrupts them even further. An evil person acting alone is much more easily thwarted than an evil person commanding the power of the state.

25. Why do libertarians seem to have simple answers to complex problems?

Libertarians do not purport to know the answer to every possible problem that will crop up if we reduce the state's power in everyday life. However, libertarians will suggest that people acting with rational self-interest can organize themselves in many unexpected ways to solve increasingly complex problems. This is an entrepreneurial process where people will take risks, make cost-benefit analyses to see what works and what doesn't, and then seek to invest in the means to solve those problems for others and gain a benefit through mutual exchange (free trade). We cannot know ahead of time what the exact outcome will be.

If libertarians did have exact answers to everything, that would suggest that one should simply put libertarians in charge of the world and have them run every aspect of society—but that would be antithetical to libertarian philosophy.

26. Doesn't libertarianism reject morals and make decisions on cost-benefit analysis?

This is a similar question to whether libertarians are merely hedonists or not (Question 22) but with a twist. It is true that there are some people who believe that government activity should be based solely on a cost-benefit analysis of a policy, but libertarians don't measure policy like that. Libertarians believe in the natural rights of every individual in person and property, and these are inviolable. Therefore, libertarians don't reject moral intuitions at all, but rather arrive at their political principles based on a particular subset of moral principles applicable to public life.

The key is that libertarians believe that moral principles do not fall away if someone suddenly becomes elected to a government position or is born into a monarchy. Libertarians say that there is no privilege of position and every individual is held to the same moral principles. That sounds rather Christian, actually!

27. Is Libertarianism an all-encompassing worldview?

Absolutely not! Libertarianism is concerned with political theory, which is certainly part of a worldview. A worldview includes, but is not limited to, views on all aspects of life including cultural, social, linguistic, ethical, and economic, but libertarianism does not purport to be the answer to life, the universe, and everything. If anything, the fact that the two major parties purport to answer all aspects of life is an erroneous extension of political theory outside its proper boundaries.

Libertarians are always more than libertarians, and the Christian libertarian especially has more to be concerned with than politics alone. We have a prior and more important commitment to serve Jesus Christ, to love and provide for our families, and to seek lasting personal fulfillment through useful work and relationships.

Understanding political theory is important, helping to inform various parts of our lives, but it is not everything. We cannot stress enough in this book that we agree with the message of the gospel and the words of the Westminster Catechism that man's chief end is "to glorify God and enjoy him forever." Part of how we glorify God is by seeking truth in all aspects of life, and getting our political theory right helps ensure that we are proper neighbors and respecters of all mankind.

Additional Resources

"Can Christians Be Libertarian?" Norman Horn debates Al Mohler. https://moodyaudio.com/products/can-christian-be-libertarian/.

Leave Me Alone and I'll Make You Rich: How the Bourgeois Deal Enriched the World by Deirdre Nansen McCloskey and Art Carden (The University of Chicago Press, 2020).

The Libertarian Theology of Freedom by Edmund A. Opitz (Hallberg Publishing Corporation, 1999).

"Myth and Truth About Libertarianism" by Murray Rothbard. 1979. https://mises.org/mises-daily/myth-and-truth-about-libertarianism/.

The Soul of Atlas by Mark David Henderson (Reason Publishing, 2013).

4

Government

"There is no such thing as Government with a capital G. There is only an arrangement which sets aside a small group of people and gives them the power to coerce all the rest of the people."
—Edmund Opitz

28. Isn't the government an institution created by God? How can a Christian square this truth with being anti-government?

Satan was originally created by God too, but we do not presume to think that makes Satan good or that everything Satan does is approved or justified by God. Consider that even in the case of Job, God was permitting Satan's actions but not approving. Likewise, we can recognize that God created everything in this world, including the state, but this fact neither makes the state a good institution nor justifies its activities.

God gives no special privileges of position to do evil or to let ends justify means (Jas 2, Rom 2:11, Rom 3:8). Therefore, we should oppose institutions that claim such power to coerce and the privilege to commit aggression against others—which is inherently what states do. This does not mean we take up arms and fight every chance we have against such institutions, but rather, we act peacefully to persuade and help people realize that there are better ways to organize ourselves and solve problems than committing acts of aggression against each other.

God has given his creation a measure of self-determination: the ability to "choose this day whom you will serve" (Josh 24:15). We see Satan as choosing to rebel against God and thus fall from grace, and God allowed it. Humans commit a similar rebellion through the institutionalization of aggressive force—that is, the formation of the state—and God allows it as well. Romans 13 gives us an idea of how to act within it, but the passage does not morally justify its existence or behaviors.

29. Okay, so maybe not all governments are established by God. But isn't the state needed to keep sinful people under control?

All people are sinful, but does this mean we need the state to control all people?

There are certainly those who would agree that people need to be controlled. One of the key philosophers who advocated this idea was Thomas Hobbes. Hobbes maintained that individuals pose a direct threat to each other, thereby making the existence of the state a necessity for maintaining order. He believed that power to govern equally distributed among individuals was a motivator for people to attack one another, and that power held centrally, by either an organization or a single person, resulted in peaceful cooperation. James Madison echoed this in his famous quip, "If men were angels, no government would be necessary."

But since libertarian Christians recognize that all people are sinful and have a propensity toward corrupting power, we disagree that the state is a necessary apparatus for tempering sinful behavior. Indeed, the last thing we want to do is concentrate monopoly power in the hands of sinners. Instead, it's the role of the church to encourage moral behavior, and the role of the Holy Spirit to sanctify us, in part, toward that end. Contrary to popular belief, "legislating morality" is outside the scope of God-ordained civil governance.

To create the conditions for human flourishing society needs civil governance. Civil governance is the administration of civil justice, which is based on the legitimate use of coercion. The initiation or first use of coercion is always illegitimate, regardless of whether it's an individual acting alone or people acting in the name of governing authority. So straight away we see that it's improper for civil governance to control anything through the initiation of force. Instead, civil governance can only be responsive, and only to previously (and thus improperly) initiated coercion.

30. Sure, the state isn't great at managing society, but surely they keep the peace, right?

It's helpful to understand what is meant by "keep the peace." This phrase has become a rather meaningless idiom. We used to call our judges "justices of the peace" and our law enforcement officers "peace officers." Supporters of law enforcement often (and, in our view, mistakenly) associate Matthew 5:9 ("blessed are the peacemakers") with law enforcement officers. But it's a contradiction to attribute "peacekeeper" to people who regularly initiate force and violence upon others.

If the state exists to keep the peace, then they sure aren't doing a very good job of it! Criminal justice reform is a regular campaign issue. On the one hand, there are problems with the administrative side: police brutality, no-knock raids, corrupt or careless judges, etc. On the other hand, there are problems with the effectiveness of the policies: high recidivism rates, mandatory minimums, overcrowding and rising cost of prisons, etc.

How much peace we enjoy today is really due to market forces and not because of (or in spite of) government policies?

There are a couple of ways we can conceive of civil governance as "keeping the peace." One classic metaphor is the "night watchman." Another is a "referee." Either way, the peacekeeping role of civil governance necessitates the impartiality of the peacekeeper in a given dispute. Historically, the difficulty has always been holding the peacekeeper accountable when disputes arise involving them. This is part of the ongoing dialogue between libertarian anarchists and libertarian minarchists (see Question 32). The aim of both, however, is that civil governance is only successful in "keeping the peace" when it's properly and effectively limited.

31. If the government doesn't make laws, how will people know what authority to obey?

The fundamental principles of self-ownership and non-aggression are self-evidently true (see Questions 14–17). In other words, people intuitively know them. In fact, you'll find that arguments against them are derived from premises which assume they're true. How can this be? God's creational order entails laws written into the fabric of reality. This involves physical laws (e.g., the law of gravity), but also involves normative laws (e.g., "you shall not murder," Exod 20:13). God's law is written on the hearts of humankind (Rom 2:15), even if they try to suppress the truth of it (Rom 1:18).

Beyond this, disputes arise as human beings come in contact and interact with one another. Along with voluntary human action comes disagreement; this is inevitable. There are two ways people would know what authority to obey if the government didn't create new law: contracts and dispute resolutions.

First, with contracts, the rules governing parties are established at the onset of the relationship. This is useful when dealing with an exchange of services (if you do this, then I'll give you that), where stipulations aren't self-evident and therefore need to be defined. But contracts cannot foresee all possible outcomes and disputes arise. For these disputes, resolutions need to be made by third-party arbitration. These might be courts or private agencies. Part of any good contract you find today is an agreement to use third-party arbitration in the event a dispute arises. So our society is already acclimated to this form of governance.

If the dispute happens to be a common problem, then the resolution could become common practice where it's effective and upholds the property rights of the parties involved. In our current system, we might refer to this as "case law." And even case law can (and would) be challenged in a libertarian society. No doubt, there will need to be a way of keeping track of effective dispute resolutions, which means there will be a market need for impartial record keeping. Some have suggested that blockchain technology could serve this purpose. But whatever the solution, the need for contracts and resolution necessitates a market response, not a monopoly response from a state government.

32. Do libertarians believe any and every government is illegitimate?

This is a tricky question. Libertarians are a diverse bunch situated across an ideological spectrum. And we have to talk about what a "government" is.

Some libertarians advocate for a government in the form of a minimal, "night watchman" state. These libertarians believe that a few things are best provided through a limited state; usual examples include so-called "public goods" like roads, national defense, and a court system. Other than those limited public functions, minarchist libertarians believe that markets can reliably serve the needs of society.

Other libertarians reject the need for the state altogether. These libertarians believe that public goods can be provided by competing enterprises operating on a voluntary, profit-motivated basis. They are pessimistic about the prospects for keeping limited states within their appointed bounds. These libertarian anarchists want markets to be entirely self-regulated.

But one thing that all libertarians do believe in is some form of governance. Libertarians all believe in keeping the peace and protecting the vulnerable. We just have different ideas about how those important functions might be carried out.

33. Wait a sec, are you saying there's a difference between governance and government?

In English, the word *government* has changed over time. The famous author and professing Christian J.R.R. Tolkien complained in a letter to his son that "Government is an abstract noun meaning the art and process of governing and it should be an offence to write it with a capital G or so as to refer to people."

Contrary to Tolkien's preferences, the word *government* in common usage more often refers to government entities, not to the process of government. It makes sense to use the term "governance" to refer to what Tolkien believed "government" should have meant all along. The distinction is important, because one refers to a noble social goal, and the other refers to a group of people who may or may not be so noble.

Governance, in essence, is about restraining injustice. Christians should care very much about justice, because we know God loves justice (see Question 12). Violent crimes like armed robbery and kidnapping are not the only sorts of injustices that we should avoid; more mundane evils are still matters of great concern to God. The Bible tells us that honest dealing is pleasing to God (Prov 16:11). He condemns those who use dishonest weights and measures (Prov 20:23, Mic 6:11). Employers who withhold just wages from workers and build up earthly palaces with dishonest gain will be judged by God (Jer 22:13–15, Jas 5:4). The ancient Israelites in the time of Amos were judged nationally, in part, for tolerating perjury against the innocent and abuse of the poor (Amos 2:6).

Punishing evildoers to avenge wrongdoing is something that Christians are ultimately called to trust God for (Rom 12:19). God does use earthly authorities as a means for punishing evildoers (Rom 13:4). He repeatedly used the pagan governments of the other nations to chasten backsliding Israel (Judg 2:20–23). However, nowhere is God's instruction to justice-hungry believers that we should use secular government to carry out our work as the body of Christ. Remember that when Gideon was given the opportunity to rule, he refused and reminded the Israelites that God was their ruler (Judg 8:22–23) Not only did Christ refuse Satan's offer of the kingdoms of the world, but Christ also resisted the Jewish Zealots who believed the coming messiah would be a political king who would overthrow Israel's oppressors.

34. Why do governments need to be limited? Shouldn't they be able to do whatever it takes to keep the peace?

If government is meant to keep the peace, that presupposes that we value peace. As Christians, we should! If we are in Christ, he gives us an internal peace even as we face the trials of this world (John 14:27). Christians should desire agreeable, peaceful relations with everyone, in part because that is how the lost can see God's love through us (Heb 12:14, 2 Cor 13:11). We are called to be peacemakers (Matt 5:9). If a member of the body is easily angered or provoked to violence, scripture warns us these character traits disqualify that person from service in church leadership (Titus 1:7–8).

A familiar quotation often attributed to George Washington warns that, "Government is not reason, it is not eloquence—it is force. Like fire it is a dangerous servant and a fearful master."

Violence is the opposite of peace. It destroys resources, relationships, and human lives. As Christian believers and followers of the Prince of Peace, we should be gravely skeptical of violence and reluctant to resort to it. If the defining characteristic of government is force, it stands to reason that government is not a tool Christians should be fond of using.

35. The government is a special entity. It sounds like you're holding it to the same ethics as individuals have to obey.

Every proper authority in society is necessarily limited. The authority of parents is limited to their own family. The authority of church officers is limited to the church. The authority of an employer is limited to the sphere of business. Government is not an exception. To treat it as an unlimited touchstone of societal order is to make an idol of it. Libertarians believe that we should evaluate questions of justice uniformly, regardless of whether a person is an agent of the state or a private individual. The American Declaration of Independence recited a radical claim about governments "deriving their just powers from the consent of the governed."

Consent is the crucial difference between competitive boxing and criminal battery. Consent is the essential ingredient that must be present in order for any government power to be just. The claim that consent is relevant even for the sovereign logically implies that justice is not just a matter of what government says. Justice is a standard not subject to modification by any mortal person.

For Christians, these claims should ring true. In Luke 16:17, Jesus tells us that God's law does not ever change. God's law of love applies equally to every person made in his image, prince and pauper alike. "God is no respecter of persons" (Acts 10:34b, KJV), which means he doesn't play favorites. Christ-followers must be opposed to the perversion of justice to recognize social station, wealth, or for any other reason (Jas 2:1–4, 8–9).

36. What sort of legal order would a libertarian support?

Libertarians prefer markets to bureaucracy. The world we live in today is largely dominated by state bureaucracies. We usually think of "law and order" as being a product of government. In spite of government courts dominating the legal market, there is a flourishing market for alternative dispute resolution services. Negotiation, mediation, and arbitration are important means for avoiding or resolving disputes that would otherwise go in front of a judge.

The efficiency of private mediation and arbitration has led to legislation in some jurisdictions that encourage or even require disputing parties to participate in mediation before asking the court to solve their problems. These services offer predictable outcomes to parties, they control costs, and they can be more private than litigation in government courts. A report published by the Economic Policy Institute in September 2017 claimed that the share of the American workforce subject to mandatory arbitration agreements had risen from about 2 percent in 1992 to over 55 percent by 2017. Purchasers of airline tickets, luxury cruise berths, and other relatively expensive consumer services will find that they, too, are subject to mandatory arbitration clauses should a dispute arise with their service provider.

A libertarian legal order would utilize these effective, private dispute resolution methods instead of relying on a centralized, monopolistic government court system. Competition between arbitration firms already exists today. In a free market in legal services, this competition would continue to promote efficiency and reach reasonable, predictable outcomes. If a party failed to honor his legal obligations, adjudication of that failure would likely impact his creditworthiness and future business prospects.

Additional Resources

Anatomy of the State by Murray Rothbard (Ludwig von Mises Institute, 2009).

Chaos Theory by Robert P. Murphy (Ludwig von Mises Institute, 2002).

"The Church of Christ and World-Powers" by David Lipscomb. ed. Norman Horn, 2020. https://libertarianchristians.com/2020/08/22/the-church-of-christ-and-world-powers/.

Civil Government: Its Origin, Mission, and Destiny, and the Christian's Relation to It by David Lipscomb (Gospel Advocate Publishing Company, 1889).

Creation in the Image of the Glory Spirit by Meredith G. Kline. https://meredithkline.com/klines-works/articles-and-essays/creation-in-the-image-of-the-glory-spirit/.

The Enterprise of Law: Justice Without the State by Bruce Benson (Independent Institute, 2013).

"The Growing Use of Mandatory Arbitration" by Alexander J.S. Colvin. https://www.epi.org/publication/the-growing-use-of-mandatory-arbitration/.

"Privatizing the Adjudication of Disputes" by Edward P. Stringham and Bryan Caplan. Theoretical Inquiries in Law, Vol. 9, No. 2, 2008. https://econfaculty.gmu.edu/bcaplan/pdfs/privatizingadjudication.pdf.

The Quest for Community by Robert Nisbet (Intercollegiate Studies Institute, 2010).

The State by Franz Oppenheimer (Black Rose Books, 2007).

5

The Limits of a Free Society

"Rightful liberty is unobstructed action according to our will within limits drawn around us by the equal rights of others. I do not add 'within the limits of the law' because law is often but the tyrant's will, and always so when it violates the rights of the individual."

—*Thomas Jefferson*

37. Shouldn't there be limits on individual freedom? People can't just do whatever they want without consequences!

As Christians, we know that sin has consequences both in this temporal life and in eternity. A person who diligently works to provide for future needs will usually receive favorable consequences from his actions: he and his family will eat! Labor is often unpleasant, but it brings the joyful reward of the harvest. "May those who sow in tears shall reap with shouts of joy! Those who go out weeping, bearing the seed for sowing, shall come home with shouts of joy, carrying their sheaves" (Ps 126:5–6).

A person who is lazy and irresponsible will eventually be both humbled and hungry (Prov 10:4, 13:4; 20:4). The sin of idleness is not just something that has consequences for the idle person.

Scripture warns that failure to provide for one's family members, especially one's own household, is a denial of the Christian faith (1 Tim 5:8).

There are many other vices that are currently treated as crimes by the state: activities related to drug and alcohol abuse, prostitution, gambling, and so forth. As Christians, we should counsel our brothers and sisters to avoid polluting their bodily temples. We should encourage wise stewardship instead of frivolous frittering away of the resources with which God entrusts us. But the Bible does not teach us to use violence to exhort others to good works. Indeed, strict, external enforcement of rules about touching, tasting, and eating forbidden things does not help to restrain sensual indulgence (Col 2:16–23). Using violence for reasons other than responding to violent aggressors is not a proportionate response to wrongdoing (Lev 24:19–21).

38. What limitations do I have as an individual under libertarianism?

Libertarianism only speaks to what is just or unjust for an individual to do. The boundary between justice and injustice is based on the ownership of property, including your own body. Libertarianism categorically rejects violations of other people's property rights as wrong. However, if an act does not violate another person's rights, it is not "unlibertarian," which is to say that it is not an injustice. Libertarians agree that the use of force against others is only permissible if they are aggressors whose actions violate the rights of others. Otherwise, libertarianism leaves the individual free to choose what to do with his time and property.

But remember, libertarianism only speaks to what should be legal. As Christian libertarians, we recognize that a thing's being lawful is not enough to make it good. Believers must also consider whether a particular choice is spiritually expedient; that is, whether it glorifies God (1 Cor 6:12, 1 Cor 10:23–29). Justice tells us what people can be compelled to do or not do. The teachings of our Lord in scripture and through the moving of the Holy Spirit show us how we ought to live in order to please and glorify him (2 Tim 3:16, 1 Cor 2:6–16).

39. What keeps others from victimizing me under libertarianism?

Governance is a lot bigger than government. There is a thriving market for a variety of accountability and protection products and services. The invention of financial bookkeeping made sophisticated financial audits possible. Computer software has made managing these records and auditing them faster and easier. Many journalists have made careers out of revealing scandals of public concern or reviewing products to expose the dangerous and unreliable ones.

Underwriters Laboratories has been a leading product safety testing and certification firm for more than a century, and it earns billions of dollars every year doing it, largely motivated by concerns of insurance companies that would lose money if policyholders suffer a loss. Burglar alarms, security cameras, fences, locks, and self-defense products are all produced by entrepreneurs serving the demand for protection against wrongdoers.

Make no mistake: we live in a fallen world. In this fallen world, we will face a variety of perils to which we apply our God-given talents and material resources. Libertarians do not promise a utopia. Libertarian Christians benefit from the insight of scripture. We know that a perfect human society is not possible so long as the world is in the thrall of sin. As Christians, we should prepare for tomorrow with prudence and diligence. We must be careful, though, to always put our trust in God, not in our own strength or in the plans of secular leaders. We do not always know how God is planning to work things out. However, we know our God is good and that he will lead us if we acknowledge him and look to him for guidance (Prov 3:5–6).

40. What if other people don't like what I do or how I live?

People often disagree with each other about what life ought to look like. As Christians, we believe that we ought to live as Christ taught us to live. Scripture tells us that the world hated Christ and that it hates Christ followers, too (John 15:18–19). Despite living in a world that hates us, we should do our best to live at peace with everyone (Rom 12:18). In his letter to the Philippian faithful, Paul reminded them of Jesus' self-humbling, self-sacrificial example. Loving peace and avoiding disputes are habits that are practically beneficial "in the midst of a crooked and perverse generation" (Phil 2:15). They allow us to "shine like stars" in a dark and sinful world (Phil 2:15–16).

We are to be so conflict-averse—and loving towards others—that Christ admonished us to respond to presumptuous demands with a charitable response that goes above and beyond what is demanded (Matt 5:38–42, Luke 6:27–36). This is commanded even towards our enemies (Matt 5:43–48; Luke 6:32–36).

Paul exhorted the faithful in Corinth to abstain from using secular courts to sue other believers (1 Cor 6:1–8). Jesus told us the appropriate steps for making a godly appeal to an offending brother or sister in Christ, and that process is in the context of a local fellowship of believers (Matt 18:16–17).

41. What about people who have more wealth? They can buy votes and rig the system in their favor!

It is true that wealthy political donors can obtain ready access to elected policymakers in a way that other people cannot. This is true despite complicated campaign finance laws and limitations on how and when money may be donated. Taxing wealthy people more cannot change that—they will still have plenty of things that others want.

Even where campaign contributions are not at issue, lobbyists often get their way for another, seemingly benign reason: lobbyists are usually experts in their policy areas. Politicians learn to rely on lobbyists to efficiently explain complex legal and policy issues to them. It should be unsurprising when the "students" later reach the same policy positions as their "teachers."

Lord Acton, a 19th century English historian, famously said that "power tends to corrupt." The libertarian solution is to rely more on markets and to rely less on political policymaking. Markets are ultimately controlled by consumer preference and the realities of business. Though individuals make mistakes sometimes, when they are engaged in market activities the personal consequences of failure naturally motivate them to exercise great care.

Economists sometimes refer to a problem called "moral hazard." Moral hazard exists when a decision-maker has an incentive to increase risk because they are not directly impacted by the consequences of that risk. For example, many libertarians are concerned that banks engage in riskier conduct because of the prospect of government bailouts. The decisions politicians make are chiefly about other people's resources, not their own. Private entrepreneurs and investors are financially accountable for their actions in a way that politicians never are.

Christians know that perverting justice, especially for money, is an abomination to God (Deut 16:18–20). Politicizing and bureaucratizing justice does not promote equality before the law. In fact, political and bureaucratic incentives can facilitate further injustice. We know this from economic theory. We also know it from scripture (Eccl 5:8–9).

Additional Resources

Anarchy, State, and Utopia by Robert Nozick (Basic Books, 2013).

The Art of Community by Spencer Heath MacCallum (Institute for Humane Studies, 1970).

Bureaucracy by Ludwig von Mises (Mises Institute, 1944).

The Free Society by Laurence Vance (Vance Publications, 2018).

Markets Without Limits by Jason Brennan and Peter M. Jaworski (Routledge, 2016).

Religion: Foundation of the Free Society by Edmund Opitz (Foundation for Economic Education, 1996).

The Voluntary City: Choice, Community, and Civil Society by David Beito, Peter Gordon, and Alex Tabarrok (University of Michigan Press, 2002).

6

Economics and the Christian

"The curious task of economics is to demonstrate to men how little they really know about what they imagine they can design."

—F. A. Hayek

42. Why should Christians be interested in economics?

Jesus calls us to love our neighbor as ourselves (Matt 22:39), and to follow this seriously means understanding how our actions affect others. Economics becomes essential, because it helps us see how our choices play out in a world of scarcity, and helps us do so with wisdom and humility. God charged humans with having dominion over the earth (Gen 1:28; 2:15). How likely are we to succeed if we do not properly understand how scarcity impacts our ability to accomplish our ends?

Christians concerned about social justice, ethical business practices, charity, environmental stewardship, and many other issues should consider economics a helpful framework because it tells us what is possible and not possible in a world of scarcity. This serves us as citizens of God's Kingdom to achieve just ends through just means (see Question 71). While economics doesn't tell us everything about the human condition (other fields can complement this pursuit), we should utilize it to our advantage when possible.

An economic understanding of human action and decision-making helps us to predict the effects of human action so we can discern how to properly respond. It informs how we can love our neighbors by preventing destructive consequences that well-meaning but economically ignorant often bring about. It helps us develop a proper understanding of the role of money in society. And it also equips Christians to promote the common good and live peaceably with others (Rom 12:18).

43. Would understanding economics make me a better Christian?

The Bible speaks often of seeking and applying wisdom to our daily lives, whether in the home, in our work, or in the public square. Jesus taught his disciples to demonstrate a life of obedience, and used economic metaphors like "estimating the cost" (Luke 14:28) and "bearing fruit" (John 15:8). Because our lives are constrained by the realities of scarcity, an economic way of thinking will help us yield better fruit and live wisely in obedience to God.

At home and in our work, our appreciation of human dignity and cooperation will deepen as we gain a better understanding of economics. This helps us understand our own contribution to the world around us, and how it connects to meeting the needs of others. This can have a powerful compounding impact when more of us see our work (and the work of others) as meaningful service to the glory of God.

In the public square, our good intentions will be held in check by a sharpening of our thinking about trade-offs and unintended consequences. It can enhance our witness by aligning our compassion and sense of justice with effectiveness. It can help guide our actions to productive service and reinforce themes like honesty, justice, and love of neighbor. In short, it can prevent us from acting naively in ways that work against human flourishing.

44. What are the consequences in society of poorly understanding and applying economic principles?

Christians have long helped shape society through missions, justice work, and even politics (see Questions 1 and 42). Whatever the endeavor, our actions must pursue good outcomes through peaceful and just means. Pursuing just outcomes through unjust means isn't just wrongheaded—it can be catastrophic. In 2020, mailing cash to households into a supply-choked economy during a pandemic kept households afloat, but helped ignite the inflation that followed.

Ideally humans will pursue just outcomes by understanding and choosing just means. Economic principles specifically help us avoid the tyranny of good intentions by comprehending how even our best plans might go awry or backfire, causing more harm than good. While this is no doubt true in all areas of life, it is doubly critical for us to pay attention to how this applies to the government.

When certain ends are pursued through state force, rather than ones that can be achieved through peaceful cooperation, distortions arise in every sphere of life. When the state intervenes to "help the poor," it often creates perverse incentives that harm the very people it was meant to serve. When officials allocate funds to "invest" in infrastructure or other causes, they skew the market in ways that produce inefficiency and injustice. And when legislators mandate outcomes through central planning, this robs individuals of moral agency. In turn, this weakens civil society and undermines human responsibility, enables abusive exploitation, and breeds dependency by shifting its burdens onto the state.

45. What are the core economic principles every Christian should know?

Economics starts with the core reality that individuals act with purpose. People set goals and take action to achieve those goals using whatever resources we have at our disposal. These decisions are guided by what we value, and because not every individual values things equally, we have to trade to achieve our ends. Out of the countless decisions we each make, order arises in society as people trade voluntarily. This coordination creates "signals" both small and large that help us discern whether our resources are being guided to useful ends that serve others or are wasted and should be redirected (see Question 49).

Understanding sound money is also crucial, as we find in several places in the Bible that just weights and measures are critical to justice (Prov 11:1, 20:10, 23). Trade reflects God's design for cooperation, as it is a key example of two or more parties agreeing to act peacefully to each other's mutual advantage. This builds trust and strengthens community bonds. However, every trade comes with the cost of opportunity: choosing one path means giving up another. This is highlighted by another principle, where people specialize in their work, which increases productivity, and we begin to rely on one another toward human flourishing. And all along the way, our behavior is shaped by incentives, because as humans we all respond naturally to rewards.

While this list is just a start, Christians can use these principles and others to better understand human action and live in ways that honor God through service to others.

46. Does the Bible teach us any economic principles that apply today?

The concern for justice and a strong consideration of the poor and marginalized should drive Christians to seek biblical and theological support for properly using economic principles. While the Bible isn't a book about economics, it is full of stories, proverbs, and even laws regarding human interactions, which are often economic in nature. We have to be very careful to not import a modern economic system into the Bible, but we can discern principles of economics from the Bible based on inference (e.g., property rights; see Questions 15–18), divine commands that are universal (e.g., don't steal), and through holistic theological study (see LCI's Core Value #1).

From the beginning, it is clear that God gave human beings agency and moral responsibility. This implies the freedom to choose, and a responsibility to steward our choices and our resources wisely (see also Luke 14:28). While an explicit theory of private property is not elaborated upon in Scripture, it is assumed to exist and we are called to respect it. That is, a system of private property provides us with the best way to think about allocation of resources as well as the stewarding of those resources. In addition to the stewardship of resources, God instructed Israel to employ just weights and measures (Lev 19:36), and chastised them for diluting money's value (Isa 1:22).

47. What does the Bible say about money?

Bible references to money, wealth, and possessions are numerous, starting with God's instructions to Abraham on the occasion of their landmark covenant (Gen 17:12–13). The Bible discusses many practical and beneficial uses for money: the purchase of land (Gen 23:9–13, 33:19), livestock (Ezra 7:17), and food commodities (Gen 47:14), the payment of wages (Exod 2:9) and civil damages (Exod 21:34), and even as a means for rebuilding the Temple of the Lord (2 Kgs 12:9–11, Ezra 3:7).

However, sin has infected all aspects of life in a fallen world, including our relationship with money. Both the Old Testament and New Testament are full of warnings against temptations related to money. People are tempted to steal money entrusted to them (Exod 22:7). We are tempted to withhold timely payment of it to our employees (Jer 22:13). We are tempted to use money to satisfy our fleshly lusts (Deut 23:18). We are tempted by bribes (Prov 17:23, Mic 3:11).

All of these misuses of money are rooted in the love of money (1 Tim 6:10), a sinful heart attitude that comes from discontentment with what God has provided (Heb 13:5). Christians need not reject the practical and beneficial uses of money. Indeed, we should be trustworthy in our handling of money (Luke 16:11) and good stewards of all that is entrusted to us (Matt 25:14–30). But all believers must always be wary about putting our trust in money or other forms of material wealth (Matt 6:19–21). We should instead emulate the widow who dramatically demonstrated a confidence in God rather than in money (Mark 12:41–44).

48. Is there a relationship between justice and money?

In addition to the moral temptations that money can present, there is a strong relationship between justice and money. When covetousness and the love of money leads a person to steal from or defraud others, those dishonest acts are not merely sinful. They also violate the rights of those other people. There are also many cases where a person may improperly damage the property of another person. These problems were present in ancient times just like they are present today. That is why God gave clear directions to the ancient Israelites in the Torah about how to go about addressing acts of injustice. Often, money played an important role in the divine prescription for righting wrongs.

Personal injuries resulting from either intentional acts (Exod 21:19) or negligence (Exod 21:32–34) could sometimes be settled by payment of money damages. When a person was caught stealing livestock, the thief who still had the stolen livestock in his possession was required to pay two-fold (Exod 22:3). The trespasser who allowed his animals to devour another's field had to pay with the proceeds from his own field (Exod 22:4). Negligent damage to a neighbor's crops (Exod 22:5) or failure to protect entrusted livestock (Exod 22:9) both required compensation. People guilty of embezzlement, other forms of theft, or any sort of fraud were required to return their ill-gotten gains and to pay an additional amount of money restitution (Lev 6:1–5), in addition to bringing certain designated sin sacrifices to the priest (Lev 6:6–7).

49. What is the role of profit in the market?

The market is where people use their scarce resources—time, land, commodities, and money—to make themselves useful in the service of others. While this requires some guesswork, this process will eventually lead to reward or failure. This is the profit and loss system at work, and it is a very effective way to know if the choices we make with our time and money are wise. Nobody wants to waste their time, money, or other resources on something that doesn't reward us, or "pay us back," in some manner.

Profits are a signal that the scarce resources we put to use were of value to others, while losses signal misallocation of scarce resources and encourage us to redirect them toward better uses. Even if someone believes there are things worth doing that sustain losses (e.g., collecting stamps or helping refugees), it cannot be overlooked that it took profits in the past to fund those efforts that are sustaining losses.

Additionally, this profit and loss system tends to steer individuals in an economy toward innovation and efficiency, allowing the accumulation of profits to be stored for future use. This is called capital formation, and it is a key component for both sustainable charity and for further job creation that enables savings and investment, which drive productivity. When many market actors are doing this peacefully, we can say that the market is cooperating toward human flourishing.

50. How is wealth created?

Modern libertarians overwhelmingly subscribe to the idea that all economic value is derived from the subjective preferences of human beings. Different people value things differently, and even the same person may value the same good differently in different contexts. Those different preferences create opportunities for the creation of wealth through exchange. When a seller exchanges goods for a buyer's money, both parties end the transaction in possession of assets that they value more highly than what they traded to get them. Voluntary exchange creates wealth because the people conducting the exchange believe that they are better off than they were before.

To operate a wealth-producing enterprise, an entrepreneur must first have some understanding of what other people want. The entrepreneur then engages in the process of production, using both labor and capital to produce and bring to market things that customers desire. If the entrepreneur is able to bring his production to market at a price that exceeds his costs, and consumers are willing to pay that price, the enterprise will produce a profit. The investments by the entrepreneur are risky. But one who invests little also receives little in return, a lesson that holds true in spiritual matters as well as in business enterprise (2 Cor 9:6).

The Bible teaches that wealth is the product of diligent planning and effort (Prov 10:4, 21:5). But scripture also clearly states that our own efforts or physical strength are not enough, and that it is God who enables us to be productive in this way. (Deut 8:17–18).

51. What about people who get rich from exploiting the labor of others?

The word *exploitation* is often treated as a synonym for abuse and is frequently slapped onto any employment scenario its critic deems substandard. The word literally means "to make full use" of something, which is something we all do in everyday life as we seek to efficiently use what is ours. In a market where labor is voluntary and competitive, deploying labor is not inherently abusive, but simply the effort of entrepreneurship and raises the living standards of all involved. The claim that value is created through extracting the labor of employees misses how value is actually formed—subjectively in the buyers' and sellers' judgments.

We should distinguish between economic gains through genuine free market competition and gains won by throttling competition—licensing cartels, regulatory favors, subsidies, and other crony arrangements. Christians may even adamantly oppose these fraudulent or rigged systems while recognizing that many people accept low wages because their alternatives are worse. These alternatives are not always the creation of other individuals or systems of oppression. Where they are, we can and should oppose them.

If we're troubled by a landscape where nobody can get a decent job, it's futile to believe the state can solve these problems effectively, because the state itself is a major source of the barriers that create these conditions. However, we can constructively choose to be part of the solution in at least two ways. We can build better opportunities ourselves by hiring, training, and investing in people, and we can roll back the barriers that make abusive exploitation possible.

52. Why did Jesus seem to have harsh words for the wealthy?

Jesus made it clear that one cannot be a loyal servant of God and a loyal servant of money at the same time (Matt 6:24). He warned of the spiritual dangers of riches (Luke 18:24–25), and rebuked those who made money their master instead of God (Matt 6:24). He affirmed generosity and faithfulness (Matt 25:21) as well as concern for the poor (Luke 18:22). He taught us to store up treasure in heaven and not in accumulated wealth (Matt 6:19–20; cf. Jas 5:4), and to give freely to those who ask (Matt 5:42). Furthermore, his tirade in the temple (Matt 21:12–13) made it clear that misuse of money in the house of the Lord was a gross injustice.

While Jesus' concern about wealth is unmistakable, the Bible tells us of many wealthy people who were not condemned or chastised simply for being wealthy. Abram (Gen 13:2), Job (Job 1), and Joseph of Arimathea (Matt 27:57–60) were wealthy yet faithful, using their resources for God's purposes.

The key to understanding Jesus' words for the wealthy can be found in understanding the economic and class structure of the first century. Being rich in first century Judea often meant exploiting the poor and collaborating with an oppressive empire rather than providing goods and services in an open market. Being poor often meant being kept from the upward mobility which free markets afford. In an extractive economy where wealth was almost always zero-sum, we would expect nothing less than for Jesus to give such warnings to the wealthy. Railing against the wealthy in Jesus' day was tantamount to excoriating exploitation by the elite!

In contrast, today's free market capitalism is a more inclusive economic system, even if imperfect in practice. Wherever exploitation exists, Jesus' admonitions stand ready as a firm confrontation against those who exploit others. For those who have wealth, the temptation may be stronger to put trust in riches, but it is also true that wealth can be put toward Kingdom purposes for the glory of God.

53. What role does capital play in an economy?

There are different reasons for saving. One may save for future consumption. Setting resources aside for future needs is praiseworthy, as seen in the case of Joseph's stewardship in Egypt (Gen 41:34–36, 46–49) and the example of the industrious ant (Prov 6:6–8). The saver may also apply his savings to some productive use, in which case they become what economists describe as "capital." Such productive use might include investments in tools, building materials, seed, worker training, wages, and research and development. Every project should begin with an attempt to understand associated costs (Luke 14:28).

The accumulation and investment of capital should not be motivated by a desire to vainly store up treasures on Earth for their own sake (Matt 6:19–21, Luke 12:16–21). Instead, it is so that we can be wise, productive stewards making use of the things temporarily entrusted to believers as servants of God (Matt 25:14–30), especially to facilitate care for our own households and for the needs of others as well (1 Tim 5:8).

54. What roles does labor play in an economy?

The human condition has been defined by toil ever since the Fall (Gen 3:19). Hard work is virtuous and necessary (Prov 10:4–5). As populations grew and developed over the course of human history, it became possible for individuals to focus on their areas of comparative advantage. Specialization and division of labor maximizes overall productivity, meaning that it is possible to satisfy more people's material needs. At the building of the Temple in Solomon's time, an international workforce of highly skilled workmen was differentiated by their respective trades (1 Chr 22:14–15). Throughout the Bible, people are often identified chiefly by their form of employment, including metalworkers (Gen 4:22), masons (2 Kgs 12:12), fishermen (Matt 4:18–22), and most notably a Nazareth-based workman who was born in Bethlehem (Mark 6:3).

The fact that people flourish when using their individual talents in cooperation with others comes as no surprise to God. Scripture uses the illustration of the human body and its diverse parts to teach about a special kind of division of labor: the kind that happens inside the Church. The Apostle Paul exhorted the Corinthian Christians to recognize that the Church is unified "in one Spirit [...] baptized into one body" (1 Cor 12:13). Despite this essential unity, the different members of that Church body are diverse in their backgrounds and worldly social standing. The different members of the body also have different functions, and by being a part of Christ's church, believers all partake in the greatest honor—that honor that God bestows (1 Cor 12:22–26, Rom 12:4–8).

55. What role does the state play in an economy?

Throughout recorded history, states have sought to create economic advantage for their inhabitants. Ideally, this might include protection from other sovereigns and enforcement of laws against stealing, murder, and other rights violations that tend to disrupt peaceful commerce and diminish profits.

But in every known case, states have gone beyond this "night watchman" role and attempted to forcibly impose restrictions on enterprises and consumers that distort the market, make it less productive, and enrich the ruling class at the expense of the people. States impose tariffs on imports, licensing fees for workers and entrepreneurs, and all manner of taxes. They may interfere with the freely negotiated contracts between parties, altering the terms of business deals and often making a good business plan uneconomic as a result.

States attempt to increase economic activity through all sorts of policies. Whether economic protectionism, monetary inflation, or special tax treatment for favored market actors, the effects of economic development policies cannot rigorously be measured, and all too often hamper entrepreneurial planning in the private sector. While voluntary exchange results in the creation of wealth, the state obtains everything that it has by violent compulsion of the rightful owners. States extract useful capital from the structure of production and use it for programs that are either less efficient than their private analogs (e.g., road construction and other civil engineering projects, government courts) or downright destructive (e.g., war, or the vast administrative state).

This diversion of capital has an opportunity cost: diminished production in the private sector and more human wants left unfulfilled. It also always involves selecting some for favorable treatment and others for unfavorable treatment, often to match the idiosyncratic vision of the rulers of the day.

56. What sort of economy should Christians advocate?

The New Testament tells Christians to eschew greed (Matt 6:24–34, 1 Tim 6:10) and live generously (Luke 6:38, 1 John 3:17). The Old Testament required theocratic Israel to tithe for the poor (Deut

14:28–29) and set aside a portion of their agricultural fields for the poor to glean from (Lev 19:9–10). As a result, Christian advocates for progressive economics have argued that a Christian approach to economics would involve heavy state redistribution from the rich to the poor.

While libertarian Christians take these inspired Old Testament commands seriously, we read them in light of the new covenant and the end of Israel's earthly theocracy (Heb 8:13). When seen through that light, libertarian Christians conclude that love for neighbors in the area of economics includes some irreducible minimums. For instance, we should not initiate force against our neighbors, even to help others we think are in greater need. We should also allow them the freedom to peacefully pursue their own goals without being interfered with, therefore giving them every opportunity to thrive and meet their own needs. Finally, we should not create artificial caps on prosperity. The greater the amount of prosperity which we create, the more our neighbors can be provided for–whether through direct trade or through the generosity of others who produce wealth.

There is only one economic system that meets all of these conditions: free market capitalism.

Additional Resources

Choice by Bob Murphy (Independent Institute, 2015).

Economics in One Lesson by Henry Hazlitt (Random House, 2014).

The Ethics of Anarcho-Capitalism by Kristopher A. Borer (2020).

Foundations of Economics by Shawn Ritenour (Wipf and Stock, 2010).

The Good of Affluence by John R. Schneider (Eerdmans, 2002).

"'Ye Cannot Service God and Mammon': An Institutional Interpretation of the Gospels," by Walker Wright. Faith & Economics, Issue 74, Fall 2019. https://christianeconomists.org/article/ye-cannot-serve-god-and-mammon-an-institutional-interpretation-of-the-gospels-walker-wright/.

Was Jesus a Friend to Big Business? By Cody Cook. https://fee.org/articles/was-jesus-a-friend-to-big-business/.

Human Action by Ludwig von Mises (Yale University Press, 1949).

Mere Economics: Lessons for and from the Ordinary Business of Life by Art Carden and Caleb S. Fuller (B&H Academic, 2025).

Strangers with Candy by Art Carden (Christians for Liberty Press, 2023).

7

Capitalism and the Christian

"I believe a man is happier, and happy in a richer way, if he has 'the freeborn mind.' But I doubt whether he can have this without economic independence, which the new society is abolishing. For economic independence allows an education not controlled by Government; and in adult life it is the man who needs, and asks, nothing of Government who can criticize its acts and snap his fingers at its ideology."

—*C.S. Lewis*

57. How can a Christian support the pursuit of profit when the Bible discourages the love of money?

Many Christians argue against the pursuit of profit, citing Paul's admonition in 1 Timothy 6:10 that "the love of money is a root of all kinds of evil." Libertarian Christians concur that the pursuit of money as an end in itself is sinful and damaging to oneself and to others. Anything good and useful that is made ultimate is a form of idolatry. It is not wrong to seek more money because you possess very little and need to make ends meet, or because you wish to provide meaningful work for others. Money used as a tool is wise stewardship. Money as an end-in-itself is where we go astray.

Economic profit-seeking and "the love of money" are not the same concept. In an economic sense, pursuing profit is another way of saying we are utilizing scarce resources to create value for ourselves and others. This does not guarantee good results, but the profit-and-loss system signals to humans that resources are being used properly, not abused.

Pursuing profit is what everyone does every day when they choose to go to work, because both parties agree that they are better off by making the trade. This includes labor. Therefore, every time we go to work, we are engaging in an exchange resulting in us profiting off of the work. From manual laborers to high-level managerial work, everybody seeks an income which covers their expenses, plus some. What is done with that "plus some" is up to each person to decide. Charity, reinvestment, savings, spending—all these are options each individual must decide is right for them (see Question 49).

58. Doesn't capitalism create winners and losers through competition and conflict?

The most popular misunderstanding about free markets results from a misunderstanding of the term competition, probably because we use it in sports where there are winners and losers in a zero-sum game. Yet not all sports are zero-sum (some competitions have various tiers of "winners"), and the free market is especially not a zero-sum game.

A better way to think about competition is that it drives people to pursue the best interests of their customers in ways that rival other businesses. That is, good businesses compete in how much better they can serve customers, and customers reward the businesses that serve them better. This is not a situation of conflict, nor is it an either/or outcome. Even the "lesser" of the two businesses can still win a different customer base. And in reality, most of us want bad businesses to fail so owners can appropriate their resources to more productive uses for society.

In reality, free competition in the market aids in creating a more vibrant and dynamic economy where the needs of everyone are met to a greater degree. When the state is involved, it doesn't create healthy competition; rather, it sows discord and breeds conflict because it causes businesses to compete for attention, favors, and special privileges. This kind of competition is a destructive force in an economy.

59. Doesn't capitalism promote consumerism and materialism?

Christians rightly oppose that which engenders greed and creates an insatiable appetite for more. Critics of capitalism believe that because businesses are always pursuing profit by trying to please consumers, both producers and consumers are always wanting more and more in an endless cycle of materialistic hedonism. They say this creates an unhealthy economy.

Yet at its heart, capitalism is about creating new and innovative ways of using scarce resources for human flourishing. The very term "capital" denotes the use, not depletion, of resources. It is unfortunate that our modern Western economy is labeled "capitalism" because there are large parts of it that depend on the demand for more. In fact, the dominant economic theory most at play is Keynesianism, which is a consumerist vision of the economy. It is inaccurately named "capitalism."

What critics of capitalism often ignore is the significantly better outcomes for human flourishing that have resulted over the past 200 years. Yes, some people are materialistic, but that isn't a guaranteed outcome. Capitalism has created a space for humans to flourish materially, and many are now ready to think about and ponder deeper spiritual realities.

60. What about the inequalities that capitalism creates?

Economic inequality has always existed wherever there have been economies. In pre-capitalist days, having wealth often (but not always) entailed exploiting others who then remained poor. This is one reason we see so many admonitions against wealth in the Bible. It is also why many early church leaders and theologians decry wealth. It is only in a free market capitalist system that being wealthy has not been associated with unjust acquisition of wealth but instead with the indication that mutually beneficial trade is occurring.

Under free market capitalism, wealth must be obtained by effectively and efficiently providing value to others in exchange for their money. Whenever inequality indicates that the few are exploiting others and leaving them worse off, we should stand against it. But under conditions where everyone is better off and some are "more better off," we can appreciate, if not applaud, the gains through exchange.

Christians are often concerned about the well-being of others, yet it is all too common that concern over inequality is not about the well-being of those with less but a suppressed envy that arises because of the perceived reasons behind the injustice.

We must be mindful that we are not suppressing our envy when we advocate for the well-being of others. All too often the concern over inequality is not about the well-being of those with less but the perceived reason behind the perceived injustice. For example, while the purchasing power of the average worker's wages has improved dramatically for several decades, the top 1% have seen even greater gains. Many have pointed out that this is the reason to institute redistributive schemes to rectify the perceived injustice of inequality, even though everyone has gained financially (see Question 61).

61. Is economic growth all libertarians care about?

Economic growth is not merely about the money in our bank accounts or the GDP of an economy. While those can be indications of prosperity or growth, they are just that: indicators. Real economic growth only occurs when scarce resources are put to use in increasing ways. This happens through free exchange, a profit-and-loss system, and innovation in labor and capital, and results in an increased material well-being.

Because libertarian Christians care about freedom from violence, we have respect for private property (see Question 14) and adhere to the non-aggression principle (see Questions 12–13). This leads us to believe that freedom of exchange should be permitted in an open market. Libertarian Christians would strongly support the idea that when individuals are free to do commerce with one another under the conditions of peace and voluntarism, we should expect the economy to grow and the well-being of individuals to improve.

62. Why are some people poor when there's so much wealth in our world?

Why some people are poor has many complicated answers which constitute a mixture of personal and social explanations. We should always reserve judgment on individuals for their circumstances in life, regardless of how much we think we know about their world. When we consider why any particular individual, family, or even community is poor, we must remember it is possible to factor in both individual responsibility and institutional injustices that contribute to the underlying reasons.

An additional layer to this question is asking, "What do you mean by 'poor'?" Absolute poverty has been falling for decades, both nationally and globally. Those who are poor by today's standards have access to or possess the types of goods and services only available to the wealthy half a century ago. This is not to make light of the plight of those on the margins, but to suggest that what constitutes poverty is a moving target.

To ask "why are people still poor" by adding "when there's so much wealth in our world" is to make an assumed connection between the wealth of some and the lack of others. There may be a connection, but assessing this requires an empirical analysis of the economies involved. But even if there is a small causal connection, this does not explain the reasons for lack in our world. It also commits what many economists call the "fixed pie fallacy."

The fixed pie fallacy is the assumption that the economy is a certain size and that the portions are distributed in such a way that a larger slice for you means a smaller slice for me. If the economy were like this, we could have cause for concern over inequality. But consider this: was the pie in 1870 as big as in 2020? Nobody would claim it's the same size pie. It's clearly a larger pie.

63. What is there to do about concentration of wealth, such as in large corporations?

Concerns about concentrated wealth in large corporations generally have two motivations: concern for the poor, or accusations of unfairness and exploitation (see question 51). The problem isn't that corporations exist, but the way state power corrupts them by creating special legal privileges that shield them from market accountability. This includes special grants of immunity for torts, government subsidies, regulatory capture, intellectual property monopolies, and central bank monetary policies. Wealth concentration isn't a problem in itself when earned through voluntary exchange, but these state distortions often result in artificial and unearned concentrations of wealth.

In contrast, a genuinely free market—stripped of these state-backed distortions—would foster a radically different economic landscape. Without state favoritism, firms would rise or fall based on their ability to serve consumers, innovate, and operate efficiently. Competition would remain dynamic and open, lowering barriers to entry and preventing the artificial entrenchment of wealth and power. Libertarians rightly oppose crony capitalism, which is essentially socialism for the rich, but this does not require opposing the natural accumulation of wealth that results from voluntary, mutually beneficial exchange.

Libertarians and Christians should reject equality of outcome as unnatural and contrary to God's design for human society. As long as wealth is gained without coercion or fraud, it is not an evil to be corrected, but a fruit of service in a free and moral society.

64. How could a free market respond to misconduct and economic crises?

Economic crises and corporate misconduct are often blamed on deregulation, but the real culprits are most frequently government-induced distortions. Take the 2008 financial crisis: while regulations like Glass-Steagall were repealed, the root causes were the Federal Reserve's artificially low interest rates and government guarantees through agencies such as the FDIC and Fannie Mae. These interventions distorted incentives, created moral hazard, and fueled unsustainable borrowing, leverage, and malinvestment—setting the stage for collapse.

Even before they were repealed, regulations such as those separating consumer banking from speculative finance acted less like cures and more like weak pharmaceuticals, temporarily managing symptoms of a deeper illness. The real disease was the Federal Reserve's cheap credit and moral hazard, which remained active and continued to slowly spread through the system. When those regulatory "drugs" were withdrawn, the disease quickly ramped up. Deregulation didn't cause the crisis; it removed the containment, allowing the damage from longstanding distortions to erupt. This nuance is often lost in mainstream narratives.

Unlike today's system, free markets do not rely on bailouts or manipulated credit. They depend on transparency, voluntary risk, and the discipline of profits and losses. Firms are held accountable by consumers and investors, not shielded by central banks or political favoritism. Without government interventions distorting signals and creating moral hazard, economic downturns would be less frequent and severe.

65. Aren't markets inherently unstable and detrimental to human flourishing?

We need to point out what the mainstream media means by markets and what we mean by markets. If you've listened to the financial talking heads on cable television news shows, you might believe markets are a reference to Wall Street, or the Stock Market. But "the market" for libertarians, are all instances of human beings making voluntary exchanges for mutually beneficial ends. This includes the Stock Market, but also includes you and me and the exchanges we make every day.

So the market is actually quite stable. Though there will always be a natural ebb and flow in the market, the real culprit of market instability is government intervention either through economic regulation or monetary policy. For example, since the establishment of the Federal Reserve Bank, the boom and bust cycle of the economy has become a normal feature. Ironically, when the economy is in the bust phase, capitalism and "free markets" are blamed, but during the boom phase, extolling the virtues of a market economy are rare. In fact, most people incorrectly believe America's current economic structure is the best example of "free market capitalism" the world has ever seen. It's really not. Investopedia correctly identifies America's economic system as a mixed economy; mixed between capitalism and socialism. Immediately blaming "the market" (or capitalism) for the problems in our economy is at best ignoring the socialist elements and at worst, a false cause fallacy. What libertarians and Austrian economists find upon closer analysis of these problems is that it's the socialist elements of the economy that are to blame for "market instability."

Intervention in the market itself is a hindrance to human flourishing. Human flourishing requires that we allow individuals to participate freely in an economy. When markets are free from interference, humans flourish.

66. This sounds great, but when we have global capitalism, don't we still need governments to regulate trade imbalances and protect the national economy through tariffs and price controls?

The word *regulate* in its original, literal sense, means to "make regular" by the imposition of relevant standards. Markets are self-regulating, and they adjust to changing conditions far more elegantly than governments do. This self-regulation is not due to altruism or consistently benevolent sentiments on the part of entrepreneurs. It is enforced by the profit motive. Abusing customers is bad for business in a free market with healthy competition and functioning courts. Of course, most problems in business are not related to wrongdoing. They are related to the efficiency of firms and both their use of technology and their internal administrative processes. Where one firm devises more efficient methods and processes, it will be able to out-compete other firms whose production is carried out in a less efficient fashion. Inefficient firms should not be protected by politicians, because there is an opportunity cost when capital is bound up in those inefficient enterprises.

Many calls for government intervention in international trade are based on superficial and erroneous beliefs about trade. Because of these, policymakers may intervene to address problems that are not even real problems.

In 2005, German economist Thorsten Polleit reacted to American public policy discussions at that time about trade deficits by arguing that the United States' trade deficit was "merely a reflection of the competitive advantage that the United States has been enjoying over the past decades.... [T]he current deficit in the United States may very well be a result of its adherence to a more efficient economic model.... In today's world of flexible exchange rates, the United States' competitive edge is reflected by a capital surplus, i.e., a trade deficit."

Additional Resources

America's Great Depression by Murray Rothbard (Mises Institute, 2000).

Economics in Christian Perspective by Victor Claar & Robin Klay (IVP Academic, 2015).

Egalitarianism as a Revolt Against Nature by Murray Rothbard (Mises Institute, 2000).

The Great Leveler by Walter Scheidel (Princeton University Press, 2017).

Money, Greed, & God by Jay Richards (HarperOne, 2019).

"The Trade Deficit: An Austrian Perspective" by Thorsten Polleit (2005, 2018), quoting Ludwig von Mises. https://mises.org/mises-daily/trade-deficit-austrian-perspective/.

8

Libertarianism and Christian Ethics

"God alone is Lord of the conscience, and hath left it free from the doctrines and commandments of men which are in anything contrary to his Word, or beside it, in matters of faith or worship. So that to believe such doctrines, or to obey such commands out of conscience, is to betray true liberty of conscience; and the requiring of an implicit faith, and an absolute and blind obedience, is to destroy liberty of conscience, and reason also."

—*Westminster Confession of Faith, Chapter XX.II - On Christian Liberty*

67. Should Christians support gun ownership?

The ownership of weapons is a particular kind of property right that is also derived from the right to self-defense. The right of self-defense flows from the biblical command to protect innocent life. Scripture affirms that life is a sacred gift from God, and that to stand by while violence destroys it is itself a moral failure. Proverbs 24:11 urges us to "rescue those being taken away to death," and Exodus 22:2 allows for defense of one's household from violent intrusion. The consistent moral principle is that force may be used to stop aggression—not to take vengeance or assert dominance, but to preserve life made in God's image.

Christians abhor aggression, but recognize that firearms are tools which, when justly used, can help believers prevent or stop aggression. The modern push for sweeping gun control, while allegedly motivated by compassion, misunderstands both morality and economics. Criminals ignore gun laws, while peaceful citizens bear the cost of compliance—not only the cost imposed by the state, but the cost imposed by crimes that might otherwise be mitigated even by merely bearing a holstered side arm. Additionally, every prohibition must ultimately be enforced by armed agents of the state—meaning that gun control depends on violence to suppress non-violent ownership. Such measures betray the alleged compassion for peaceful people that gun control proponents claim to advocate for.

History shows that gun confiscation has often paved the way for tyranny. The British disarmed the Irish to maintain control, the U.S. government disarmed Africans and Native peoples to subdue them, and regimes like the Soviet Union, Communist China, and the Khmer Rouge confiscated weapons to secure total power. Each instance left populations defenseless against State violence. In contrast, a society that respects the right to self-defense discourages both personal and political aggression. Christians who value peace must also value liberty, recognizing that a well-armed and virtuous people are among the strongest deterrents to tyranny and the surest guardians of human dignity.

68. Does that mean there should be no restrictions on who can own guns or what kinds of guns can be owned?

The right to self-defense belongs to every moral agent created in God's image. That right does not vanish because some misuse it; rather, justice demands that only those who violate others' rights lose liberty through due process. A violent offender serving a sentence, or someone who is threatening or committing aggression, may be justly restrained. But outside those narrow circumstances, moral law grants no authority to preemptively disarm peaceful people.

The right to self-defense and property ownership includes the freedom to possess the means necessary for that defense. On principle, no firearm or "weapon of war" is unlawful or immoral for an individual to *own*. The objections to this view stem from misconceptions about legitimate use of violence, or from ignorance of the functionality of different weapons. The term "assault weapon," for example, is a meaningless propaganda phrase (viz "assault") designed to blur distinctions between civilian and military firearms. An AR-15 is simply a popular semi-automatic rifle—mechanically identical in function to countless hunting and sporting arms owned by millions of peaceful citizens. Any so-called "assault weapons ban" would inevitably amount to the mass confiscation of ordinary semi-automatic firearms. This is because laws have to define a thing by what it does, not what it looks like, thereby criminalizing responsible ownership without reducing crime.

The truth is even automatic weapons bans accomplish little because state-sponsored weapons sales, black markets, and illegal modifications make them easy to bypass. In truth, there is little evidence that gun control measures reduce overall violent crime rates in the states and countries that pass them. True public safety arises not from coercive disarmament, but from a society where individuals retain the moral and practical means to defend themselves and others from aggression.

69. Wouldn't I have to endorse prostitution if I'm a libertarian?

No. Just because a behavior is legal doesn't make it moral or something anyone should condone. For those who might balk at the idea of legal prostitution, consider how we draw the distinction on abortion. It's easy for us to see how something can be legal and not moral. (Obviously this becomes disanalogous when we understand why abortion should not be legal either; see Chapter 11.)

Libertarianism draws a much sharper line between legality and morality—and not because we seek a more licentious society, as some have claimed. Many Christians believe the role of government is to legislate morality—that is, to prescribe moral rules for society over and above rights violations. Romans 13:4 is often used to hit home the idea that the role of government is to promote what is morally good and punish that which is morally wrong. Christian libertarians would certainly agree that all rights violations are morally wrong, but that's where we stop. Why?

Those behaviors that are morally wrong but are not rights violations in themselves, like prostitution, drug addiction, or suicide, are indicative of social ills or health problems that can be addressed by the free market (and the gospel). Prostitution, which is often connected to human trafficking (which is a rights violation), usually occurs when women are in desperate situations. And often when they seek to escape prostitution, they wind up punished and exploited by the criminal justice system.

Alternatively, women who choose prostitution voluntarily cannot seek justice for rape, often because the authorities believe they deserved to be raped. Is that justice? We don't think so. So while Christian libertarians wouldn't endorse prostitution, we do believe that legalizing it will help women who want out to escape it, and women who want to stay in to at least get justice when rights violations occur.

70. If addictive/harmful drugs are legalized, doesn't that mean more people will use them?

It's true that people will use drugs if they're legal, but it's also true that drugs are used while they're illegal. Libertarianism doesn't deny that human beings are plagued with vices, but it does deny that vices (non-aggressive immorality) rise to the level of criminal activity.

This, of course, doesn't answer the question of how society should handle vices like drug addiction. But just because libertarians don't want the government to handle drug addiction doesn't mean we don't want anything done about it at all. Quite the contrary. Instead, non-aggressive problems require non-aggressive solutions which are provided for by the market.

There is a necessary distinction between government and other societal spheres. Often the objection to decriminalization stems from a moral question, not a legal one. If the goal is to reduce the use of drugs and our legal system doesn't consider drug use a crime, then drug addicts are free to seek market services to help them overcome their addiction.

Criminalizing drug use activity makes it more difficult for drug addicted users to get help. Criminalization doesn't prevent use. Studying it (rather than merely accosting the immorality of it), we find that decriminalization doesn't encourage more use; it encourages addiction recovery. Isn't that what we want in our society?

As Christians, we're called to respond to the world with grace and compassion (Zech 7:9–10, 2 Cor 1:3–4, Gal 6:2, Eph 4:32, Col 3:12). Since criminalization of drug use only compounds the problem and doesn't achieve the ultimate goal, it stands to reason that the Christian response is through means that are proven to achieve the original intent of criminalization—the reduction of drug use in society—and that means decriminalization and promotion of market services for recovery.

71. What does a libertarian Christian suggest to keep greed in check in a truly free market?

Libertarianism is sometimes perceived to advocate for allowing people to do anything they want, regardless of the consequences. In most people's minds, this means letting people with a lot of money and power do things that disadvantage or oppress those who are not in those same positions.

What advocates of state-regulated markets claim is that government intervention is needed to keep greedy capitalists in check. That is, without some government interventions, the top 1 percent of earners would run roughshod over the 99 percent. What we find, however, is that the government regulatory agencies actually favor and protect the elite few in their regulatory measures. In other words, the regulations intended to keep greed in check actually enable it for those who cozy up to lawmakers and bureaucrats.

We're often left with the impression that a lack of government regulations means a lack of any regulation in the market. But this isn't so. The consumer acts to regulate the market by their normal economizing. When a consumer purchases a good or service, they send signals to producers that the good or service is a market need. When consumers see unethical business practice and stop purchasing from a particular producer, they are sending a signal that they won't tolerate said practice.

If anything, libertarians are keenly aware of the dangers of economic elitists, but we also understand how these elites exploit regulatory agencies for their own gain. What we see is that the most efficient regulator of the market is the consumer, and an unregulated market really does level the playing field.

72. How do libertarian Christians account for gay rights or women's rights?

Libertarians don't demarcate rights based on group identity; there are only human rights. And as human beings, we all have the same rights. One reason group identity politics have become a problem is because of systemic rights violations related to particular groups of people. Women have had their rights systematically violated throughout history. That said, not all "rights" advocated for by these groups are indeed rights. When we treat rights this way, groups are set against each other. This is essentially how we get class warfare, except now it might be more accurate to call it social or identitarian warfare.

By reaffirming that all human beings have equal rights by virtue of their humanity, we resolve the conflict between these groups. Those groups who have been oppressed should have their human rights recognized. Those groups who claim that which are not rights can be peacefully corrected. The libertarian concept of human rights is the equalling of the playing field for all.

73. Should the government play a protective role with marriage licenses?

While governments have long recorded marriages for legal purposes, in the United States marriage licenses were also used as a tool to enforce racist anti-miscegenation laws which allowed the state to deny legal recognition to interracial couples. Thus, the license functioned not as a record or sacred seal but as an instrument of state control, and needs not be defended to protect marriage in any meaningful sense.

A Christian marriage is a lifelong covenant between a man, a woman, and God. A marriage *license* is a temporal contract between you, your spouse, and the state.

The government has no legitimate authority to grant permission to voluntary adult relationships, despite their having asserted themselves to the contrary. The practical matters of marriage can be handled through contract law, essentially a kind of prenuptial agreement. Third party dispute agencies or the local magistrates can adjudicate these contracts should the need arise. But state-issued licensing is not a bastion of freedom; it's a tool of oppression. In fact, clergy who cooperate with marriage licensing turn out to be unpaid agents of the state, enforcing a rule that is extra-biblical.

Even if some condone homosexual marriage, true equality means not having to ask the government permission to exercise your rights. Regardless of where you stand on gay marriage, the most optimal option is to abolish the marriage license altogether. We don't need the government's permission to enter into a covenant with God, and God will sort in his eyes who is married and who is not.

74. If society becomes more libertarian, won't this mean a cultural collapse into hedonism?

There will always be those who attempt to demoralize society. That's a fact of life, and it exists because we live in a fallen, sinful world. Where immorality exists as vices and not violations of the non-aggression principle, society still has the opportunity to use the market to persuade and provide social services to reduce the incidence of immoral cultural vices.

There is also ample evidence that the benefits of the economic policies that libertarians favor create societies in which individuals seek to serve one another through the market, thereby enriching one another and creating greater prosperity for all. More open and economically liberal societies create abundance both materially and spiritually.

This isn't to say that society will be cured of its cultural ills. That won't happen until Christ returns. But the free market and libertarian legal order gives us the greatest opportunity to deal peacefully, creatively, and compassionately with these issues.

75. Do libertarians support the right to kill oneself?

The right to kill oneself is rooted in self-ownership and the right to do with our bodies what we want. This is not to say that we (libertarian Christians) see suicide as moral, desirable, or a social good. As Christians, we affirm that killing oneself is sinful (Exod 20:13). Again, it's helpful to look beyond the act to the social ills contributing to one's desire for suicide. By treating suicide as a health issue to be solved by the free market, solutions present themselves that may actually dissuade an individual from suicide and help them get onto a path of flourishing in life. Isn't that what we want? By contrast, punishing a person for attempting suicide only reinforces in their mind the utter despair and hopelessness in which they suffer. In fact, our criminal justice system magnifies this despair and hopelessness.

Another issue related to this is voluntary doctor-assisted suicide. Again, we would set aside the moral conundrum—because it is a conundrum (the movie *Me Before You* offers a sense of the moral conundrum). Sometimes it's a little too easy for Christians to offer up platitudes of God's plan and purpose. Tell that to a person who's suffered their whole life and struggled with the idea that God's plan was to bring them into the world to torture them. Though we would disagree with this caricature, it's definitely the wrong way to encourage a person in the depths of despair.

What libertarianism offers in this case is a free market with creative and innovative options to help those struggling to see the value of life, whether that despair be health related, job related, relationship related, or spiritually related. By allowing suicide to be legal, the idea is destigmatized in such a way that it's safe to talk about and safe to get help for. And, God forbid, should it happen, we can grieve it for what it should be grieved as—a tragedy, not a crime.

76. How can a libertarian expect a free society without a safety net to provide for the poor?

Christians have a personal obligation to look out for the poor, either through direct care or supporting those who provide direct care. In addition to this, libertarian Christians ask a broader question: how can we help those who are poor get to the point they are no longer poor or require others for support? This adds an important dimension to the "charity versus welfare" debate.

Many Christians against the welfare state claim that the Church and charitable individuals are charged with caring for the poor. Christians in favor of the welfare state claim that churches and charitable organizations cannot possibly meet the needs of all who are poor. Libertarian Christians point out that this is a false choice and that a third option is not only important but has proven to be effective: free markets with stable property rights for all individuals, regardless of social status.

In the end, libertarian Christians want to see a society where the need for charity and safety nets is nearly nonexistent because of the economic gains made by all in society. Only a free society with stable property rights can achieve this end.

77. How can a Christian fulfill Jesus' command to care for the poor in a free society?

When Jesus said in Matthew 26:11, "For you always have the poor with you," he was describing the kind of people his followers would be: ones who attracted the poor because of their love and care for them. Yet while Christians are to signal to the world that we are the community who loves and takes care of the poor, the signaling itself is not the purpose. The real purpose is to meet the needs of the poor.

We must resist the idea that the poorest are the only people who need our attention. Because there are varying levels of need and various types of poverty, we must be on the lookout for people we can help who are in need at whatever level. For example, the father who just got fired because of an addiction might not qualify in our minds as "very poor," but he and his family are in need.

Through personal responsibility, Christians can and should participate in or fund endeavors committed to the well-being of those on the margins. This well-being should not merely be about the charity of feeding empty stomachs or sheltering the homeless, but about the empowerment of human beings with untapped talents, skills, and something to offer their fellow human beings.

Care for the poor is often misunderstood as charity for those who lack, but a much broader vision of care is needed if we are to pursue human flourishing. We must seek to empower those on the margins because it is physically and spiritually nurturing to them.

Additional Resources

The Abolition of Man by C.S. Lewis (Oxford University Press, 1943).

For the Least of These: A Biblical Answer to Poverty, eds. Anne Bradley and Arthur Lindsley (Zondervan, 2015).

"Want to Win the War on Drugs? Portugal Might Have the Answer" by Naina Bajekal. *Time*, August 2018. https://time.com/5336871/portugal-drug-use-decriminalization/.

The War on Drugs is a War on Freedom by Laurence Vance (Vance Publications, 2012).

When Helping Hurts by Steve Corbett and Brian Fikkert (Moody Publishers, 2014).

9

Public Goods and Services

"Socialism, like the ancient ideas from which it springs, confuses the distinction between government and society. As a result of this, every time we object to a thing being done by government, the socialists conclude that we object to its being done at all."

—Frederic Bastiat

78. Without the state, who will build the roads?

While this question may at first seem like a trump card against the idea of privatization in general, it is readily answerable from both a theoretical and historical point of view. Simply put, roads would be produced both by companies and individuals. Their operations would be funded by tolls (for highways), subscription fees (for local roads), and neighborhood dues (for streets like those in front of your house). Throughout history, roads have been built privately and even continue to be built this way today. Most roads are not actually produced by the state but by private companies as contractors. The libertarian argument is to suggest that this should be expanded even further and not have the state involved in the first place.

79. Wouldn't it be inefficient for all roads to be tolled?

Even if all roads were privatized, not all roads would be toll roads. Your neighborhood probably would rather not operate that kind of system even if it were a gated community. Businesses desire people to frequent their establishments and therefore may invest in the road system around them in order to make it more appealing to go there. But ultimately, it is up to entrepreneurs to experiment and find ways to serve their road-going customers most effectively.

We could turn this question and ask if government-run road operations are efficient, safe, and cost-effective? Our experience in the United States, at least, suggests that such qualities are near non-existent on government roads. Think about it: if any business had to answer for nearly 40,000 people per year dying while using their goods or services, they'd probably be out of business in two seconds flat. Yet that is the reality of government roads. It's high time to get rid of road socialism.

80. Who will educate our children? Isn't public education a cornerstone of the American Experiment?

It was Thomas Jefferson who advocated for public education as a necessity to maintain a free society. But what Jefferson meant, and the way it's practiced today, are two wildly different things. Public education advocates appeal to the Massachusetts model.

Legal compulsory child education in America goes back to 1642. Ironically, the non-libertarian, non-Christian practice of religious establishmentarianism is its root. It yields one of the most authoritarian-progressive states today. The Massachusetts model infringes on liberty by molding citizens to state patterns, a form of idolatry substituting government for God. Conversely, Jefferson's 1778 merit-based concept aligns with God's impartial gifting of talents, promoting a "natural aristocracy" to safeguard liberties without state coercion, echoing Paul's call to use one's freedom wisely.

Libertarian-friendly elements appear in decentralized, choice-driven education, like Rhode Island's resistance to centralization. Jefferson's hybrid model funded the basics while encouraging privately-funded extensions for promising students. Christian libertarianism views education as a distinct sphere with God-given norms, polycentrically ordered and free from state control, rejecting coercive regulations. The free market complements this. It emphasizes entrepreneurial innovation of diverse methods via subjective value and market signals. This fosters spontaneous order in not only the basics, but adapts to the mutual needs of both students and the evolving market.

State-centralized public education relies on coercive taxation while breeding wealth inequality. It enables administrative bloat with dismal outcomes for students. Jefferson's ideal can be promoted by libertarians while also pursuing more suitable solutions than tax-payer funding.

81. Who will protect children from child abuse, or rescue abused children?

The remedy offered to us today are Child Protective Services departments provided for by the state. These services rely on concerned citizens calling in to report suspected abuse. The problem with these services, as they exist, is that they're monopolized through the state. This has resulted in rampant abuse within CPS departments and foster care systems. One need only search Google to find endless reports of CPS failures, corruption of power, and foster abuse to see there's a problem.

This is no solution to child abuse! Children deserve better, and free market services could vastly improve responses to child abuse. And in fact, there are already some market choices available including Safe Families and Bethany Christian Services. These organizations provide services to troubled families and families in crisis. And being left to the free market and the natural regulation of the consumer, abuse within these protective services would be mitigated.

82. Who will catch the criminals?

It can be hard for some people to imagine anyone other than the government being responsible for protecting us from criminals. "Crime" is something defined in modern society by the laws that state institutions have crafted, and it seems natural that state institutions would enforce these laws. In a libertarian society, there would be far fewer crimes and far fewer criminals by definition. Legal writers use two Latin phrases to distinguish between categories of crimes: criminal acts that are evil in themselves (*malum in se*) and acts that are crimes purely because the state has chosen to legally prohibit them (*malum prohibitum*). Libertarians generally reject the proposition that *malum prohibitum* crimes should be crimes at all.

That still leaves *malum in se* crimes to deal with. Generally speaking, everyone wishes to avoid being murdered, being the victim of theft, and so on. There is a strong demand in society for security services. The principal argument for public police forces is based on the idea that public safety is a public good that is not efficiently produced by markets.

Historically, public police forces have been created to carry out a number of different functions: keeping public order, controlling crime, performing various public safety services, and suppressing and controlling of undesirables. Government police forces win support within government because they reliably enforce the will of the sovereign, and they win business support because they socialize some of the cost of private security. Some of the origins of police in America are undeniably sinister. From the colonial period until the Civil War, slavers expended substantial resources in catching runaway slaves. The creation of the earliest government-funded police forces in Southern and mid-Atlantic American colonies circa the

1700s, largely revolved around socializing these costs of maintaining slave patrols.

Libertarians have a lot of different ideas about how security services would be provided in a libertarian society. One belief is shared by almost all libertarians: private companies should be doing a lot more, and government police would be doing a lot less.

83. Who will regulate air traffic or prevent future terrorist attacks?

Having government agencies like the Federal Aviation Administration (FAA) in charge of airplane safety and maintenance and the Transportation Security Administration (TSA) in charge of security at airports might make some people feel safer. Libertarians believe that private firms would be more successful than government bureaucracies at stopping dangerous cargo—and more efficient, too. It is not clear that the TSA is very good at what it does. Penetration testing of TSA security measures has shown that these measures are highly porous. While it is possible that these measures have deterred some bad acts, there is clearly much room for improvement in airport security. Many passengers pay extra for pre-screening credentials, suggesting that there is demand for more efficient, less burdensome security screening measures.

Crashing planes into each other is just as horrifying a prospect as losing them in a terrorist attack. Coordination of aircraft across space and time is essential for avoiding such a calamity. But there is no reason that this coordination must be done by the state. In 1996 in Canada, air traffic control was privatized and placed in the hands of profit-making enterprises instead of a public bureaucracy. Canada's private system is now recognized as one of the best in the world by industry watchdogs, and a model for other nations to imitate.

It is also important to remember that passengers are not the only people with a stake in safe air travel. Airplanes are expensive machines. Losing an airplane is expensive and disruptive to an airline, and the reputational costs of a deadly disaster can be even more damaging. Even if the FAA and TSA ceased operation tomorrow, airlines, their insurers, and their customers would all have a strong interest in making air travel safe. There are already airports operating today with private security screening, but they must use TSA protocols and TSA-approved equipment. Instead of a government bureaucracy providing a one-size-fits-all solution, libertarians promote competition in security services.

84. Some libertarians say public safety should be handled by insurance companies. What about people who aren't policyholders?

Many libertarians believe that insurance companies should play an even more important part in providing for security and dispute resolution services than they do today. But what about the uninsured? The good news is that insured and uninsured people have many interests in common. For example, my insurance company has a strong interest in fires on neighboring properties being extinguished quickly. If fires are allowed to spread, insurance companies will receive more claims and pay out more money. If fires are quickly extinguished, insurance companies will not receive these claims and will enjoy higher profits.

Even today, in a world where fire departments are heavily funded with tax dollars, insurance companies voluntarily expend many millions of dollars both directly and through grant-making foundations (including the Allstate Foundation, the State Farm Insurance Grant Program, and the Fireman's Fund Heritage in Action Program), to support fire departments of all sizes across the United States. While companies typically distribute grant money to areas where they market insurance products, most residents in the areas benefiting from these grants are not actually customers of the individual company offering the grant.

Libertarian writer Gil Guillory is one of the leading scholars on the feasibility of a subscription-based patrol and restitution service. In his work, he calculated that he would only need to sign up a tiny fraction of the residents in a subdivision to profitably patrol the entire area, reducing the incidence of crime for policyholders and non-policyholders alike.

Privatization of public safety functions does not disadvantage those who cannot pay or choose not to pay for these services. Many people would benefit from the free functioning of a private market for public safety services without paying any fee at all.

85. How would parks exist if not for the state?

It might initially seem like the state is necessary to protect certain kinds of natural resources, but how can we expect a government that mismanages practically everything to maintain a complex ecosystem? We can observe from the history of state-managed ecology projects that the government is far better at destroying than preserving. Besides, private parks already exist in various forms. From small private campsites to massive amusement parks (hey, they call them parks for a reason!), we can see that private ownership of land and the freedom to use it in entrepreneurial ways can surely allow for the development of the equivalent of any "government" park. Some parks, like Bryant Park in New York City, will be open to the public and run by private foundations, funded by donations from individuals and businesses. Some will be attached to businesses to encourage people to become customers of that business and to serve the community. Some will have subscription services or entry fees like a country club. The state is simply not necessary to ensure that parks stay solvent and operational.

86. What about people who can't afford to pay for these privatized services?

The beautiful thing about the free market is that competition tends to drive down prices of goods and services—especially those considered essential. State management, in contrast, trends exactly the opposite.

Take roads, for example. We would expect that competition amongst road producers would ultimately drive prices downward or even have multiple pricing tiers for different sections of the road. Nonetheless, there will likely be many options available for lower income individuals, especially as more competition arises in public transportation (since cities would no longer monopolize those services). We need to keep in mind that the government effectively has a legalized monopoly position on the roads of greatest concern here. Opening up competition eliminates that monopoly and allows more options at lower cost.

Besides driving costs down, free markets also drive prosperity through production. With greater prosperity, widespread poverty inevitably decreases in turn. Availability of services becomes less and less of an issue. Greater prosperity will also lead to greater charity activity. We already see private charity stepping up to fill the voids because of government mismanagement. There may always be those less fortunate who need help, but the state is not the best solution.

87. But surely libraries should be handled by the government, right?

Libraries were initially created because books were scarce and expensive. A wonderful aspect of our modern era is that books are far more plentiful and inexpensive than in the past. The advent of the internet age has changed the nature of the modern library, and the availability of information is greater than ever before in the history of the world.

Yes, libraries are wonderful, but they do not need to be funded by forced taxation. Of course, communities can still come together and create lending libraries that will look just like what occurs today. Perhaps they will have subscription fees, perhaps not, but we can be certain that books are not going away. In fact, people are doing this in a decentralized fashion right now through the "Little Free Library" movement. So don't worry; libertarians love books and love the dissemination of knowledge. We believe free people are able to organize efforts to spread knowledge in a multitude of effective ways, and do so better than the state, voluntarily.

Additional Resources

Chaos Theory by Robert P. Murphy (Mises Institute, 2018).

Failure: the Federal Miseducation of America's Children by Vicki E. Alger (Independent Institute, 2016).

For a New Liberty: The Libertarian Manifesto by Murray N. Rothbard (Mises Institute, 2020).

Land Use without Zoning by Bernard H. Siegan (Mercatus, 2020).

Order Without Law: How Neighbors Settle Disputes by Robert Ellickson (Harvard University Press, 1994).

The Privatization of Roads and Highways by Walter Block (Mises Institute, 2009).

To Serve and Protect: Privatization and Community in Criminal Justice by Bruce L. Benson (Independent Institute, 1998).

10

Democracy, Voting, War, and Patriotism

"The State is the great fictitious entity by which everyone expects to live at the expense of everyone else."

—*Frederic Bastiat*

"Political democracy is a method for deciding (directly or indirectly) when, how, and in what ways a government will threaten people with violence."

—*Jason Brennan*

88. Should Christians have a favorable view of democratic government?

Christians believe that God cares deeply about how we treat one another. For that reason, the way governments act, and the ways we allow ourselves to be governed, carry real moral weight. Modern political discourse often assumes as a given that democratic government is good. Before we can talk about democracy being good or bad, though, we should first identify what democracy is. The word *democracy* is often used as a synonym for majority rule. In this sense, there is no good reason for Christians or libertarians to be particularly democratic, especially when it comes to questions of right or wrong. A majority of people may indeed hold to a view that is abhorrent and advocates the violation of rights.

The word *democracy* comes from the Greek language and denotes, literally, rule by the people. It has often been used to describe something that is the opposite of autocratic authoritarianism, and implies a social structure where decision-making authority is more decentralized. Ludwig von Mises described this sort of democracy as referring to "the right of self-determination both of individuals and of nations." However, Mises also warned that "Majorities are no less exposed to error and frustration than kings and dictators."

While we are rightfully wary of appeals to simple majoritarianism, libertarian Christians view decentralized authority favorably. This is consistent with the injunction of Jesus to not behave like the rulers of this world (Matt 20:25), and instead practice servant leadership like the early church did in the book of Acts.

89. How should a Christian approach the idea of political participation?

Because our allegiance is to Christ and his Kingdom, the struggle of Christians in every age has been to live faithfully and proclaim the gospel while navigating worldly powers (Eph 6:12). With a broader understanding of politics (see Questions 1-2), Christians best engage the world when we reflect the image of God to the world as exemplified by Christ himself.

Humans were created to bear the image of God and reflect God throughout creation. Israel was chosen to be a people ruled directly by God in contrast to surrounding kingdoms and cultures. When it failed in this vocation, God raised up prophets to speak truth to those in power and to call the nation to repentance. During exile, God called a faithful remnant whose role was to maintain a distinct identity as God's people.

The Kingdom of God is the culmination of this theme, establishing a community who uses the message of the gospel to stand in contrast to the kingdoms of this world. Instead of power and control, we pursue love and service. We choose persuasion over coercion. We refuse to be a mouthpiece for state power, and instead use a prophetic voice to speak against the powers of domination and violence.

In this way, libertarianism and Christianity share an ethos, resisting injustice by declaring what is morally right. This carries on the important tradition of living an ethic from an "upside down" Kingdom. We must resist having our imaginations shaped by political discourse, but instead be "transformed by the renewing of the mind, so that you may discern what is the will of God—what is good and acceptable and perfect" (Rom 12:2). This will help us remain a light in a world of darkness (see Question 224).

90. Should Christians seek positions in government office because having believers in office will have better outcomes for Christians and for society?

It seems like a good thing for a police officer to be a Christian police officer, or for a politician to be a Christian politician. But as a police officer, a person is obliged to enforce the laws, including laws that may be unjust. That enforcement occurs by the credible threat and use of physical violence, sometimes deadly violence. Peter was warned by Jesus of the dangers of living by the sword (Matt 26:52), and the early church took that to mean that faithful followers of Jesus should not be soldiers or to participate in retaliatory violence.

Being a faithful politician or bureaucrat is tricky, because all too often a politician can only make progress by trading favors, by voting for things that are wrong or destructive in order to build support for their own proposals. There are, however, examples in the Bible of faithful people who came into positions of high influence within government. Trapped by his jealous brothers and sold into slavery, then falsely accused by Potiphar's wife and imprisoned, Joseph's divinely granted discernment was apparent to Pharaoh.

At thirty years old, Joseph came to be the second most powerful person in the Egyptian empire, and as Pharaoh's crisis manager obtained a great amount of money, livestock, and land for Pharaoh while also preserving his own father Jacob's whole family.

Daniel was taken as a slave and probably made a eunuch by Babylonian captors (2 Kgs 20:18, Isa 39:7, Dan 1:3), but his God-given discernment soon came to the attention of the king. Daniel came to serve as the ruler of the province of Babylon and as chief advisor to Nebuchadnezzar and his successors, and he held similar authority in the Medo-Persian empire that conquered Babylon. Daniel's career in government spanned the reigns of three Babylonian kings and the succeeding Persian administration.

Christians should be wary of undertaking any course of conduct that could involve sinful acts. It is sin to do evil so that good may come (Rom. 3:8). Providing godly counsel to a ruler is permissible and even praiseworthy. Seeking and using power to dominate others, engage in vengeance, or commit injustice is wrong.

91. How should Christians view the practice of voting?

Voting is sometimes regarded as a civil sacrament in American culture. Many activists across the political spectrum, opposed in nearly every policy area, will nonetheless agree to the secular "article of faith" that voting is inherently good, and that everyone should vote no matter what!

Christians should be wary of the quasi-sacred treatment received by ballots and elections in popular culture. In a way, politics is like two neighbors wrestling in the front yard over a loaded gun. The state is a violent enterprise (see Question 34), and voting is designed to allow a polity to decide which candidate to entrust control of that violent organization.

Some libertarians claim that casting a ballot somehow signals consent to the government under which the election is taking place. The abolitionist Lysander Spooner famously argued that under a government you never chose and can't escape, voting is mainly an act of self-defense, not a genuine sign that you consent to be ruled.

It may be the case that a Christian prayerfully concludes that one candidate is more dangerous than the other to justice and peace. We often hear about voting for the lesser of two evils. The basic problem with that is that it leaves the voter supporting some kind of evil in the end. If a vote might injure a Christian's conscience or public witness as a believer it is best for the believer to abstain from attempting to influence the outcome of that election through voting. Eternal things are simply more important than transient concerns of a particular time in history.

92. Don't governments need to follow the will of the people?

The political philosophy of democracy supposes that governments ought to be directed by the people.

Under normal circumstances, most people intuitively accept the idea that a property owner is the one who decides how to use a particular asset. For the Christian, this should be even more obvious, because divinely inspired scripture clearly commands us to observe property rights by abstaining from stealing (Exod 20:15, 1 Cor 6:10), negligent or malicious damaging of property (Exod 21:33–34, 22:5–6), and compensation for its use (Exod 22:14–15).

The theory of democracy supposes that property rights may be abridged when a great many people vote to do so. That is in contrast with the way that God ordered the nation of Israel, a covenant community formed by consent (Exod 24:3), and based on a system of familial and individual property rights. It is wrong for a king to exempt himself from his own laws (Deut 17:18–20), and even divinely appointed rulers are accountable under God's immutable standards of justice (2 Sam 12:7–14). If King David was subject to God's law, so too is the population at large, majority or not.

If the will of the people is contrary to the will of God, it is wrong to follow the will of the people. Throughout scripture, we see examples where the will of the people did violate God's commandments: Aaron's fashioning of a golden calf at the people's urging (Exod 32), the demand by Israel's elders to Samuel for a king (1 Sam 8), and Pilate's capitulation to the people when he ordered the crucifixion of Christ (Mark 15:15).

Henry David Thoreau famously wrote, "Any man more right than his neighbor constitutes a majority of one already." Simon Peter said it better when he said, "We must obey God rather than any human authority" (Acts 5:29).

93. Don't countries have the right to self-determination?

Countries have a right to self-determination, the ability to choose their own destiny independent of other countries, inasmuch as the individuals do that make it up.

Self-determination for the individual is, essentially, a slightly different way of stating the non-aggression principle. Individuals have the right to do as they will, assuming that they do not commit aggression in their activities. Likewise, groups of individuals (such as a country) can act together, so long as they don't commit aggression. Remember, an action that is considered sinful, violent, or repugnant for an individual does not suddenly change its status if it is tacitly permitted by a group of people.

It is also valuable to recognize that "countries" do not have thoughts, but their people do. Economists from the Austrian School emphasize something they call "methodological individualism," which is the idea that the economist must analyze social phenomena based on individual actions, not an imagined corporate or social will. Organizations, including governments, may take collective action, but the motives and desires of the people making up those organizations may vary widely. It is also important to recognize this principle when analyzing ethical questions. Individuals have certain rights inherently, and they cannot confer any greater rights whether to another person or to a group of people organized together.

94. Doesn't a country need a common defense?

Individuals have a right to protect themselves from violence, and, thus, groups of people have the right to do so as well. But that doesn't mean every person everywhere needs the backing of a military from their native country.

The United States was never supposed to have a standing army, and plenty of countries do fine without them. In fact, more than twenty countries, such as Andorra and Liechtenstein, currently have no nationalized military apparatus at all. Acting from a position of neutrality often prevents antagonizing relationships from developing in the first place. Recall that Thomas Jefferson said in his first inaugural address, "Peace, commerce, and honest friendship with all nations... entangling alliances with none." Countries would do well to remember that free trade and friendship with others is far preferable to war. Libertarians often say, "When goods and services do not cross country borders, armies eventually will."

95. Can a Christian serve in the military?

Just like any major decision, we should always take into account all of the factors and weigh the benefits and costs. A Christian who joins the military should not only weigh the benefits to joining (to themselves, to the military, and to the nation it serves), but also the personal and wider costs associated.

When considering a moral choice of such importance, most of the considerations are imbalanced. For example, a young person considering joining might look at the skill development, leadership training, mind-body improvements, and educational opportunities afforded them by joining. The trade-offs might only be considered in comparison to what they are giving up: traditional college, private employment, extended time away from loved ones, the possible compromise of one's morals through the obligation to follow orders, traumatic physical and mental injury such as PTSD, and potentially losing one's life.

As disciples of Jesus, Christians are obligated to consider far weightier things in their decisions. Does this path obligate me to kill another human being if I'm commanded to? Does this path build character qualities that run counter to Christian values? Does this choice make it impossible for me to conscientiously object to acts I am commanded to do that go against the love of Christ? Will I be participating in an institution that thrives on loss of life and profits from conflict and war? Does this life choice compromise my duty to "love my neighbor as myself"?

With few exceptions, libertarian Christians believe that serving in the military obligates the Christian to unquestionably obey orders, some of which may command actions that run contrary to the principles of the Kingdom of God. Remember that first-century Roman soldiers who converted to Christianity often left their military positions because they could no longer morally justify what they did. The call to eschew violence then was too strong, and their example should still inform us today.

So what would be the exception? It's tough to say, but perhaps if there were an active and present threat to the well-being of our fellow citizens, it might be acceptable to join the military in order to help stop the aggression. Even in these circumstances, however, Christians can do many other things other than participate in war to protect, serve, and love their neighbors. At the very least, abstaining from promoting and cheering "our side" of a war conflict should be the first step in showing Christian love to one's neighbor.

It should be noted that one of the co-authors of this book, Kerry Baldwin, has served in the U.S. military and fully agrees with the above statement.

96. Shouldn't Christians honor those who sacrifice their lives for their countrymen?

Jesus said to his disciples that "No one has greater love than this, to lay down one's life for one's friends" (John 15:13). Clearly dying on behalf of others, as Christ did for the world, indicates the greatest kind of love one could have for another.

Many American Christians attribute these qualities to those who join a branch of the military. Those individuals who join, it is supposed, believe they are defending the freedoms of their loved ones and of strangers. In short, they are willing to die on behalf of others.

However, simply because a soldier dies while on active duty does not mean they died on behalf of their countrymen. To truly know this, we must understand why the soldier is fighting, not why he thinks he's fighting. Dying in combat for the operations of the United States military has rarely meant sacrificing on behalf of fellow countrymen (though that's how the state markets it), but it always means participating in acts of aggression against others.

We should commend any individual willing to make life-changing decisions that indicate sacrifice. In fact, we should all want to become people who are known for willingness to lay down our life for others (or other sacrificial endeavors less severe). But joining the military as a signal of one's willingness to sacrifice is but one way to indicate a character quality worth celebrating. Not only are there other ways to do this, serving in the military brings with it other conflicts for the Christian.

97. Should Christians say the Pledge of Allegiance?

The question of pledging allegiance isn't about flags or rituals as much as it is about loyalty. Allegiance, by its nature, implies devotion to a ruler or kingdom. In Scripture, that devotion belongs wholly to Christ. To call Jesus "Lord" is to declare that no other authority—nation, ruler, or ideology—commands our ultimate loyalty. Christians may love their homeland, care for its people, and work for its good, but that affection is not the same as allegiance.

The apostle Paul expressed deep concern for his own people, the Jews (Rom 9:2), even as his mission was to the Gentiles (Rom 11:13, Gal 1:15–16, Eph 3:8). His love for his nation did not compete with his allegiance to Christ. Likewise, there's nothing sinful about gratitude for one's country or culture, so long as it never crosses into nationalism—the belief that one's nation stands above others or deserves loyalty beyond what Christ allows.

Still, because allegiance is a public declaration, it carries meaning beyond private intent. Paul's teaching about meat offered to idols (1 Cor 8) reminds us that even if we personally know the idol is nothing, others may see our participation as worship. In the same way, pledging allegiance can signal a kind of worship of the state, even if that's not our heart's intent.

Our citizenship is in heaven (Phil 3:20). Every earthly loyalty must remain subordinate to that truth. For the Christian, allegiance belongs to one King alone.

98. Should Christians be thankful to live in a free country?

Christians have been transformed by Christ, according to 1 Thessalonians 5:18, to "give thanks in all circumstances." That would certainly include where you reside! But thankfulness for your homeland and the good qualities it has does not mean you cannot or should not criticize its culture, behavior, and especially its state apparatus. We can respect the ways in which the United States has maintained liberty while simultaneously saying that the state is at odds with crucial liberty principles. The ways in which the state ever promotes liberty, in fact, are incidental and not fundamental to its being, since the state's existence is predicated on the threat of violence in the first place.

Additional Resources

A Century of War by John V. Denson (Mises Institute, 2017).

A Change of Allegiance by Dean Taylor (Radical Reformation Books, 2008).

Christian Views on Voting: Why Vote at All? By Doug Douma. https://libertarianchristians.com/2021/07/23/voting-conscientious-objection/.

Democracy: The God That Failed by Hans-Hermann Hoppe (Transaction Publishers, 2001).

The Early Christian Attitude to War by Cecil John Cadoux (Headley Brothers, 1919).

Electing Not to Vote: Christian Reflections on Reasons for Not Voting by Ted Lewis (Wipf and Stock, 2008).

The Ethics of Voting by Jason Brennan (Princeton University Press, 2012).

Exiles: The Church in the Shadow of Empire by Preston Sprinkle (David C. Cook, 2024).

Farewell to Mars by Brian Zahnd (David C. Cook, 2014).

It Is Not Lawful for Me to Fight: Early Christian Attitudes toward War, Violence, and the State by Jean-Michel Hornus (Wipf & Stock, 2009).

The Myth of a Christian Nation: How the Quest for Political Power Is Destroying the Church by Gregory Boyd (Zondervan, 2007).

Myth of the Rational Voter: Why Democracies Choose Bad Policies by Bryan Caplan (Princeton University Press, 2011).

The Problem of Political Authority by Michael Huemer (Palgrave Macmillan, 2012).

Swords into Plowshares: A Life in Wartime and a Future of Peace and Prosperity by Ron Paul (Ron Paul Institute for Peace and Prosperity, 2015).

War, Christianity, and the State: Essays on the Follies of Christian Militarism by Laurence Vance (Vance Publications, 2013).

(Mises quotes from Nation, State, and Economy, p. 131 and Omnipotent Government, p. 47.)

11

Social Justice

"Like so much that is done in the quest for cosmic justice, it makes observers feel better about themselves—and provides no incentives for those observers to scrutinize the consequences of their actions on the ostensible beneficiaries. As in other cases, human beings are sacrificed to the tyranny of visions because those sacrificed are not the same as those exhilarated by the vision."

—*Thomas Sowell*

99. Shouldn't human flourishing be the goal of good government?

Human flourishing should be the goal of any human-based institution, both private and public, so long as it is done within its sphere of capacity and ability.

Christians who believe the state should guide or lead us to human flourishing usually have in mind initiatives and programs that force individuals and businesses to behave in certain ways they view as conducive to human flourishing. Yet they fail to recognize that governments are particularly bad at guiding free human beings in ways that yield certain results. When governments try to pick winners and losers through subsidies and special privileges, they almost always fail.

As an institution on the monopoly of violence in society, the state's narrow role should be to enable human flourishing through means that actually achieve human flourishing. That is, if the state's role is to protect private property by enabling free exchange, not only would the economy grow, individuals and communities would flourish not because of the state but because the state was in its proper role in society.

100. Private charity can't cover everyone's needs, so don't we need government?

Most people compare what the government spends on welfare for the poor to the private charity dollars spent on the poor, arriving at the conclusion that private charity organizations could not bear the burden of providing for the poor if the welfare state were simply removed. However, this comparison is unfair for two reasons. First, it does not account for the fact that private charity organizations, on average, have far less bureaucratic overhead than government-run ones. Money spent through private charities is often more effective than government-run welfare programs.

Second, and more importantly, it ignores a third but very prominent anti-poverty measure that doesn't require government at all: free market capitalism. People achieved prosperity in the past 200 years not through welfare programs but through free markets. Oftentimes, governments have regulated the market in such a way that it creates the conditions for higher unemployment, increased prices for goods and services, and other factors that burden the poor.

Charity is only a short-term solution to the direct symptoms of poverty, not its causes. A robust society addresses the root problems to poverty by looking at a variety of issues.

Libertarian Christians believe that because work is essential to our life and our well-being, being recipients of the fruit of other people's labor (whether private or public) can only go so far. What those in poverty want and need is the fruit of their own labor.

101. Didn't Jesus care about the poor? Isn't that really what social justice is all about?

Of course Jesus cared deeply about the poor. When he said, "the poor you will always have with you" (Matt 26:11), it was a character marker of the type of people who were attracted to Jesus and his followers: those who were impoverished. So when we apply this characteristic of Christlikeness broadly to society, it is easy to believe that social justice is all about caring for the poor.

Yet social justice should consider a set of conditions, not a particular set of outcomes. Too often we evaluate the state of justice based on perceived outcomes without assessing the institutions that produce those outcomes. For example, those who lament wealth inequality rarely decry the central banking system which creates vast inequalities of both opportunity and government privilege. Because they are formed by human beings, institutions are also flawed and in regular need of reform. Social justice requires us to think about what is properly "social" as well as what is "just." The poor are far better served when they are treated as legal equals in a society rather than persons to be pitied. Christians should demand equal treatment under the law, freedom of enterprise, secure private property rights, access to adequate defense, expedient justice in courts, and a host of other institutional arrangements under which conditions the poor can flourish along with the rest of society.

102. If the early church in Acts shared all things in common, is this a good model for society?

The early church community in Acts is an example of what can happen when people voluntarily come together for a common purpose and mission. However, this should not make us want to emulate the scenario without first asking ourselves helpful and important questions. What conditions and cultural situations made it possible for them to succeed? Was this done out of necessity, survival, or prudence? Was this a common practice among other sects? How large was the community, and how did that contribute to its success?

When we step back and ask why something "works" in the Bible, we must take into account questions like the ones above. A few key observations should warrant skepticism toward applying this scenario to an entire modern economy: all who belonged chose to belong, and nobody was forced to participate; their community was neither large-scale nor a nation-state; its participants were committed to the same mission; they were not a pluralistic society.

It is natural for humans to want to belong to a community that makes us feel like one big happy family. This is why many Christians pine after socialism: it feels really good. But as such situations scale to include larger numbers of individuals, that cozy feeling of belonging dissipates, the voluntary nature disappears, and a different sort of socio-political context emerges.

103. How do libertarian Christians propose addressing racism, both as a personal moral issue and as a systemic social concern?

While racism has been defined so broadly by those who wish to use it as an explanation for every disparity, the reality exists that everything from personal bias to overt hatred persists among individuals, influencing society in ways that, while not always violations of rights, still reflect moral failings that affect others. It is also incorrect to say America has completely put racism in the rearview mirror.

Specific injustices done to individuals should be dealt with through a justice system, but this does not mean that racism is a political problem with a political solution. Racism is a sin problem, and the starting point for addressing any sin, both personal and social, is to repent of that sin where it resides in our own hearts, and seek reconciliation with others with whom we have wronged. Political solutions to racism have often exacerbated the issue or stunted the progress of real reconciliation in society.

Christians should advocate legal equality because present racism will never be solved with future racism, a bizarre claim made by so-called "anti-racist" thought leaders. State-enforced programs such as Diversity, Equity, & Inclusion initiatives or Affirmative Action will do little to affect the root causes of racism, and are arguably driven by the very racism they purport to oppose. The solution is to create a bottom-up cultural transformation that begins with recognizing the value that people bring in spite of, or perhaps because of, their particular ethnic or regional backgrounds. And sharing with them the mutual benefit of a free society.

104. Isn't government necessary to protect people from predatory and dangerous business practices?

Business operators do sometimes violate the rights of others. Whether it is through deception and fraud, or carelessness, or failure to deliver on a contract, sometimes people do need some recourse against an unscrupulous businessman. Where persuasion and social pressure fail to secure a remedy, a judicial solution may be the only practical answer.

However, many business practices that are described as predatory are anything but predatory. Many of the government policies that are touted as protecting consumers from mustache-twisting capitalist villains actually serve to disrupt an important market function.

Take, for example, price-gouging laws. When a natural disaster strikes, such as a hurricane or flood, there is often a shortage of goods relating to the preparation for and response to a disaster. This is because of a sharp increase in demand for batteries, duct tape, contractor bags, tarps, plywood, bottled water, shelf-stable food, baby formula, ice, propane, and gasoline. That dramatic spike in demand collides with logistical challenges in resupplying local merchants. The storekeeper facing those conditions has two choices: continue to sell at the previously prevailing market prices, or adjust prices to reflect the new, temporary scarcity.

If the storekeeper chooses the first option, he is likely to experience a brief buying spree which will cause him to sell out of inventory quickly. If the storekeeper chooses the second option and raises his prices, individual buyers will tend to buy smaller quantities of the hotly demanded goods, which will in turn leave some inventory available to satisfy the needs of later buyers, or buyers who value the goods more highly. While the first course of action may seem to be more altruistic, it is the merchant who raises his prices who actually performs the greater service, because that adjustment in prices creates a strong profit incentive for suppliers to bring more goods to this temporarily hot local market, so that consumers will get relief from the shortage and the supplier will be rewarded with greater profit. Laws forbidding price gouging actually slow the market's response to crisis conditions and prolong the suffering.

105. Are there historical examples where libertarian principles have successfully led to economic prosperity and social welfare?

The consistent trend in settled societies throughout history has been for the powerful to centralize wealth and manage economies through force. The result of this trend has been predictable—poverty, death, and disease with the occasional minor jump and inevitable fall in progress and productivity.

This changed suddenly and rapidly with the advent of the ideas associated with what we call "classical liberalism" today, most significantly that each human being has a right to liberty and is, from a human perspective, a "self-owner" who is free to work and trade with anyone he sees fit. Once these ideas caught on, what Deirdre

McCloskey has termed "the Great Enrichment" was inevitable, and its effects might even be described as miraculous. After little to no consistent growth for millennia, the world's economy grew more than a hundredfold starting in 1820—and this growth didn't only benefit the super-rich. The estimate of the world's population suffering in extreme poverty was nearly 84% in 1820; by 2018 it had fallen to 8.6%.

Starting in early 2024, the world has been observing a smaller "miracle" story in Argentina. Its new president, self-described libertarian Javier Milei, was elected because Argentina was experiencing rapid inflation, growing poverty, deficit spending, and a significant housing shortage. Since Milei took office and pro-market policies were implemented, all of those markers have shown significant improvement. If Argentina maintains the same course, it will be much better prepared than its socialist-leaning neighbors to weather any potential economic storms.

106. How should we then think about global and social issues such as immigration or the environment?

Christianity is, in a very real sense, a global community. To think globally, then, is to at least indicate that our concern should not be primarily for those in close proximity or who belong to our in-group, but to all people, regardless of race, ethnicity, nationality, or place of origin.

Christians affirm that as divine image-bearers, humans are assigned to steward creation and to care for those around us. We also believe that sin has infected creation and that God is actively at work in restoring creation and human relationships to their original goodness.

Global human flourishing can only be achieved through economic freedom and trade. So in order to "think globally," we must adopt a posture of openness, which means examining our attitude towards others and the policies that restrict the free movement of people (we treat this in detail in Chapter 13) and our cooperation with others about our shared planet.

Politicians want to make immigration about "us versus them." Christians should consider the issue from an individual level and ask, "How can we coexist and live peacefully with one another to mutual advantage?" We should champion policies and practices that foster mutual benefit and extend hospitality—even when that openness runs against prevailing cultural instincts.

Environmentalism or creation care, a legitimate biblical concept, flows from humanity's responsibility to steward creation. God's gift of dominion was neither a license for exploitation nor a ban on human impact. Faithful stewardship requires understanding property rights, embracing innovation, and applying wisdom to weigh trade-offs—considering both short- and long-term consequences in order to promote human flourishing (see Chapter 15).

Additional Resources

Christian Faith and Social Justice: Five Views, ed. Vic McCracken (Bloomsbury Academic, 2014).

The End of Race Politics: Arguments for a Colorblind America by Coleman Hughes (Thesis, 2024)

A Conflict of Visions: Ideological Origins of Political Struggles by Thomas Sowell (Basic Books, 2007).

Healing Our World: The Compassion of Libertarianism by Mary J. Ruwart (Sunstar Press, 2015).

The Maker Versus the Takers: What Jesus Really Said About Social Justice and Economics by Jerry Bowyer (Fidelis Books, 2020).

On Social Justice by Saint Basil the Great.

On Wealth and Poverty by St. John Chrysostom.

Productive Christians in an Age of Guilt Manipulators: A Biblical Response to Ronald J. Sider by David Chilton (Institute for Christian Economics, 1982).

The Quest for Cosmic Justice by Thomas Sowell (Free Press, 2002).

Ten Global Trends Every Smart Person Should Know: And Many Others You Will Find Interesting by Ronald Bailey and Marian L. Tupy (Cato Institute, 2020).

Was Jesus a Socialist?, Lawrence W. Reed (Intercollegiate Studies Institute, 2020).

When All Else Fails: The Ethics of Resistance to State Injustice by Jason Brennan (Princeton University Press, 2018).

12

The War on Drugs

"Those acts by which a man harms himself or his property are those acts by which one man harms the person or property of another."

—Lysander Spooner

107. Why do libertarians oppose prohibition, including the War on Drugs? Are you saying all drugs should be legal?

There are two primary reasons why libertarians oppose prohibition laws. The first reason is that enforcement of such laws violate people's property rights. The second is that these laws tend to do more harm than good and fail to address the root problem of substance abuse.

When laws are adopted that impose punishments on people for selling, possessing, or using drugs, the enforcement of these laws requires the use of violence to stop people from doing what they want with their own money and their own bodies. It is inappropriate to use violence to prevent a person from doing something merely because some third party believes that thing is harmful or immoral. Such rules are "simply human commands and teachings" (Col 2:22) and "have indeed an appearance of wisdom in promoting self-imposed piety, humility, and severe treatment of the body, but they are of no value in checking self-indulgence" (Col 2:23). Instead of this sort of legalism, Christians recognize that we are under a directive to exercise self-control. We are called to wisely abstain from things that, while within the realm of our possible choices, are not edifying, or even worse, may enslave us or cause another to stumble (1 Cor 6:12, 10:23).

Apart from this moral and philosophical analysis, there is also the question of whether prohibition works. It does not. In fact, drug prohibition tends to result in more concentrated, dangerous drugs, greater associated criminality, more overdoses, and less legal accountability for faulty or adulterated products. And the progress of both alcohol prohibition and the drug war have been accompanied by the abuse of civil liberties through expanded use of warrantless seizures, civil asset forfeiture, broader surveillance by police, and infringements on the right to keep and bear arms such as the National Firearms Act of 1934, the passage of which was made possible by rhetoric about prohibition-related gang violence.

108. How would drug legalization reduce problems associated with drug smuggling, including empowering cartels, gang violence, and human trafficking?

Any time there is high demand for a good or service, there is a profit-making opportunity in delivering that good or service. Prohibition creates new types of risks for the prohibited enterprise, and black market entrepreneurs plan accordingly.

In a legal market, competitors may compete for market share, but they typically do not do so through direct violence against each other. They compete based on price, quality, and other factors focusing on appealing to consumers. If an employee or contractor embezzles from the firm, that wrong is addressed in a legal proceeding in the courts.

In a prohibited market, manufacturers, distributors, and vendors all face the constant danger of government violence, confiscation of business and personal assets, and the arrest and imprisonment of their workers. This means that only individuals with a large appetite for risk-taking are likely to participate. It also means that when these individuals have disputes over market share or fulfillment of a contract, there is no legal means available for dispute resolution. This incentivizes violent reprisals instead of peaceful, civilized modes of addressing these conflicts.

Gangs typically develop as a response to a collective defense problem. Rather than fall prey to competing black market actors who want to acquire market share or low-cost inventory quickly through violence, people who are familiar to each other due to previous friendly acquaintance, family connection, or simple physical proximity may band together to provide for their common defense. People who perceive that they are in danger will often do dangerous things. And once accustomed to lawless living, these people are more likely to participate in other forms of unlawful but profitable victimization, like human trafficking, utilizing the smuggling and protection infrastructure that they have already established.

109. If drugs were legalized, wouldn't that lead to more drug use, more drug abuse, and more deaths by drug overdose?

It is hard to say whether drug legalization would lead to elevated drug use. It might. Legalization might even lead to more drug abuse. But when it comes to overdoses, it seems to be the case that most drug overdoses occur because of a dangerous combination of variable potency of black market drugs and the unwise choices of multi-drug users. Most drug users take drugs to feel good, not to die. According to data reported by the United States National Center for Health Statistics, most of the approximately 100,000 fatal overdoses per year, roughly 85–95 percent, are unintentional (NCHS Data Brief, Number 457. Dec. 2022).

A major cause of these unintentional overdoses is the great variability in the potency of black market drugs. Opioid drugs are the leading drugs found to be responsible for fatal drug overdoses. The original recreational opiate—opium—was introduced to the American market as a drug that could be smoked or eaten, and while addiction was common, fatal overdoses were rare. Smoked opium would usually render the user insensate far before he could consume enough to overdose. Opium-smoking was associated in the popular press with Chinese immigrants, and in 1875 one of the first local laws banning opium dens was passed in San Francisco. Seven years later, the Chinese Exclusion Act of 1882 was passed in the U. S. Congress, driven in large part by a stereotypical association of Chinese immigrants with opium.

With the rise of legal and social stigma, some fatal overdoses began to occur as liquid opiate preparations became more common, including laudanum and various patent medicines. While opium was stigmatized and made harder to legally acquire, opioid users started injecting morphine, thanks to the recent invention of the hypodermic needle. Barely two decades after the first anti-opium laws, the Bayer Company began marketing diacetylmorphine (heroin) as a "non-addictive" alternative to morphine. In the early twentieth century, federal law continued to focus on prohibition of the safer, but more "foreign" smoked version of opium, while only requiring accurate labeling of injectable or oral opioids. The Harrison Narcotics Tax Acts of 1914 then outlawed legal opioids for most addicts and sent them to the black market to feed their addictions.

A succession of synthesized opioids were subsequently developed, and while many users started addictions with legal pharmaceutical drugs, they maintained their addiction through the purchase of illicit pills, including counterfeit drugs, that were available on the street. Progressing from codeine to oxycodone to fentanyl, the therapeutic dose became tinier and so too did the lethal dose. Overdoses are now commonly attributed to pills that are designed to appear like legitimate pharmaceuticals while actually containing fentanyl. Even though fentanyl is more dangerous, drug smugglers are incentivized to traffic in it instead of safer, less potent opioids, because the risk of smuggling is better rewarded when the contraband is more concentrated and represents more individual doses for sale in the prohibited market. Thus, it is prohibitionist policies that have driven the drug overdose problem.

110. If drugs were legalized, how would a libertarian approach handle the social harms caused by drug use?

Libertarians believe in personal responsibility, and personal responsibility is the best remedy for destructive personal vices. Under modern states, policymakers attempt to address social problems relating to addiction in a number of ways that they characterize as "harm reduction." These programs may include problem-solving courts, needle exchanges, controlled distribution of allegedly safer drugs like methadone, and taxpayer-funded support of drug rehabilitation programming. Libertarians reject the compulsory socialization of the costs of drug abuse.

Instead, many libertarians would argue that being left to face the consequences of poor personal decisions would be a better alternative. Other libertarians favor solutions that appear to be similar to those listed above, but which are paid for through voluntary charity or family funds. Rather than threatening criminal punishment while granting taxpayer-financed welfare benefits, recourse to private charity replaces legal entitlement with voluntary assistance, something that the evidence shows results in stronger community and peer support, lower overall costs, and an element of spiritual growth instead of a purely secular public health approach.

Other symptoms of drug abuse may include homelessness and petty crimes that would cease to be a significant problem under a private property regime as proposed by libertarians. Government managed "public property" often becomes a haven for drug addicts, enabling self-destructive behaviors by providing a location for incorrigible abusers to congregate and live out their addictions. Private property owners can remove such people from their grounds, while governments are often unable or unwilling to dissipate homeless camps that are set up on public property.

111. If drugs were legalized, how can we be sure our communities won't be overwhelmed by addiction and its consequences?

No one can guarantee that any solution to addiction will totally eliminate it from society. However, we can minimize the extent to which well-meaning government policies incentivize and enable this sort of destructive behavior. We live in a fallen world, and sin is a part of that world. Those of us who are strong are called to bear with the weak and build them up despite their infirmities, and to seek their good pleasure rather than our own (Rom 15:1–3, Phil 2:3–4).

In such an environment, rather than relying on government sanctions to make temptation impossible—a strategy which does not seem to be working anyway—we would instead be called to demonstrate self control, not merely for our own sake but to help the weaker brother not to stumble (1 Cor 8). Taking personal responsibility and choosing to take care of the needs of others seems harder than relying on external restraints, but by following Jesus' example, we can aid the weak and serve them far more effectively than government ever will (Gal 5:13, 1 Thess 5:14).

112. Perhaps these policy ideas make sense to a libertarian, but why should a Christian accept them? Are you saying you want to treat the health matter of drug abuse separate from the legal matter of drug abuse?

More than the secular libertarian, libertarian Christians should be able to recognize that drug abuse and addiction are symptoms of a spiritual problem, not merely a physical health problem or a criminal matter for courts to sort out. Anyone who serves a master other than Jesus is guilty of idolatry, and drug addiction can be one of the more visible forms of that ancient sin. As believers, we recognize that all have sinned, and that all need to repent and believe in Jesus.

Rather than holding disdain in our hearts for drug addicts, as Christians we should have compassion for them and a desire to help them escape the consequences of sin through the gift of salvation. As Christians, each of us has come to the realization that we are not enough in ourselves, but that we can be more than enough in Jesus. That hope—a hope that is absurd and impossible according to the world's wisdom—should give us a boldness in reaching out to other sinners who have yet to repent of their sins and seek the only lasting escape from them through our Lord and Savior. This compassion is in keeping with the great commandments of Jesus and honors him.

113. Are there real-life examples of how shifting to a treatment-oriented or social-oriented approach toward addiction improves outcomes for people?

Yes, there are examples in recent memory that show this approach has merit.

Portugal adopted a policy of drug decriminalization in 2001. That policy shift was followed by a dramatic drop in Portugal's overdose deaths, which are now five times lower than the European average. New HIV diagnoses dropped by over 90 percent among drug users most at risk of infection—those who use injectable drugs. More people entered treatment. Despite the reduced criminal penalties, drug use does not seem to have significantly increased among young people in Portugal since that time.

Switzerland implemented a health-focused drug policy in the 1980s and 1990s, involving public education campaigns, therapy and treatment, and harm reduction strategies like clean needle exchanges and even medically supervised use for the addicts who were deepest in addiction. These policies resulted in a massive reduction in Swiss crime, as fewer addicts were stealing to support their addictions. Homelessness fell, employment increased, overdoses fell, and HIV rates dropped. There was not a discernible increase in new users, and the addict population seems to be getting older, suggesting that fewer young people are becoming newly addicted.

Additional Resources

Curious: A Foster Mom's Discovery of an Unexpected Solution to Drugs and Addiction by Christina Dent (Thorne Publishing Group, 2023).

The Economics of Prohibition by Mark Thornton (University of Utah Press, 1991).

Vices Are Not Crimes: A Vindication of Moral Liberty by Lysander Spooner (1875).

13

Immigration

"When innocent people seek to interact with willing others in ways that are productive and mutually beneficial, justice does not ordinarily allow other people to set up barriers between them."

—Jason Brennan & Bas van der Vossen

114. What does the Bible have to say about immigration?

The Bible tells immigrant story after immigrant story: Adam and Eve were exiled from the Garden of Eden, made refugees by their own sin. Joseph was the victim of fraternal violence and was sold into bondage in the strange land of Egypt. Israel made its exodus from Egypt to the then-unfamiliar Promised Land. Ruth was a foreigner who immigrated to Israel. Christ traveled in foreign lands as an infant fleeing for safety from Herod the Great's Massacre of the Innocents. Our savior identified with the immigrant, and he included the "stranger" as one of the groups whom he called the "least of these" (Matt 25:34–46).

Scripture speaks clearly on the topic of how God's faithful are to treat immigrants. The Bible tells us that foreigners who come to our country must be afforded equal legal rights to people who are native-born (Exod 12:49, Lev 24:22). More than that, we are to love them as we love ourselves (Lev 19:33–34). Immigrants are a segment of the community who are worthy objects of our charity (Deut 10:14–22). Indeed, it is an outward mark of a righteous man that his door is "always open to the traveler" (Job 31:32). Israel was reminded by God of its heritage as a people who were once strangers in a strange land, and instructed that it would be hypocritical for them to mistreat the alien (Deut 24:19–22). God warns of judgment for those who "deprive aliens of justice" (Mal 3:5, Deut 27:19). Widespread mistreatment of immigrants can lead to national judgment (Ezek 22:7, 29–31; Jer 22:3–5). Treating immigrants justly was one of the conditions for Israel's continuing to enjoy the blessings of the Promised Land (Jer 7:6–7).

115. Didn't God establish nations to keep people separate?

The nations described in the Bible were not nation-states in the modern sense, but rather extended family groups or tribes who shared a common language and culture. The original division of nations occurred early in post-deluge history. Nations are first mentioned in the Bible in Genesis 10, in a passage naming the first generations born after the great flood subsided: the offspring of Japheth, Ham, and Shem. Genesis 11 then focuses on the particular events that led to the division of the nations by language and physical distance. The efforts of a united humanity to construct a tower to their own glory ("let us make a name for ourselves," v. 4) displeased God. God responded by confounding their language, leading them to abandon their construction project and "scattered them abroad over the face of all the Earth" (Gen 11:8–9).

The children of Israel were selected as a nation set apart as God's chosen people, and they were commanded to keep away from the corruption and idol worship of other nations. Even before that, the first great order of separation for Israel was an internal schism.

Moses separated the wandering people of Israel into groups of faithful and reprobate before the Lord caused the earth to swallow up the followers of Korah, Dathan, and Abiram (Num 16:23–35).

The good news is that national divisions that came about due to sin and corruption can be overcome by the grace of God. Foreigners who worshipped the one true God were to be welcomed by the nation of Israel (Isa 56:1–8). In the Great Commission, Christ commanded his followers to go to all nations teaching his commands (Matt 28:19–20). Peter preached that God had revealed to him that he "should not call any man common or unclean," and told his listeners about a faith that offered hope to God-fearing people of all nations (Acts 10:28; 35). National divisions are a consequence of sin. Everyone who repents and believes in Christ can join the eternal, holy nation of God (1 Pet 2:9–10).

116. How does immigration affect a country's economy, culture, and social stability?

From the economic point of view, laborers who migrate from a low wage area to a high wage area are performing an arbitrage and making the market function more efficiently in the satisfaction of human wants. But human beings are not merely laborers, and they bring with them more than labor hours.

Immigrants bring with them their own experiences and customs, and often their own languages. It is true that a culturally heterogeneous population can experience social friction because different cultures can dictate dramatically different expectations from one another. For example, in some cultures, direct eye contact may be considered presumptuous and aggressive. In others, *avoiding* eye contact may be viewed with suspicion. This is not only true of international immigration. Cultural differences may also be present within different populations in the same nation-state, such as those between New Englanders and southerners in the United States.

People as social creatures are also immensely adaptable. Customs can be consciously learned, and linguistic features are often acquired without conscious effort or awareness. Every person grows and changes over their lifetime, including in their customary behaviors and language, and they will adapt to their environment.

While some traditions and customs may indeed be ancient in origin, local culture is by its nature a transient and dynamic thing. Attempts to freeze a culture in time to preserve it are based on the mistaken idea that culture is static and stable. It is not. Even if some cultural clashes may greatly annoy adults, such displeasure need not persist in succeeding generations. Indeed, combinations of previously unacquainted peoples have sometimes resulted in explosions of cultural creativity, such as the innovative jazz and blues styles of music that developed in the culturally complex Mississippi Delta region.

117. If open immigration policies raise concerns, what solutions do libertarians propose to address them effectively?

It's important to recognize that free migration isn't destined for conflict (see Question 116). People are adaptable, and markets reward peaceful cooperation. Yet open immigration under modern state conditions can create unintended challenges, since governments control land, welfare, and public property—distortions that lead to forced association and perverse incentives. In a free society, migration is regulated by the market. State interventions in borders, welfare, drug policy, and the economy disrupt the market dynamics that would otherwise harmonize migration with demand.

The more we decentralize government, the closer we get to a true polycentric order where society is shaped by markets and local decision-making, not central planners. Rather than federal bureaucracies managing welfare programs or vast tracts of public land, those functions should devolve to the local level—or better yet, to private ownership and market institutions. Local and private stewardship ties decisions to those who bear their costs and benefits, curbing waste, reducing moral hazard, and aligning incentives with genuine community needs. Decentralization and privatization directly reduce the friction and fear associated with open immigration by replacing coercive, one-size-fits-all systems with voluntary cooperation rooted in consent and property rights.

Inflationary policies, taxes, and regulations erode prosperity and drive up housing costs, trapping both natives and newcomers in artificial scarcity that breeds resentment. Likewise, ending the War on Drugs and U.S. military interventions abroad would remove major sources of violence, displacement, and black-market chaos that fuel mass migration. Freer markets and a peaceful foreign policy allow people to move, build, and work where demand exists, turning competition into cooperation. When paired with a fair justice system that neither discriminates against newcomers nor excuses crime, these reforms foster trust, opportunity, and liberty.

118. If libertarians affirm property rights, isn't a nation's borders an analog to personal property?

No. It is true that libertarians firmly believe in property rights. A property boundary marks where one owner's claim begins and another's ends. That boundary should only be enforceable if the owner really owns the tract of land within. But that is where the analogy comparing government borders to private property breaks down. Government does not own all of the property within its borders. Though government-held lands are extensive in the United States, the majority of American ground is privately owned. Not all of these private owners agree about how to enforce the national borders, or even the idea that they should be enforced by government at all.

Libertarians would agree that a person should not trespass on another person's property. But unlawful immigrants usually are not trespassers. The vast majority (approximately two-thirds) of such immigrants enter their destination country legally and simply overstay their entry visa. This means that they do not enter by trespassing. Instead, they enter the country by the same means as any other traveler. These immigrants then rent apartments from willing landlords, obtain employment from eager employers, and buy goods from eager retailers. The accusation that they are trespassers is simply false. A person who moves from Mexico to Texas is no more a trespasser than a person who moves from Georgia to Texas, whether they have government approval or not.

Aggressive border enforcement encroaches on private property and disrupts the normal movement of labor and capital. It also creates dangerous black markets in transportation, housing, and employment. Even worse, restrictive immigration policies interfere with the performance of our Christian duty to be charitable to immigrants and to reach all nations with the good news of the gospel.

119. What is the best libertarian position on immigration?

The best libertarian position on immigration is non-aggression, which is the core principle of libertarian ethics. If a person emigrates to a new place, is respectful of his new neighbors and their property, works hard, buys goods and services from willing buyers and sellers, and lives peacefully, it is hard to find any libertarian basis for violent action against that person. If a person moves in and lives a life of thievery and violence, that is no more and no less blameworthy for a person who came from another country than it is for a person from another location within the same country. The same measures that would be properly employed against a domestic criminal would also be applicable to an aggressor from someplace else.

Libertarians who reject socialist central-planning of the economy should not abandon their skepticism when it comes to planning the optimal size and composition of a local population. If the local bureaucracy cannot rigorously determine the appropriate quantity and qualities of bread production, how much more likely is it to be successful in determining the composition of the local workforce?

Libertarians should be suspicious of all government programs that attempt to restrict natural, voluntary immigration. These interventions disrupt normal market processes and hamper economic growth.

Libertarians should also be suspicious of government programs that attempt to drive mass migrations for political reasons. Many of the greatest migrations in human history were instigated through government action, including the expulsion of Jews from Spain in 1492, the Huguenot persecution in France in the 16th and 17th centuries, the Trail of Tears in the mid-19th century, the Jim Crow system in the post-war American South, and the Partition of India in 1947.

120. Why do some libertarians disagree with the classical open borders position?

Libertarians should be skeptical of both state-restricted and state-engineered migration, since both distort natural market processes. In a libertarian society, movement is not an entitlement but emerges from the interplay of property rights and market forces. Thus, while open borders remove government aggression against migrants, they do not inherently produce a truly market-mediated pattern of movement.

Some also contend that open borders create forced association by compelling taxpayers to support and interact with people involuntarily. They question whether coercively funded systems should be made universally accessible. Another concern is that rapid influxes of immigrants (as seen in parts of Europe and during the Biden administration) can destabilize communities, strain infrastructure, and hinder integration. These libertarians suggest that importing large numbers from regions less friendly to liberty may have significant consequences, while still acknowledging that immigrants are never a monolith and that the desire for all immigrants is to integrate well and flourish in their new society.

To be clear, these libertarians support free trade. Many are anarchists who want to abolish the state and borders entirely, but they stress that the order of transitional steps taken to dismantle state powers shouldn't be ignored. Proposed alternatives include private sponsorship or invitee systems, "Ellis Island" style entry points, decentralizing authority to states, or limiting access to public services until those systems can be privatized or decentralized.

121. Without tough border restrictions, how do we protect people from foreign threats?

There is a popular perception of constant danger at borders. Unfortunately, such dangers do exist, and they are largely a consequence of the immigration controls and the War on Drugs (see Chapter 12). The opportunity to conduct a lucrative arbitrage is a powerful motivator to break the law. Human traffickers and drug cartel hitmen are largely the creatures of government prohibition.

If border restrictions were to be lifted, dangers currently associated with international borders would largely evaporate as well. The current restrictions focus a great deal on smuggling of contraband. Without such distractions, the line between hostile invaders and peaceful travelers would be much easier to discern. Libertarians generally believe that there is a real need for security services both locally and regionally.

Many liberty-minded writers have discussed how markets might produce security services (some are mentioned in the "Additional Resources" list at the end of this chapter). As a practical question, there can be no doubt that private firms are capable of going to war. Global mercenary operations in the years following the war in Vietnam demonstrated that private firms are more efficient at ending short-term conflicts and stabilizing an area of operations than government forces. Many thousands of military contractors were used in American operations during the Iraq and Afghanistan wars. Private contractors made up as much as one-fifth of the total occupation force in Iraq.

122. Is immigration to the United States to blame for drug smuggling and addiction crises?

It is a mistake to claim that drug smuggling and addiction are causally related to immigration. Immigrants to the United States have significantly lower rates of drug abuse and addiction than the native-born population. Domestic demand for drugs, not foreign influence, is what makes the illicit drug trade profitable.

The real connection between immigration and drugs is that transnational criminal organizations profit from smuggling both human beings and illegal drugs. The way to sever this connection entirely, and to defund criminal enterprises, is to end the War on Drugs and to end policies that severely limit immigration. So long as gangs can enjoy an effective monopoly on making money from smuggling contraband, they will continue to operate and create the other social problems attendant to organized crime, including crimes of violence.

These criminal enterprises are not only a threat to destination countries, which are typically wealthy and enjoy relatively low crime rates. They are an even greater threat to residents of the regions where the smuggled contraband originates and is transported on its way to export markets in North America and Europe. For example, Ecuador saw its homicide rate increase by more than 500 percent between 2020 and 2023, with prison massacres and targeted assassinations on the rise, as narcotics traffickers sought out new territory with locations for storing, processing, and exporting drugs.

123. Wouldn't allowing poor immigrant laborers into the country permit others to take advantage of their status as poor?

As Christians, we can and should be concerned about human labor exploitation, especially when the situation involves predatory behavior.

Allowing immigrants from a relatively poor country into a relatively wealthy country does not inherently exploit the situation of the poor. To know whether such behavior is happening, we need to assess relevant information, and we don't always have what we need. If an immigrant travels across the border to perform work, he is doing so because he is choosing his best known available opportunity for work. If he were restricted to his own country, he would have fewer options. It is an unjust situation for this poor person to be restricted from voluntarily offering his labor to a willing employer.

Some object that this situation is suboptimal, and they would be right. It would be nice if everybody had the skills to perform high-value labor and the employers had the profit margins to pay top-dollar wages. But the world we live in is one of limited knowledge that increases through discovery, and it is up to us to discover how to best cooperate and exchange within the parameters of peaceful, voluntary work.

Lastly, we ought to be very careful to not assume that we know what is better for the lives of immigrants than they do for themselves.

124. Shouldn't we abolish the welfare state before we allow open immigration?

Many who favor libertarian politics but oppose open immigration use the existence of a welfare system as a reason to not favor open immigration. Setting aside the reality that most non-natives are not eligible for most welfare benefits, the argument has emotional appeal. It seems unfair to give non-citizens benefits that citizens pay for through tax dollars and that may raise citizens' taxes. If you abolish the welfare state, these opponents say, they would favor open immigration. But even this acknowledges that open immigration is the default libertarian position, since their argument is to overcome the default with a justifiable restriction on human liberty.

Their position ignores that a restrictive border necessitates highway checkpoints, an immigration police state, warrantless searches of property, forcible separation of children and their parents, and a host of other egregious practices.

The reality is that most immigrants do not come to take advantage of the welfare state, nor is the federal government required to provide aid to foreigners. In fact, some economists have calculated that open immigration actually reduces the burden of the welfare state.

While this argument has some initial emotional appeal (and because Milton Friedman said it), this appears to be yet another ad hoc reason to oppose the free movement of people and deny them their right to flourish.

125. How would a mass number of immigrants effectively integrate into their new host country?

This question is predicated on two false beliefs: First, that open immigration would immediately result in mass immigration, a possible but not likely outcome. Second, that "effectively integrated" should be the goal of permitting more immigrants.

If the federal government were to open its borders tomorrow morning, there would likely be an initial influx of new immigrants, which would fairly quickly increase the costs of moving for those who weren't quite as quick to immigrate. Markets would adjust, and immigration would stabilize.

Whether or not those immigrants would effectively integrate into their new host country depends on a lot of variables. While immigrants themselves sometimes struggle to adapt to their new society beyond survival, their children often thrive, and third-generation immigrants are quite well-integrated into society. While the "how" is an important question, it seems that American culture has proven for centuries that it can handle the adjustment many immigrants bring.

126. Wouldn't allowing open borders create a "brain drain," where the able and intelligent in poor countries leave the poorest of the poor behind?

In reality, it is restrictive immigration policy that permits only the best from other nations that creates a "brain drain" where the least-productive workers are left behind in their native country to survive. In an open borders situation, the poorest would be permitted to immigrate, and would be better off.

Many critics of open immigration are concerned that the GDP of the sending countries would reduce, creating a spiral of even more poverty. But this way of thinking only considers countries, and we should be thinking about people.

Aside from the moral problem of treating the wealthy more favorably than the poor, forbidding poor people in other countries from migrating essentially keeps them from making choices that they believe would improve their lives while cooperating with others in a broader economy. Additionally, poor people are often poor because they lack the opportunity to become more skilled and therefore relatively wealthier. The best example of open immigration benefiting not only the immigrants but the receiving areas is the expansion of the United States westward. Not only were free people able to improve their lives and the areas to which they moved, they were free to avoid harsh and unsatisfactory regions because no state was forcing them to remain.

In short, free movement of labor enriches, not impoverishes.

Additional Resources

The God Who Sees: Immigrants, the Bible, and the Journey to Belong by Karen González (Herald Press, 2019).

The Immigration Crisis: Immigrants, Aliens, and the Bible by James K. Hoffmeier (Crossway, 2009).

In Defense of Openness: Why Global Freedom is the Humane Solution to Global Poverty by Jason Brennan and Bas van der Vossen (Oxford University Press, 2018).

Open Borders: The Science and Ethics of Immigration by Bryan Caplan and Zach Weinersmith (First Second, 2019).

"The Private Production of Defense" by Hans-Hermann Hoppe. *Journal of Libertarian Studies, Vol. 14, No. 1*, 1999. https://mises.org/library/book/private-production-defense.

The Production of Security by Gustave de Molinari (Mises Institute, 1849).

Hussey, J. M., Hallfors, D. D., Waller, M. W., et al. (2007). "Sexual behavior and substance use among first-generation and native-born adolescent children of immigrants." *Journal of Immigrant and Minority Health*, 9(2), 93–103.

"What the Bible Says About Immigrants" by Norman Horn. *Libertarian Christian Institute*, 2014. https://libertarianchristians.com/2014/05/28/what-the-bible-says-about-immigrants/.

Wretched Refuse? by Ben Powell and Alex Nowrasteh (Cambridge University Press, 2020).

Sources

Alegría, M., Canino, G., Shrout, P. E., et al. (2008). "Prevalence of mental illness in immigrant and non-immigrant U.S. Latino groups." American Journal of Psychiatry, 165(3), 359–369.

14

Abortion

"Abortion on demand is the ultimate State tyranny; the State simply declares that certain classes of human beings are not persons, and therefore not entitled to the protection of the law. The State protects the 'right' of some people to kill others, just as the courts protected the 'property rights' of slave masters in their slaves. Moreover, by this method the State achieves a goal common to all totalitarian regimes: it sets us against each other, so that our energies are spent in the struggle between State-created classes, rather than in freeing all individuals from the State."

—*Ron Paul*

127. Does abortion violate the Non-Aggression Principle?

Since murder is prohibited by the NAP (see Question 12), then the question is whether abortion constitutes a form of murder. Prior to *Roe v. Wade*, U.S. jurisprudence didn't explicitly outlaw abortion per se, however, Leah Savas explains in her book, *A Street Level History of Abortion*, that abortion was legally prohibited as a form of murder. This is supported by Joseph W. Dellapenna's, *Dispelling the Myths of Abortion History*.

Abortion violates the NAP insofar as it ends the life of a human. So when does new human life begin? Many people muddle this question with philosophical personhood (see Question 135) as if some living humans can't be considered persons. However, this is the same distorted rationale used to argue against the rights of all sorts of marginalized groups. The beginning of new human life is not an enigma; science answers the question for us.

LCI's Kerry Baldwin argues for fetal self-ownership, recognizing that a new, unique, living, human exists from the moment conception is complete, *and is therefore a rights-bearer*. This is slightly different from the conventional pro-life argument that life begins at fertilization. But only upon completion of the process of conception (which takes approximately three days) do you have a unique DNA differentiated from both mother and father. Additionally, it is at the completion of conception that fetal development begins as "autonomous and self-organizing." In other words, the woman's body is a passive participant in the activity of fetal development. It is fetal DNA giving instructions for development.

Self-ownership (see Questions 14 and 15), the necessary antecedent of the NAP, requires two criteria: you must be human, and you must have possession (direct and immediate control) over your own body. The first time we see this is upon completion of conception; the DNA of the fetus indicates it is human, and the autonomous and self-organizing processes indicate direct and immediate control by the fetus' body. Therefore, self-ownership is established at completion of conception, and initiating aggression on these new self-owners constitutes a rights violation. Abortion is an act of aggression that results in the death of the fetus, therefore abortion is a violation of the NAP.

128. Why are some libertarians pro-choice if abortion violates the NAP?

Since libertarianism is predicated on the concept of self-ownership, many pro-choice libertarians believe that a right to abortion falls under a woman's bodily autonomy and so, in their view, does not violate the NAP. For them, human rights aren't expressed until some other stage (viability, birth, etc.). Though libertarianism recognizes human rights in terms of property rights, the ongoing debate relevant to abortion concerns when those rights begin.

Various figures throughout history have offered different answers. But even among pro-choice libertarians, this is still a contested point. Some simply hold to the feminist view of abortion, which says that even if the fetus has some measure of rights, no one has the right to live unbidden on another, and that includes the fetus. In this view, a fetus has human rights but doesn't have an inherent right to live, unwanted, in their mother's womb.

Another view, known as Evictionism, argues that the mother (like any other property owner) is legally permitted to evict, not kill, her unwanted fetus. Nuances of this position do permit lethal eviction (abortion) prior to viability. However, lethal eviction is impermissible where it's possible for the fetus to live outside the womb. So technological improvements, such as artificial womb technology, could conceivably render abortion obsolete in this view (and therefore legally prohibited) in the future. However, the Evictionist view is not the pro-choice argument for abortion. Many pro-choice libertarians disagree with Evictionism, arguing the state shouldn't have a legal interest in human life until after birth.

What this really shows is that the abortion debate is not a settled issue for libertarians, and it's our position that pro-life libertarians have a much stronger response to pro-choice libertarians than conservative pro-lifers.

129. Are there pro-life libertarians?

Yes! There are many pro-life libertarians; with approximately a third pro-life, a third pro-choice, and a third who are otherwise ambivalent. One of the first groups to organize was Libertarians for Life, founded in 1976 by Doris Gordon. Gordon, a non-theistic libertarian, cited various scientific and philosophical arguments for a right to life. Like pro-choice libertarians, most pro-life libertarians simply hold to their respective conventional views, often defending conventional arguments in libertarian terms.

In response to evictionism, Baldwin has developed an alternative libertarian pro-life perspective. In Baldwin's view, the intractability of the abortion debate is due to both sides compromising rights: pro-choicers compromise the rights of the fetus in favor of the woman, and pro-lifers compromise the rights of the woman in favor of the fetus. Baldwin makes an argument from the principle of self-ownership, using science to illuminate the facts of nature which support the argument that self-ownership begins upon completion of conception (see Question 127). She argues against the pro-choice position that abortion is an act of self-defense; doing so violates the principle of proportionality—that is, abortion is a lethal response and is only justified if the fetus poses a corresponding credibly imminent *lethal* threat to the mother.

Her view takes into account not only the legality of abortion but also the problem of enforcement, demonstrating that an authoritarian enforcement of abortion prohibition is untenable in a truly just legal order. A just prohibition of abortion, she argues, requires both a libertarian legal system and a freed market that empowers women to make life-affirming choices.

130. How is fetal self-ownership reconciled with the mother's prior claim to bodily autonomy?

Fetal self-ownership is not a violation of the woman's self-ownership or her bodily autonomy. Those who object bear the burden of proof that a fetus is initiating aggression against the woman. Here, I will explain how it cannot be.

Pro-choice analogies always fail.

- Trespass fails: the fetus doesn't enter from outside or cross any boundary; it comes into existence inside the only place human life ever begins.
- Thomson's violinist fails: no third party kidnaps you and plugs in a stranger; instead, a new person is created through the woman's own body in the one organ biologically ordered to that very purpose.

There is literally no analogous situation in nature or ethics. The womb is not a house that can be burgled or a hospital bed that can be hijacked—it is the sole natural site for the origin of a new human being. Analogies therefore cannot disprove fetal rights; they only reveal how unique pregnancy actually is.

Fetal self-ownership doesn't conflict with the woman's self-ownership—it's a natural consequence of her own voluntary choices. She alone controls the act that can create a new person and can abstain or use contraception to reduce (but never eliminate) that risk. When her choice results in a new rights-bearer, she is responsible for the outcome, just as she would be for any other foreseeable consequence of her actions.

Whether conception takes place intentionally or accidentally, the fetus thereby acquires a proprietary interest in continued life-support from the mother (and the father too). This interest simultaneously creates:

a. an enforceable positive duty on both parents to provide or arrange life-support until the child reaches independence, and
b. a corresponding parental right in both parents to direct the manner of that support (custody, medical decisions, upbringing, etc.), consistent with the NAP and the child's rights.

Abortion is not a way to "reclaim bodily autonomy" because in voluntary intercourse, there's no autonomy to reclaim. Abortion is aggression against an innocent rights-bearer and violates the NAP. The next obvious question is, what about the case where she has no voluntary choice over sexual intercourse? What about rape?

131. How does the case of rape affect the argument about fetal and maternal self-ownership?

In rape-caused pregnancy, the fetus remains completely innocent—its presence is never aggression, so abortion is impermissible, exactly as in voluntary cases.

The rapist, by his violence, commits grave rights-violations against two victims and forfeits all parental rights:

- Against the mother: rape plus nine months of non-consensual occupation and use of her body.
- Against the child: forcibly creating a dependent rights-bearer in trauma and foreseeable jeopardy, making the fetus a co-victim and rendering the rape itself an act of child abuse.

Consequently, the fetus's normal proprietary interest in parental life-support is altered: it now runs exclusively against the rapist as an enforceable debt, in addition to tort restitution he owes the child for the abuse inherent in violent conception.

Separately, the rapist owes the mother massive tort restitution covering the rape and the entire non-consensual gestation, birth, and adoption process; including full compensation for every physical, emotional, medical, and opportunity cost. Because safe removal before birth is currently impossible, every day the pregnancy continues counts as part of the rapist's ongoing tortious trespass against her body.

The mother, never having consented to creating this dependent rights-bearer, owes the fetus no positive duty; only the universal negative duty not to aggress against it. Continued gestation is biologically unavoidable today, but it is legally classified as part of the rapist's ongoing tort against her, for which she is owed massive restitution. She is therefore free at birth (or earlier if technology permits) to relinquish the child to adoption or to raise it herself if she chooses; either way, the rapist's independent tort and proprietary liabilities remain undiminished.

To guarantee she receives prompt and certain restitution even if the rapist is unknown or judgment-proof, private rape-pregnancy restitution insurance can pay out immediately (or over time) upon verified rape-conception, then subrogate both the mother's tort claim and the child's proprietary claim against the perpetrator.

A major aspect of reconciling the rights between the woman and the fetus, is coming to terms with judicial malfeasance in our existing system for sexual violence against women and girls.

132. How do you reconcile fetal self-ownership with its dependence on the mother?

The "dependence violates autonomy" argument for abortion collapses immediately: if total dependence justified killing, parents could lawfully kill born children whenever they become burdensome—financially, emotionally, or otherwise. No one accepts that consequence, so the argument fails.

In consensual sex, the parents' voluntary act foreseeably creates a new rights-bearer who is helplessly dependent on them. That child therefore acquires a legitimate proprietary interest in continued life-support from both parents—before and after birth—exactly like the restitution you owe if your voluntary action damages someone else's property. Killing the child to escape that duty is straightforward aggression.

In rape, the rapist alone bears responsibility. He commits rights-violations against both mother and child (rape + non-consensual bodily occupation against her; child abuse against the fetus by violently originating its life in trauma and jeopardy). He forfeits all parental rights and becomes solely liable for massive tort damages to the mother and full proprietary support of the child. The mother owes the fetus no positive duty; any continued gestation is simply part of the rapist's ongoing tort against her, for which she is owed massive restitution.

Dependence, therefore, never justifies abortion. Children are dependent on adults by nature until independence. The real solution is to make rape the single most expensive crime imaginable—massive financial obligation for the rapist—creating genuine deterrence while fully compensating both victims. Unlike retributive justice policies, retributive policies, such as Jessica's Law (see "Examining the Influence of Jessica's Law on Reported Forcible Rape"), show little to no deterrence against sexual violence.

Anything less is judicial malfeasance that pits women's and children's rights against each other instead of protecting both.

133. Does being a libertarian mean I should be personally opposed to abortion but favor legal abortion?

Criminalizing something involves two distinctions: (1) codifying the reason why it should be illegal; and (2) the manner of enforcement. What happens more often than not, especially in society today, is that we confuse these two distinctions. One can favor abortion prohibition and oppose certain forms of enforcement that are themselves unjust. In fact, the Christian libertarian view is that civil governance may not act unjustly even when attempting to exact justice.

A major element of the abortion debate (which Baldwin believes is the most divisive) deals with enforcement of abortion prohibition. For many pro-life libertarians, authoritarian enforcement of abortion prohibition proves to be draconian and therefore not a genuinely pro-life (or libertarian) alternative.

Concerns over draconian enforcement result in the ever growing number of "moderates" on both sides, who feel left with no other option than the "safe, legal, and rare" position. Other pro-lifers insist that abortion is morally outrageous enough to justify an authoritarian approach to enforcement. But it is the case with many issues concerning criminal justice that an authoritarian punitive system is unjust even for violent crimes that are already illicit.

So a libertarian pro-life position must take into account the criminal justice system as well. We are opposed to cruel and unusual punishment. The manner in which we deal with rights violators is a reflection of our views of the value of human life.

Libertarianism still involves many classical liberal principles that we take for granted: presumption of innocence, being secure in our persons and property, proof beyond a reasonable doubt, and others that necessarily exclude a number of current efforts to either incrementally decrease or abolish outright the practice of abortion.

Libertarians can rightly say something should be illegal, and even work towards legal prohibition of it, while also maintaining certain methods of enforcement and/or punishment should be in no way permissible.

134. How does the libertarian approach justify abortion restrictions in non-rape cases?

Many people believe that if abortion were illegal, that it would change all sorts of things. And it definitely could if abortion were outlawed by authoritarian (not libertarian) means. To be clear, we oppose the authoritarian enforcement of abortion prohibition. This is explained further in questions 137 and 138.

The libertarian approach is simply to treat abortion as though it's murder; this was the way abortion was treated per Leah Savas as mentioned previously. In other words, if you suspected someone committed murder (abortion), you could bring charges and present a case of evidence. The woman is presumed innocent until proven guilty, so you cannot violate her rights in an effort to find and substantiate that evidence. She has a right to not incriminate herself, to remain silent, secure in her body and property, and so forth. You'd have to demonstrate *mens rea* (criminal intent)—so miscarriage doesn't count. The hired hitman (abortionist) could be charged as well; both are responsible.

A cornerstone of common law was Blackstone's Ratio: "It is better that ten guilty persons escape than that one innocent suffer." Deference can be given in the case of duress (see Question 141), if the accused woman could demonstrate coercion into the crime.

In other words, libertarian enforcement of abortion prohibition looks like libertarian enforcement of any prohibition of violence in terms of the court of law: with regard for individual human rights and high standard of evidence to justify revoking the rights of the accused.

So would a libertarian legal order outlaw certain medical procedures or pharmaceuticals? No. We don't advocate outlawing things and behaviors simply because they are life threatening when used in particular ways. If we did, we'd have to endorse gun control laws. It may be the case that their use falls out of practice voluntarily, or are a tell-tale sign a crime has probably taken place, but bans on things just compound the problem of justice, they don't facilitate it.

135. Do personhood laws enacted by the state protect unborn lives?

We don't want the government defining personhood. It should only recognize that all living humans are also persons and, as such, the rights of the unborn should already be protected by the 14th Amendment to the U.S. Constitution. This was the fundamental problem with the now-overturned Roe v. Wade decision, where the Supreme Court declared that pre-viable fetuses do not qualify for 14th Amendment protection.

There simply is not a good reason why "human" shouldn't already equal "person," and another attempt at a government-imposed definition will make it worse. Every attempt to separate humanity from personhood results in privileged statuses, class warfare, racism, and eugenics. This is antithetical to a free society. While philosophical debates over what constitutes personhood are intriguing and educational, no philosopher or philosophical system of thought has successfully separated personhood from humanity in a way that doesn't ultimately result in a draconian and dystopian view of society.

The state doesn't have a good track record of protecting the rights of women either. In fact, *Roe v. Wade* also determined that a woman's bodily autonomy is subject first to state interest. So *her* rights are not really protected, either. If the existence of the state means protecting human rights of both women and the unborn, then why aren't they doing it? Why are they acting contrary to the 14th Amendment?

The unfortunate reality is that personhood has been defined—and redefined—to fit particular agendas. And in an authoritarian system of government, especially one which has so monopolized power, we are left with a system that has no incentive to uphold already existing laws that don't serve state interest. A libertarian system doesn't need a definition of personhood. Self-ownership, established at the completion of conception, is sufficient for protecting universal human rights.

136. If libertarians oppose state intervention, how can they protect the unborn while also supporting women in crisis pregnancies? Would this approach work without authoritarian enforcement?

There is an implied assumption that the most important problems in society must be solved, or facilitated, by the state. Not only is this a baseless assumption, the implications of such an assumption proves to be counterproductive. The libertarian approach not only is better suited for women in crisis pregnancies, it's more effective than authoritarian enforcement. Why?

The state eventually finds its role in preserving societal order unrewarding, expensive, and time-consuming (see Gerard Casey). Bored with its primary duties, it distracts by curtailing citizens' lives, liberty, and property more devastatingly than ordinary criminals. Ironically, this dubiously moral entity (the state) inefficiently provides essential services while presuming to guard public morals. Abortion is an emotionally volatile topic and advocacy against it is strongly driven by a sentiment of guarding public morals. While we agree abortion should legally count as murder, authoritarianism sets us up to tyrannizing and controlling women, especially mothers, all in the name of guarding public morality. This is the opposite of justice!

When it comes to libertarian enforcement of rights violations, we support the administration of legitimate justice. This excludes many measures that authoritarian pro-lifers believe are necessary to end abortion. When it comes to supporting women in crisis, we believe our strongest tool for ending the practice of abortion is the freed market.

If abortion and its associated culture are no longer subsidized through tax dollars and are addressed politically through a consistent approach to human rights, then by leaving the market to solve the myriad problems associated with unwanted or unplanned pregnancies, we'll discover a plethora of pro-woman, pro-child solutions that are both effective and cost-efficient.

Culture *is* the product of the market. The market will naturally mitigate against solutions that are dangerous, expensive, or disregard human rights (see Question 139).

Will a libertarian approach to prohibiting abortion be effective in adjudicating fetal rights violations when abortions do occur? Yes, various judicial remedies can be leveraged to produce effective deterrence and reduce recidivism. We have three in mind: tort, restorative, and retributive (see Question 138). A libertarian approach is flexible enough to match the form of justice more effectively to the crime.

137. Why don't libertarian Christians take the simpler approach, which is to call abortion sin and demand repentance?

Conservative pro-lifers are also not settled on how to end abortion, and this seemingly simpler approach, unfortunately, causes a lot of infighting; It's one reason why pro-lifers are often labeled religious fanatics, and not taken seriously. The moral argument concerning abortion is not in dispute. Theological arguments, however, are.

We affirm the transformative work of the Holy Spirit through the preaching of the gospel. We also affirm the call to Christians to live out and share the gospel in a fallen world. This positively impacts the culture around us. Though we would never discourage street preaching or persuasion through theological arguments, we do remember the church has always lived in a fallen world.

That said, there is immense value to the pro-life argument when we can address the issue from multiple angles. Having a sharp understanding of the science and drilling down with precision and accuracy, bolsters our claims that life (and rights) begin from conception. Understanding how the economy, and economic and monetary policy, negatively impacts women and mothers bolsters our claims that pro-lifers care about women after their baby is born. It puts us in the best position to understand what real solutions are, rather than spiritualizing it.

The mission of pro-lifers should be the same regardless of the legal status of abortion. We are to always, "do justice, love mercy, and walk humbly with our God" (Mic 6:8, NIV). We are to act as free people by serving one another humbly and in love, not covering evil (Gal 5:13, 1 Pet 2:16). Because as Christians, we're called to "be imitators of God … walk in love, just as Christ loved us" (Eph 5:2) … and doing so "while we were still sinners" (Rom 5:8). And we are to leave vengeance of evil to God (Rom 12:19).

138. What should be done with women who have an abortion?

It's necessary for pro-lifers to maintain a consistent strategy on this question regardless of the legality. Our aim with abortion should always be to save lives and uphold legitimate rights.

In a society that legally permits abortion:

Many pro-lifers are led to believe that a society that legally permits abortion is a hopeless situation for the unborn, when really the hopelessness comes from the polarization of the topic and not the legality of it.

A free market is something pro-life and pro-choice libertarians strive for. In fact, it is likely the free market is more important to the pro-life cause than legal prohibition of abortion. Why? In a free market, pro-life and pro-choice services would compete, especially if the government has deregulated the industry (we know this sounds ominous, but bear with us).

Crisis pregnancy centers (CPCs) already compete with abortion clinics, and abortion clinics are largely subsidized. There are more CPCs now than abortion clinics, and CPCs provide more services to women with unwanted pregnancies than abortion clinics. The key to dealing with abortion where it's legally permissible is to be both innovative and persuasive. Providing better, less expensive, life-affirming options results in more women voluntarily making life-affirming choices (whatever those may be). And really, even in a society where abortion is legally prohibited, we still need women voluntarily making life-affirming choices.

This has less to do with amping up polemics and more to do with innovation and the specialization of labor. In a free market society, some people are motivated to prevent unwanted pregnancies, and some are motivated to provide life-affirming options when unwanted pregnancies occur. We need both of these aspects of the market! This would leave a relatively small percentage motivated to provide a dangerous, expensive, and immoral service, like abortion. There's a great deal that can be done with women seeking to free themselves from an unwanted pregnancy, so long as there is a free market.

In a society that does not legally permit abortion:

In addition to what we mentioned above about free market remedies, we now add the layer of criminal justice. Unlike an authoritarian enforcement of abortion, a libertarian enforcement provides restitution, recompense, and effectively reduces recidivism rates. This could be **tort**; monetary restitution to a family member who has charged a woman with abortion. Or it could be **restorative**; wherein the woman learns the impact of her decision on family, friends, and even society. Or perhaps she obtains services to help her avoid circumstances of an unwanted pregnancy in the future. Or, in extreme cases where a woman, with *mens rea,* has gone beyond an act done in fear to an act done in outright hostility, **retributive** justice would still be an option. While we're under no illusions that retributive justice mitigates recidivism (it doesn't) we recognize there are some crimes heinous enough to warrant a stronger punishment.

The aim of a libertarian legal order is to administer genuine civil justice while avoiding cruel and unusual punishment.

139. What should be done with doctors who perform abortions?

In a society that legally permits abortion:

Many people believe that where abortion is legally permissible, the majority of society will embrace it. But this isn't necessarily the case. Much of what drives a pro-abortion orientation of our health care system is bureaucratic regulation and licensing. If we consider this, one might see why pro-life incrementalism (regulating the abortion industry to limit access) is a tactic used by conventional pro-lifers.

Both pro-lifers and pro-choicers fail to take into account the influence that bureaucratic regulation plays in promoting abortion. But a freed market, absent the regulations of bureaucratic agencies and legislators, wouldn't necessarily result in the abortion free-for-all that one might imagine.

Abortion providers would be subject to market forces just like any other service. If a free market in life-affirming options, both pro-choice and pro-life, were to occur, then the profession of abortionist becomes dangerous, expensive, and an immoral service. Malpractice insurers could be disincentivized to insure providers. Abortion alternatives would compete with abortion providers, and innovations would occur (on both sides) as a result. Both would also be subject to principles known as "creative destruction," where the market finds less expensive, more effective alternatives that render older options obsolete.

While it's hard to say where the market would land on this, it seems that much of the polarization of the abortion issue stems directly from the politicization of it. Depoliticizing it means the market can work sans the perverse incentive of politics. If these market forces can do things like lift the entire world out of abject poverty (which is mutually beneficial for all), then it's likely market forces will promote life-affirming options to women with unwanted pregnancies, and abortion providers would become an archaic, cruel, and expensive service incompatible with a free society.

In a society that does not legally permit abortion:

Given that a freed market would likely push abortion out as an acceptable means of dealing with unwanted pregnancies, then abortion service providers would likely be much fewer than we would imagine now. Nonetheless, abortion isn't likely to be completely eliminated by the market. So, if we operated in a free society where abortion was legally prohibited, it's not difficult to imagine what would happen to abortion providers. They would be subject to the same sort of criminal justice system described in Question 138. We still wouldn't need an authoritarian legal system to deal with illicit abortion services.

140. Post-Dobbs, how can you balance supporting state abortion bans despite those bans also including language that violates a woman's self-ownership?

The key thing is to be consistent. Simply banning abortion doesn't actually comport with a consistent view that abortion is a form of murder. Bans on abortion criminalize procedures or drugs, which necessitate authoritarian enforcement (see Questions 128, 134, and 135). Despite the emotional appeal bans on abortion bring, they should be opposed as a miscarriage of justice. Firearms advocates know this all too well—it's not the procedure or the tool that is on trial, it's the aggressor of one's person or property who is.

A libertarian enforcement of abortion prohibition would simply involve amending current state-level criminal codes to include abortion in the definition of murder. It's really uncomplicated. Advocacy is a big deal toward this end. Passing laws banning abortion just to claim political victory risks our rights, and expands state power when focused on the means and not the crime itself. In fact, should these kinds of bans on abortion stand, it will create the very legal precedent needed for similar bans on firearms, or anything else that can end life.

Many pro-lifers will object saying that unlike firearms, abortion procedures and medication have no net positive purposes. Actually, that's not true. The medications used for abortion can also be prescribed in cases of Cushing's syndrome (under the name Korlym) and is being researched as a potential remedy for cancer. Misoprostol can be used to aid labor induction in a full term (wanted) pregnancy, and various surgical procedures are used in cases of incomplete miscarriage and other female reproductive ailments such as uterine fibroids, endometrial hyperplasia, and others.

This is, in part, what has contributed to mass confusion on the left about abortion bans on procedures rather than being consistent, and changing the definition of murder to include abortion.

A pro-life libertarian position doesn't throw the baby out with the bath water, simply because this issue has (rightly) conjured up strong emotions. But we must act in response in a logical, level-headed, and philosophically consistent manner if we are to maintain a proper sense of justice. (And that notwithstanding the major overhaul our criminal justice system needs in the first place).

141. How does the libertarian Christian approach differ from the Abolitionist approach to abortion?

We agree with abolitionists that abortion constitutes murder (see Question 127), and civil governments must protect the rights of the unborn without exception. Additionally, we agree this issue should be handled at the state level. However, we disagree on the necessity of "personhood" laws (see Question 135), how to categorize the degree of abortive murder, their use of moral outrage as justice, and the Abolitionists' religious grounding of their views.

First, the libertarian argument does not depend on the 14th Amendment; it depends upon (God-given) self-ownership established at conception and corresponding non-aggression (see Question 127). Consequently, pro-life libertarianism upholds fetal rights even if the U.S. Constitution or Bill of Rights prove inadequate.

Second, not all women seeking abortions possess the premeditation and *mens rea* required for first-degree murder; making it more akin to manslaughter. Many are misled by propaganda claiming the fetus is mere tissue, only later realizing the truth and feeling horror. This lack of intent undermines claims that abortion equates to premeditated murder. Furthermore, abortions obtained under duress (e.g., threats from partners or family) warrant duress as a valid exonerating defense; instead, those coercing the woman should face charges.

Third, many abortions stem from economic pressures like high living costs and healthcare expenses. While these do not justify abortion, moral outrage should target the interventionist policies inflating those costs, not the women facing them. Advancing free-market reforms to foster prosperity and reduce economic stressors offers a far more effective path to ending abortion.

Finally, we reject the abolitionists' religious claim of national blessing and curse—an arguably unbiblical notion that frames abortion prohibition as a means to avert God's wrath on the nation for the sins of abortive women. This view imposes collective blood guilt on all Americans, particularly pro-life Christians, and attributes national hardships to divine curse. While God's law serves as a tutor revealing sin, man's misapplication or misappropriation of it does not. Retributive justice has proven ineffective at deterring crime or reducing recidivism, whereas tort and restorative approaches yield better outcomes (see Question 138). Insisting on punitive measures to vent moral outrage amounts to forbidden revenge, not justice.

We agree with abolitionists that abortion is murder and governments must protect unborn rights without exception (ideally at the state level), but differ on personhood laws, equating all abortions to first-degree murder, punishing women retributively, and invoking unbiblical national curse or collective blood guilt. As Murray Rothbard highlighted, drawing on William Lloyd Garrison's abolitionism: urge immediate abolition earnestly, for "it will, alas! be gradual abolition in the end"—yet "gradualism in theory is perpetuity in practice." Thus, principled immediatism, paired with practical gradualism, offers the surest path to ending abortion without compromising justice.

142. How can the libertarian Christian view avoid alienating potential allies among other pro-life supporters and other libertarians?

Alienation on this topic exists because the loudest, most militant voices compromise on a radically consistent approach to human rights. Those on the right compromise women's rights in favor of the fetus. And on the left, they compromise fetal rights in favor of the woman. It's this polarization that is alienating.

Pro-life libertarianism diffuses alienation on both sides of this debate. The loudest, most militant voices on the topic are in the minority. The majority exist in the expansive middle and encompass people who recognize both the complexity and the gravity of the issue and feel otherwise helpless to offer solutions. They may lean to one side or the other, but they reject militancy. This is the demographic we've found are more intrigued by pro-life libertarianism, as articulated by Baldwin.

Pro-life libertarianism doesn't pit the rights of one against the other; it reconciles them. This respects the self-ownership and bodily autonomy of both the woman and the fetus. Through radical consistency on human rights, in all stages of human life, we find the failures and weaknesses in our criminal justice system, our economy, and indeed, our very social fabric. We recognize that civil governance has one job, and subsidizing or propping up either side of this debate, or leveraging the power of the state against the market, leads to all sorts of injustices and abuses. We do not need to sacrifice some rights for the good of the rest. This is a false paradigm. If a theory of human rights is not radically consistent across all stages of human life, it is falsified and should be discarded.

Abortion is a canary in the coalmine; it is indicative of social, economic, and judicial ailments that as a society we keep turning a blind eye to. But if we face it, head on, we can solve a plethora of problems, holding human rights across the board in high regard. Pro-life libertarianism has the potential to be unifying.

143. Shouldn't I vote for a party or candidate that is pro-life? I just can't stomach voting for a pro-choice candidate!

What constitutes a pro-life party or candidate, though? The party normally associated with being pro-life, the Republican Party, removed their abortion plank and shifted to a safe, legal, and rare vision with Melania Trump's self-titled memoir. They may prefer heavily regulating it, but their interest is the same as that of the Supreme Court: to protect their reputation in the eyes of mainstream voters.

If we understand the abortion issue in three parts, then we can begin to see how pro-lifers might reconsider their vote:

1. The legal rights aspect
2. The legal enforcement aspect, and
3. The praxeological (or economic) aspect.

However, pro-life Republicans only agree on point one, and disagree on points two and three. Pro-life Republicans can't even agree on how to move forward. Since the party no longer represents their voice, even if the GOP only gave lip service before.

Libertarians have more common ground on abortion. Both pro-life libertarians and pro-choice libertarians agree on points two and three. And there is still an internal debate on point one, even among pro-choice libertarians. In 2022, the abortion plank of the Libertarian Party was repealed since pro-life libertarians make up a larger demographic of the party than previously believed. The beauty of the libertarian approach to abortion is that we agree on the practical application of legal enforcement and economics, even if we disagree on the legal rights aspect causing us to live in a legally pro-choice society. Pro-lifers can do more with that situation to end abortion than they can with a pro-life authoritarian party or candidate. In other words, even a pro-choice libertarian is more pro-life than a pro-life Republican.

The pro-life libertarian view is not one of control, but one of empowerment of the individual. So yes, you can vote for personally pro-choice libertarian candidates.

144. If you can be libertarian and pro-life, how does the Libertarian Party address abortion?

In 2022, the Libertarian Party removed the abortion plank entirely, and effectively became neutral on abortion. The aim of the party platform should reflect what the Party has consensus on, while recognizing the ongoing internal debate. The fact is, pro-choice and pro-life libertarians are unified on a lot more regarding abortion than non-libertarian factions are.

First, we all agree that tax dollars should not be used to subsidize abortion. A bedrock tenet of both the Party and libertarian philosophy is that taxation is theft, and governments should not be using it to subsidize anything, anyway, including abortion.

Second, both pro-life and pro-choice libertarians believe the free market is best equipped to provide options for women who aim to avoid unwanted and/or resolve crisis pregnancies. We also believe in the self-ownership of women (and therefore their bodily autonomy) that affords them the right to make decisions about their own bodies and reproductive goals.

Where we disagree is whether one of the plethora of options available to women should include abortion and whether self-ownership of the woman extends over the body of the fetus. Neither one of these disagreements should supersede our agreement that a free market economy and self-ownership are foundational to our views.

We argue that a consistent libertarian position on abortion doesn't compromise the rights of either the fetus or the woman. We still can work together with pro-choice libertarians toward the common goal of a free society, knowing that the logic and principles are on the side of the pro-life argument and that our friends will see the error of their position in time.

Additional Resources

"Kerry Baldwin and Walter Block Debate Abortion" by Kerry Baldwin. *Mere Liberty*, 19 Dec. 2019. https://mereliberty.com/philosophy/kerry-baldwin-and-walter-block-debate-abortion/.

"Libertarianism, Abortion, And Fetal Self-Ownership (1 of 2)" by Kerry Baldwin. *Mere Liberty*, 2025. https://mereliberty.com/podcasts/libertarianism-abortion-fetal-self-ownership/.

"Libertarianism, Abortion, And Fetal Self-Ownership (2 of 2)" by Kerry Baldwin. *Mere Liberty*, 2025. https://mereliberty.com/podcasts/libertarianism-abortion-an d-fetal-self-ownership-2-of-2/.

"Life vs Personhood and Abortion: The Metaphysical Distinction without a Legal Difference" by Kerry Baldwin. *Libertarian Christian Institute*, 9 Aug. 2022. https://libertarianchristians.com/2022/08/09/life-vs-personhood-abortion/.

"Mere Liberty: On Abortion" by Kerry Baldwin. *Mere Liberty*. https://mereliberty.com/tag/abortion/.

"The Libertarian Party is Officially Silent on Abortion" by Kerry Baldwin. *Libertarian Christian Institute*, 2 June 2022. https://libertarianchristians.com/2022/06/02/the-libertarian-party-is-officially-silent-on-abortion/.

"Meddling in Other Men's Affairs: The Case for Anarchy" by Gerard Casey. *Academia.edu*, 2007. https://www.academia.edu/332844/Meddling_In_Other_Mens_Affairs_The_Case_for_Anarchy.

"Examining the Influence of Jessica's Law on Reported Forcible Rape: A Time-Series Analysis" by Rick Dierenfeldt and Jennifer Varriale Carson. *Criminal Justice Policy Review*, vol. 28, no. 1, Feb. 2017, pp. 87–101. https://doi.org/10.1177/0887403414563139.

"Ep. 218 Kerry Baldwin Uses Property Rights to Correct Both Sides in the Abortion Debate." *Bob Murphy Show*, 18 Oct. 2021. https://www.bobmurphyshow.com/episodes/ep-218-kerry-baldwin-uses-property-rights-to-correct-both-sides-in-the-abortion-debate/.

Challenge to Liberty: Coming to Grips with the Abortion Issue by Ron Paul. (Ron Paul Enterprises, 1990).

"Ron Paul Explains His Anti-Abortion Position" by Ron Paul. *Reason*, 27 Apr. 2011. https://reason.com/2011/04/27/ron-paul-explains-his-anti-abo/.

The Early Church on Killing: A Comprehensive Sourcebook on War, Abortion, and Capital Punishment by Ronald J. Sider. (Baker Academic, 2012).

Abortion: A Rational Look at an Emotional Issue by R. C. Sproul. (NavPress, 1990).

"What's The Correct Libertarian Position on Abortion? A Soho Forum Debate." *YouTube*, uploaded by ReasonTV, 19 Dec. 2019. https://www.youtube.com/watch?v=OKU_xutF-eQ.

15

Environmental Stewardship

"Animals are forced to adjust themselves to the natural consequences of their environment; if they do not succeed in this process of adjustment, they are wiped out. Man is the only animal that is able—within definable limits—to adjust his environment purposively to suit him better."

—Ludwig von Mises

145. What does the Bible say about our responsibility to the earth's well-being?

God said in Genesis 1:28 to "Be fruitful and increase in number; fill the earth and subdue it." This is sometimes called the "dominion mandate." God created the world "good" in all its wonders, but it was also created to be built upon. We are given many stories and parables in the Bible that describe cultivation and caretaking of resources. The natural world in the beginning is described as a garden. Gardens are meant to be worked, and that work inherently means that the garden is incomplete. God's intent from the beginning was for humanity to work the earth, discover it, improve it, and create value from it. That work is a partnership with the one who created it all.

Therefore, the destiny of the whole earth is not pure wildland, but cultivation by its inhabitants. We are those cultivators. Utilizing the earth's resources for economic activity is what we were intended to do. Now, that does not mean we should be utterly wasteful and foolish with those resources, but it also means we do not have the right to assume we know better than our neighbor how he can use those resources that he rightfully owns. We can cooperate and trade to be more efficient and effective in the consumption of resources. In fact, history bears out that private ownership and free trade actually improve the environment overall!

146. What is the best way to understand our relationship to the environment?

The natural environment and the resources in it are great blessings that have been entrusted to us. That same environment also presents us with challenges that we must overcome in order to survive. Since the Fall, mankind has lived in a state of natural poverty and decay (Rom 8:18–21). Rather than the abundance and safety of the Garden of Eden, the fallen world constantly presents us with such dangers as starvation, exposure, and disease. In his mercy, God has provided people the tools that we need to face these challenges, starting with the first garments he fashioned for Adam and Eve from animal skins (Gen 3:21). God told Adam then that life after sin would require hard work (Gen 3:17–19, 23).

Though the world groans under the bonds of sin (Rom 8:22), it was not created as a cruel obstacle course to torment sinners. In fact, everywhere we look we can see visible wonders that point us to the glory of God (Ps 19). Abraham was the first to refer to God as the one who provides (Gen 22:14). As we use the resources that God has seen fit to grant us, we should use them as mindful stewards of a divine blessing (Matt 25:14–30). The righteous take care to leave something of value for future generations (Prov 13:22).

147. How could a free society protect the environment?

A free society is one where property rights are respected. Property owners have a much stronger incentive than politicians to protect natural resources because preserving precious capital provides for future opportunities to profit (see Question 148).

When property boundaries are clear and unambiguous, neighbors can more readily hold each other accountable. If a neighbor begins emitting toxic materials into a waterway, people downstream whose property is damaged should have a legal right to seek damages. Too often, in a system where environmental regulation is provided through government, political decision-making can lead to wasted resources. Under modern environmental regulatory regimes, polluters and other bad actors may even be able to defend their harmful actions legally by pointing to government licensure and compliance with relevant regulations.

In a free society, property owners would have a better chance at holding others accountable for the environmental damage that they cause. When environmental waste is priced into market behavior, market actors will seek to avoid that source of liability.

Finally, it is important to point out that governments do not just fail to protect the environment; in fact, they are among the worst polluters. A 2020 report concluded that the United States military is the "largest single institutional consumer of hydrocarbons in the world," and that American military spending artificially induces greater reliance on dirty fuel sources. As a society relies more on accountable market institutions and less on wasteful bureaucratic ones, it is reasonable to expect more careful environmental stewardship to result.

148. Doesn't the corporate drive for profit come at the expense of the environment?

Profit and preservation of resources are not necessarily at odds with each other. In fact, private property owners have a strong incentive to conserve their privately owned resources. Unfortunately, when government owns and manages natural resources, there is an incentive for private parties to attempt to get as much as they can until the resource is exhausted.

From time to time, we see news articles about a politician controversially opening up government-held lands to mineral extraction, logging, or some other potentially destructive private use. In these cases, the most basic incentive for conservation is missing: private ownership. It is rational to maximize profits, and for as long as human beings live in a fallen world with scarce resources, they will seek to do so.

If we wish to conserve natural resources, society must be ordered in a way that aligns the profit motive and self-interest with conservation. The most obvious reason that a forester would plant trees is that he expects someday to reap a benefit from that planting. Property rights are required for that expectation to make sense. Consumer preferences can drive even the largest companies to consciously work to reduce the negative environmental impacts of their enterprise, not because of government regulations, but because they want to be seen by consumers as environmentally responsible.

149. Even if we are improving the planet, what about adverse effects like pollution?

We must recognize that some pollution is inevitable simply because of entropy—energy consumed is never 100 percent efficient, and some wastage will occur in the form of emissions or lost heat.

The bigger concern, though, is hazardous waste. Is it possible that someone will pollute land? Yes, absolutely. And to the extent they own that land, then that is technically theirs to do with as they will. The moment, however, that they damage someone else with their pollutant, they are then liable for those damages in the form of a tort (a civil lawsuit). The polluter would have to pay restitution for those damages and restore the property (or health) of the claimant. But these people will be few, and those who act so foolishly will not own much.

Strong property rights and restitution end up protecting the environment far better than states ever do. Keep in mind as well that the top polluter in the United States is, ironically enough, the United States federal government.

150. What is the free market solution to climate change?

Many people argue that climate change is a problem that requires a global, collective effort to solve. Assuming that climate change is really happening and is anthropogenic in nature, a unilateral collective solution handed down from an organization like the United Nations is a bad idea.

The data looking back does not necessitate a forward look that is catastrophic. Models of the future are massively uncertain, and their predictions of global climates and the need to "fix" the predicted issues are dangerous at best and unjust to billions at worst. Forcing the world economy to use less energy not only will likely not have the intended effect but also will guarantee a tremendous loss of future economic growth that would benefit the impoverished across the world. A free market solution is to adhere to strong property rights and privatize transportation systems (see Questions 78–79).

In energy markets, nuclear power plants are without a doubt the most cost-effective and cleanest way to produce power, and governments that claim to care about the environment yet shackle nuclear energy with unending regulations are doing the world a terrible disservice. The most recent nuclear reactor to come online in the U.S. was installed in Tennessee—in 2016. The next most recent came online in 1996. Why is this? Regulatory burden. Ultimately, free markets are life-bringing ventures and restricting their operations by fiat will take that life away.

151. Since many in the world do not accept libertarianism, are there legitimate compromises that libertarians can make that would be considered good stewardship?

The first thing libertarians can do is to take personal responsibility for themselves and their businesses. It's a good thing, of course, not to litter and follow the general guidelines of their community with respect to waste disposal. Being mindful of appropriate reclamation of hazardous waste is essential. Libertarians should support the improvement of property rights laws as they pertain to pollution as well. Encourage efforts that move land and resources into private hands rather than the state. Remember, the environment's worst enemy is statism, not the free market.

Additional Resources

"Can the Government Solve Transportation Pollution?" by Norman Horn. *Ethics, Place, & Environment, Vol. 12, No. 2*, 2009. https://www.tandfonline.com/doi/abs/10.1080/13668790902863374.

Energy: The Master Resource by Jr. Robert L. Bradley and Richard W. Fulmer (Kendall Hunt Publishing, 2004).

Environmental Stewardship in the Judeo-Christian Tradition by Jay Richards and Robert Sirico (Acton Institute, 2007).

Fossil Future by Alex Epstein (Portfolio, 2022).

"Law, Property Rights, and Air Pollution" by Murray N. Rothbard. *Cato Journal, Vol. 2, No. 1*, 1982.

The Moral Case for Fossil Fuels by Alex Epstein (Portfolio, 2014).

Nature Unbound: Bureaucracy vs. the Environment by Randy T. Simmons, Ryan M. Yonk, and Kenneth J. Sim (Independent Institute, 2016).

"Our Stewardship Mandate" by Robert A. Sirico. *Acton Institute*, 2010. https://www.acton.org/pub/religion-liberty/volume-7-number-2/our-stewardship-mandate.

"Property Rights vs. Environmental Ruin" by David Theroux. *Independent Institute*, 1994. https://www.independent.org/article/1994/08/01/property-rights-vs-environmental-ruin/.

Prosperity and Poverty: The Compassionate Use of Resources in a World of Scarcity by E. Calvin Beisner (Wipf & Stock, 2001).

Salvation Means Creation Healed: The Ecology of Sin and Grace by Howard A. Snyder and Joel Scandrett (Cascade Books, 2011).

16

The American Revolution and the U.S. Constitution

"[T]he history of human events is, for better or worse, the history of men and women acting according to a conception of what they think is good, right, just, and true."

—C. Bradley Thompson

"That our story begins with Americans falling short of the ideals embedded in the Founding is not an indictment of the ideas; it is testament to the nobility of America's story arc."

—Jonah Goldberg

152. If libertarians emphasize freedom from government, can the American Revolution be considered a libertarian movement?

As described in the Declaration of Independence, many of the motives of the American Revolution were indeed recognizable as libertarian, including objections to King George's obstruction of immigration to the American colonies, his use of judges who were effectively controlled by him through their pay and the threat of their removal from office, his commissioning of swarms of bureaucrats to harass Americans, his maintenance of occupying armies, his subjugation of courts to martial authorities, his quartering of troops in private homes, his effective grant of civil and criminal immunity to his soldiers, his interference with international trade, his imposition of taxes on Americans, his extradition of political enemies for foreign trial, and his use of barbaric mercenaries against his former subjects, among others.

Other complaints were about the English king's interference with local governments established in the states. Those complaints were not strictly about libertarian concerns, but rather about local rulers being frustrated by a foreign ruler.

Even if we assume for the sake of argument that these latter concerns about American self-government were adjacent to and compatible with libertarianism, it is still the case that judging the motives of the Revolution is insufficient to conclude that the Revolution itself was libertarian. In furtherance of the war, the Continental Congress used inflationary money, forcible conscription at the state and local level, and impressment of private property into military use. This last practice, which amounted to the government's forcible taking of private property in exchange for practically worthless scrip, financially ruined many of the farmers and merchants whose property was appropriated for public use. George Washington wrote in a 1780 letter that this taking was evil but was nonetheless justified as a lesser evil than the collapse of his army.

In conclusion, many of the stated causes of the Revolution were undeniably compatible with libertarian thinking. However, the unlibertarian means used to conduct the war gravely violated the rights of the very same people it was supposedly waged to defend.

153. Did the American Revolutionaries, many who claimed to be Christian, violate Romans 13 or Jesus' teachings about turning the other cheek?

Romans 13 is sometimes raised as a blanket condemnation of any kind of political resistance, but Paul is not actually arguing that obedience to evil or corrupt rulers is always required. Romans 13 presumes that governing authorities are acting as God's servants for good by punishing wrongdoers and protecting the innocent. When they don't, this raises the possibility of civil disobedience.

On the other hand, while Christian traditions have interpreted Jesus' command to turn the other cheek (Matt 5:38–39) in different ways, it seems to fit into a broader New Testament ethic that it is better to suffer indignity than to respond with violence (see also 1 Pet 2:11–25, 1 Tim 2:1–2). This principle is true for Christians even though humans have a natural right to resist aggression.

Thus, even if one grants that the colonists had cause for resistance, were the constraints (arguably minimal by today's standards of big government encroachment) placed on them from across an ocean truly grave enough to justify a bloody war? Were other options still available? And if not, would it have been more Christlike to endure the indignity of British rule while seeking freedom by peaceful means?

Libertarian Christians answer these questions differently. While many Founders advanced liberty in profound ways, few libertarians would say they always got it right. Principled Christians will side with them when they did, and critique them when they didn't.

154. Did the Revolutionary War meet the criteria of just war theory?

Just war theory is traditionally framed around three criteria:

- *jus ad bellum* (justice in going to war, or a just cause)
- *jus in bello* (justice in the conduct of war)
- *jus post bellum* (justice after war)

Under *jus ad bellum*, the Revolution's defenders cited taxation without representation, infringements on natural rights, and the quartering of troops in peacetime. However, while many colonists agreed with these grievances, plenty remained loyal to Britain. Motives were mixed—quests for liberty coexisted with ambitions for land, commerce, and power. The necessity of war was questionable: Britain committed injustices but was far from a wholly despotic regime. Options like prolonged diplomacy or economic resistance may not have been fully tried. Whether the gains outweighed the immense human cost remains disputed.

Measured against *jus in bello* and *jus post bellum*, the Revolution's record is uneven. While combatants and civilians were sometimes distinguished, Loyalists and Native tribes endured persecution, displacement, and severe losses. Proportionality and discrimination were inconsistently upheld by both sides. After the war, lingering hostilities divided communities, Loyalists were driven into exile, and many Native allies of Britain lost their lands. Reconciliation efforts were scarce, and some even argue the new government was more centralized than before. Most wars—even revolutions—are morally complex. We can value the progress that resulted from America's Revolution while resisting the temptation to whitewash its flaws or mythologize its story.

155. In what ways might the American Revolution conflict with libertarian principles like non-aggression and voluntary association?

Just war theory asks whether a conflict is morally justified; libertarian principles go further, asking whether the Revolution adhered to non-aggression and voluntarism. By those standards, the Revolution reveals tensions. Britain committed genuine wrongs, but revolutionary actions often crossed the line from defense into aggression. Property destruction, mob violence, and reprisals against dissenters violated the NAP.

The principle of voluntary association also fared poorly. Many who wished to remain loyal to Britain—or simply avoid the conflict altogether—were dispossessed or exiled. Native American tribes were dragged into a war not of their choosing and punished regardless of which side they supported. Enslaved Africans remained in bondage even as colonists invoked arguments grounded in liberty and natural rights. In all these cases, individuals were denied the freedom to live without coerced allegiance.

Finally, while Loyalists had no right to impose British rule on those who resisted, neither did revolutionaries and their state representatives have the right to impose a new government on dissenters. Leaving aside that democracy is not a legitimate substitute for consent, even on its own terms the ratifying conventions relied on restricted suffrage, excluding women, slaves, Native Americans, and many poor free men. At best, a narrow slice of society consented, yet their decision was treated as binding on everyone—including future generations who never agreed. From a libertarian perspective, that is no more legitimate than Britain's earlier claim to rule the colonies.

156. How did Christian leaders during the American Revolution use the Bible to support liberty and independence?

Christian pastors played a critical role in providing a moral basis for the war to secede from the British monarchy. At the end of 1750, long before the War for Independence, Boston pastor Jonathan Mayhew preached an influential sermon asserting that rebellion against a tyrant was not sinful and was in fact "glorious struggle" and a sacred duty. In his "Discourse Concerning Unlimited Submission and Non-Resistance to the Higher Powers," Mayhew discussed Romans 13, asserting that where tyrannical rulers frustrated the biblically enumerated purposes of civil government by encouraging the bad and discouraging the good, submission is not commanded, because such submission would bring about "the ruin and misery of society."

In 1776, a Lutheran pastor living in Virginia, Peter Muhlenberg, taught from Ecclesiastes 3, concluding that there was "a time to preach and a time to fight," after which he doffed his clerical robe to reveal a Continental Army officer's uniform beneath it.

Other Christian ministers followed in this line of reasoning and during the Revolution came to be described as the "Black-Robed Regiment" because of the important role they played in fomenting rebellion against King George. Some used the example of resistance to Pharaoh prior to the Exodus to demonstrate that rebellion against unjust rulers was morally permissible. Others argued that monarchy was fundamentally in opposition to God, citing Israel's rebellious institution of the monarchy in 1 Samuel 8.

157. How libertarian is the United States Constitution?

The United States Constitution created a more powerful and more centralized national government than the one that came before it under the Articles of Confederation. In the view of many of its Framers, the inability to levy national taxes, regulate interstate commerce, and enforce national laws directly were untenable flaws in the national government that had operated since 1777.

The product of the Philadelphia convention was a founding document for a new federal government with national taxing power, the enumerated authority to regulate interstate and international commerce, and an executive branch to carry out and enforce national policy.

The Framers of the Constitution understood that they were creating a dangerous new instrumentality, and they attempted to embed in its design a system of checks and balances to restrain the different elements of the new government, or at least slow the progress of tyranny. The Bill of Rights was even more explicit in placing clear limits on the powers of the federal government to prevent future violations of fundamental rights.

Many lament that America has increasingly drifted away from its constitutional moorings. Some founders made this observation long ago and questioned whether the Constitution would effectively restrain the government that it had created. Prominent Virginian George Mason, for instance, warned about an "elective monarchy," an unchecked federal judiciary, and the dangers of the Necessary and Proper Clause, ultimately refusing to sign the Constitution. Eighty years after the convention in Philadelphia, Lysander Spooner wrote of the Constitution that "it has either authorized such a government as we have had, or has been powerless to prevent it."

158. Would returning to the original intent of the Constitution move us closer to a more libertarian society?

There are certainly examples where the Constitution has been used in the courts to restrain government. The Constitution, on its face, created a limited form of government with certain, enumerated powers. The Bill of Rights provided even greater detail on certain proscriptions that the Framers at Philadelphia may have believed were implicit in the original document. Legal appeals based in the text of the Constitution have worked to protect the interests of people relying on their constitutional rights to free speech, free assembly, free religious practice, keeping and bearing arms, freedom from unlawful searches and seizures, jury trial, refusing to self-incriminate, and many other freedoms worth defending.

However, it is a mistake to ascribe a single, unified intent to the whole Constitution. Although there was some agreement between those at the convention about their purposes, more than fifty men were involved, and they disagreed on a number of important topics. The actual meaning of their work product was the subject of disagreement almost immediately after adjournment, and those men voting on particular language may have understood and intended it to mean different things at the time that they were debating and voting on changes to the text.

Furthermore, modern attempts to divine the text's original intent rather than to understand the original meaning of the words used create a risk of overlaying modern wishful thinking on the text itself and potentially leading to an interpretation that goes against what the document actually says, based on claims about what certain of the Framers wanted it to say.

159. Does the presence of slavery in the founding era complicate the libertarian and Christian perspective on the American founding?

The famous 19th century abolitionist William Lloyd Garrison pointed out that the Constitution did not outlaw slavery or even condemn it. While some of the framers wanted such a declaration, others (largely of the southern states) would have immediately left the proceedings if such an idea had been seriously considered. As a result, Garrison saw the Constitution as an immoral, slavery-supporting document that compromised on truth.

Frederick Douglass, the 19th century runaway slave, intellectual, and anti-slavery activist, initially agreed, writing that the Constitution supported slavery and was thus a "covenant with death and an agreement with hell."

But after reflecting on the arguments of abolitionists Lysander Spooner and Gerrit Smith, Douglass eventually had to admit, and did so publicly, that the Constitution could and should "be wielded in behalf of emancipation." This was not only because the Constitution provided for the end of the trade in 1808 (Article 1, Section 9), but because the principles it espoused—like equality, consent, and self-governance—pointed to slavery's abolition.

While some would be inclined to sacralize America's founders and treat their words as infallible, and others are intent on demonizing them and rubbishing their insights, a more nuanced assessment like Douglass' is required. Since, as Douglass argued, "Liberty and Slavery–opposite as Heaven and Hell–are both in the

Constitution," we must stand on the shoulders of these men when they saw the world through the light of truth and set aside their guidance when it would pull us back toward unchristian and anti-liberty practices and ideas.

Additional Resources

America's Revolutionary Mind by C. Bradley Thompson, et al. (Encounter, 2019).

Conceived in Liberty (Vols. 3 & 4) by Murray Rothbard (Ludwig von Mises Institute, 2011).

The Great Contradiction: The Tragic Side of the American Founding by Joseph Ellis (Knopf, 2025).

In God We Don't Trust by David Bercot (Scroll, 2011).

The Magdeburg Confession (1550)

Politically Incorrect Guide to American History by Jr. Thomas E. Woods (Regnery, 2004).

The Spirit of '76 by Alexander Salter (American Institute for Economic Research, 2023).

Suicide of the West by Jonah Goldberg (Crown Forum, 2018).

Vindiciae Contra Tyrannos (A Defense of Liberty Against Tyrants) by Stephen Junius Brutus (1579).

17

Healthcare

"When we give government the power to make medical decisions for us, we in essence accept that the state owns our bodies."
—Dr. Ron Paul, former Congressman

160. How would people acquire healthcare in a free society?

In a free society, healthcare products and services would be produced in the marketplace in accordance with the laws of supply and demand just like all other goods and services. Even now, the modern U.S. healthcare system is market driven in many cases, but the processes are often distorted by heavy government intervention in both the provision of the healthcare products and services themselves (such as primary care doctors, surgeries, and pharmaceutical drugs) as well as the provision of the financial services of insurance (and insurance-adjacent services). Government regulation of insurance services reduces competition and decreases efficiencies that would lower premiums and make healthcare more affordable for everyone.

Regulations such as the Affordable Care Act were passed under the guise of making healthcare less expensive, yet total national health expenditures grew from 17.1% of GDP in 2009 to 17.6% in 2023, with projections reaching 20.3% by 2033 despite slower per capita growth post-ACA. Instead of lowering costs, we continue to see growth of government intervention and regulation. This is not sustainable, and the answer is to allow for a truly free market in healthcare and insurance services.

When markets are allowed to work, we would see a proliferation of useful alternative models for provision of care. For instance, even now "health sharing ministries" offer an alternative to commercial insurance and managed care that works well for many people. The important thing to remember is that there isn't a one-size-fits-all approach in nearly any market, and government control leads to consolidation and restriction of choice rather than enabling people to determine what they need and find a means to receive care. In addition, charity has always been an important part of healthcare, and it will continue to be so.

161. If healthcare is a basic human need, is it really something the free market should handle like any other service?

Our contention is that what many call "basic human needs" are not the legitimate purview of civil governance. Food, clothing, and shelter are certainly considered basic human needs, yet free markets and charitable services meet those needs far better than political rationing. Healthcare is important, but that does not give moral license to initiate aggression against others to provide it. In fact, when the government manages basic human needs, what results is inflation, shortages, and reduced access by those who need them most. Bureaucracy slows innovation, it doesn't provoke it. It's more accurate to say that basic human needs, to include health care, are too important to be left to the government to provide.

Christians ought to readily affirm the distinction that though we have a moral duty to help those in need, that duty does not create a legal claim upon our neighbor allowing confiscation of their property. Coerced "compassion" undermines dignity and consent. Scripture commends the Good Samaritan for freely aiding the injured man, not for forcing others to pay for his charity. As Paul says, God loves a cheerful giver (2 Cor 9:7), not an extorted one.

Practically, markets excel at matching diverse needs with diverse solutions. When prices are visible and entry is open, innovation flourishes and enables a variety of answers to healthcare problems. Centralized systems, by contrast, over-standardize and then ration, often putting bureaucracy over patients.

A free society treats healthcare as morally special yet economically normal. There will be a variety of services available, at a variety of price levels, serving people voluntarily and profitably, with protections in place enabling charitable provision to those in need.

162. Won't the free market result in higher costs and unequal access to healthcare services?

Today's high costs are not a market failure but the result of anti-market design: hidden prices, third-party payment that severs buyer from seller, mandated benefits, licensing cartels, and certificate-of-need laws that restrict supply. When prices are visible and entry is open, costs tend to fall and service improves. Consider medical providers outside of the typical system, like LASIK, many imaging centers, and direct primary care businesses. Their prices have been stable or declining while quality and convenience rose because these providers must win patients, not kowtow to regulators.

Access also broadens when delivery models diversify. Retail clinics, telehealth, mobile units, transparent surgical bundles, nonprofit and faith-based clinics, and small local practices meet different needs at different price points. Removing barriers that prevent nurse practitioners, pharmacists, and other clinicians from practicing to the top of their training expands capacity quickly, especially in underserved areas.

Markets do not automatically erase every inequality or price increase, but they shrink the problems gradually by lowering baseline costs and multiplying options. The remaining gaps are best met by voluntary tools: health sharing communities, church benevolence funds, philanthropic hospitals, and targeted local charity. Overall, freedom in medicine is a path that makes care more affordable and more humane.

163. How would a free-market approach keep health insurance costs in check if companies are still driven by profit?

Consumer willingness to pay determines prices, not profit margins. High costs in health insurance are a result of government intervention setting prices, mandating what services insurance must cover, and requiring consumers to purchase regardless of their own demands. To fix these problems today, insurance needs to function not as prepaid medical care that does everything, but rather as a real risk-mitigation service covering expensive, rare, unpredictable events. Pair catastrophic policies with competition for routine care, and insurance premiums will begin to reflect real risk rather than prepaid conveniences.

Costs fall further when competition in insurance happens freely and people can switch their insurance easily. Repeal anti-competitive regulations, allow interstate portability of insurance policies, and stop preventing price comparisons of plans and treatments. Remove regulations that mandate one-size-fits-all policies, bloated with services many do not want, and that will free up the market for insurance to compete on price.

Stability in healthcare services will come from sound risk tools rather than political micromanagement. As it is, the actual customer for medical care often ends up being the insurance company rather than the patient. Freer underwriting with clear, upfront rules that include anti-fraud and quality controls will make it possible to repair the broken relationship of insurer to patient, and patient to provider. Insurers and providers that don't work well with their customers—the patients—will ultimately lose business.

164. Without government regulation, how would proper medical standards and patient safety be guaranteed?

Standards do not require a political monopoly, and safety is upheld through layered, overlapping institutions that answer to the marketplace rather than government. The frameworks already exist in many respects, but they often rely too heavily on the approval and permission of the state to operate. Licensing laws end up restricting supply, rather than encourage innovation and broader availability of services. Accreditation, however, isn't the same as licensing laws. Even now, private accreditation bodies evaluate hospitals, labs, and clinics against rigorous protocols. Board certifications signal physician competence, and specialty colleges update standards as knowledge advances. Malpractice carriers and insurers demand risk-reducing practices because their capital is on the line; poor performers pay higher premiums or lose coverage. Tort law also remains as a backstop for negligence.

The United States actually has considerable means of doing this already through groups like Leapfrog, the Patient-Centered Outcomes Research Institute, the Facility Guidelines Institute, and more. Granted, many of these institutions have close ties to government agencies and receive monies from the government, but the structures are in place to further separate medicine and state. Clearly, what's needed is to go farther in these directions, rather than centralize medical practice within government bodies. Competition among standard-setters is an advantage and feature, not a bug. Multiple bodies can innovate in methods and respond faster than a one-size bureaucracy.

165. How could a libertarian approach meet the needs of the poor and uninsured without relying on mandatory insurance or government programs?

High costs are the result of government interference in the marketplace. Lowering the baseline price of care occurs when free markets are allowed to work and competition in services is the norm. As prices fall, many services become affordable without subsidies. Furthermore, decreasing costs makes every charitable dollar go further. Health sharing communities, church benevolence funds, and local foundations can fund care directly, with fewer administrative costs on average.

But it won't stop there, as many other means that even now operate on the periphery will be elevated as, once again, lower costs make it even easier to supply extra needs. Hospitals and clinics can pledge a set portion of charity care, or compete with discounts for cash payments for services to lower the costs even more. Physicians can offer pro bono clinics coordinated with churches and nonprofit partners, much like medical missions do. Community clinics, mobile units, and telehealth can expand access in underserved areas at modest, scalable cost. Opportunities will exist when innovation is not bound up through regulation.

A free society that honors voluntary exchange and private charity can care for the vulnerable with greater dignity, flexibility, and effectiveness.

166. How would malpractice and medical negligence be addressed?

Sometimes professionals do not deliver a good work product to their clients. While this may in many cases be through no fault of the professional service providers, a person who has had extensive training, testing, and experience in the field may make a mistake out of negligence or recklessness.

The standard of care in a particular profession can be dynamic. In the field of medicine, where scientific understanding is continuously advancing, standards of care can shift dramatically in a few years. For example, at the turn of the twenty-first century, cancers were primarily treated based on their location and stage of progression, whereas cancer treatment today is much more greatly influenced by information gleaned from the genomic sequencing of tumors. An oncologist in the year 2000 might have followed a course of treatment that would be considered negligent and sub-standard just a couple of decades later. Similar rapid advances have occurred in recent years in the management of ischemic strokes, Hepatitis C, and even Type 2 Diabetes.

Even today, in the government court system, professional malpractice cases are largely dictated by standards of care that are developed and implemented through a polycentric process involving numerous medical institutions across the globe all involved in practicing and advancing medical science. These subject matter experts are far better situated than politicians to determine what constitutes malpractice. An agreement on how to arbitrate any claim arising from a course of medical care could be part of the intake procedures at doctors offices and hospitals, just like arbitration agreements exist in the fine print on cruise ship tickets.

Political attempts to put a thumb on the scale in favor of plaintiffs ("pro-victim") or in favor of professionals ("pro-business") can distort the litigation process and result in less just outcomes, either subjecting business to excessive liability or capping recoverable damages for victims. These policies may also discourage development of a particular profession due to the political risk involved in any future investment.

167. What role should personal responsibility play in a libertarian approach to healthcare and public health?

To understand this, we begin with the principles of self-ownership and non-aggression. You own yourself; you are responsible for your own life. Additionally, you may not initiate physical coercion against the person or property of others.

So, your health and well-being is a major facet of your life, and since you are responsible for your life, you are responsible for your health and well-being. This is not to say that you exist on an island, or in some way isolated from other people. Of course, other people and things have touchpoints in your life that can positively, or negatively, impact it. But so long as that impact is not the result of initiatory coercion against you, your response may not involve coercion. That doesn't mean some decision or action doesn't need to happen, it only means what you decide must be non-coercive.

In matters of public health, especially in terms of infectious disease, the dominant assumption is that someone else (an expert, or governing official) must dictate the decisions made by the mass populace in order to ensure the greatest good for the greatest number. Therefore, in this view, initiatory coercion is permissible because some people will make decisions that might contribute to the spread of infection. But, then, people become subject to poor decisions and even ulterior motives of those initiating coercion in the name of public health.

When the responsibility over your life and liberty is removed from you, your right is as well. Libertarianism holds that individuals are in the best position to make the best possible decisions. It doesn't guarantee that they will make the best decisions, but no one else is in the position to do so. Knowing this, not only do you have a right and responsibility to make decisions about your own health and well-being, but it behooves you to account for the possible, and realistically likely, that other people's poor decisions may impact you, and so your health and well-being involves a sort of pre-emptive defense to protect yourself and mitigate against spread of infection.

As a general rule, simply existing as an infected person does not constitute an act of aggression, and so a coercive response to an infected person is not justified. There are certainly ways to weaponize infection, but it's the action of weaponization that justifies a coercive response, not the mere existence of it.

168. How would mental health and addiction treatment be handled in a society without state-run healthcare?

A humane approach requires us to destigmatize, diversify options, and decriminalize. It starts by treating people as individuals and neighbors. Addiction should be addressed as a health issue, not a criminal issue. Ending the War on Drugs (see Chapter 12) is crucial, and will free resources for treatment, recovery housing, and family support. Once we move past the old thinking that addiction and mental health issues require the aggression of the state to solve, progress begins.

Church ministries, twelve-step groups, and other community programs can partner with medical providers for detox and medication-assisted treatment when appropriate. Community responder teams and health professionals can handle many behavioral health crises far more safely than jail or an ER hallway. Mental health care is already moving forward in many ways in spite of government actions, and it's clear that government agencies always lag behind the important innovations in psychiatric research and treatments. If we really care about helping people, rather than just locking them up, then removing the state from this side of health care is essential.

169. Should parents have the legal right to refuse life-saving medical treatment for their children?

Children rely on parents for their health and well-being, as they lack the developmental capacity to manage it themselves. Parents, in turn, seek guidance from various sources to make the best decisions possible. When a child is ill, these choices carry significant weight.

A key issue with the question of mandating "life-saving" treatments is defining what truly qualifies as life-saving and how benefits stack up against risks. Many assume such interventions guarantee only positive outcomes, but most medical treatments involve trade-offs. Risks can vary greatly depending on the child's or family's medical history. Moreover, different health traditions may offer viable alternatives to conventional approaches.

Highlighting these complexities underscores that the gravity of a decision does not strip parents of their right to make it. As Thomas Sowell observed, there are no solutions—only trade-offs. F. A. Hayek emphasized that knowledge is dispersed throughout society. A specialist may know more about a specific disease than a parent, but the doctor lacks full insight into the family's unique circumstances, values, or alternative perspectives. A physician's expertise deserves respect, but it is not infallible, nor the sole valid option. Crucially, doctors do not bear the legal right or responsibility for the final decision—parents do.

On the other hand, negligence is a legitimate concern. While most libertarians reject the notion that parents have a right to neglect their children, Murray Rothbard's extreme view—that no enforceable positive obligations exist, permitting neglect without criminality—represents a flawed outlier in libertarian thought. However, pursuing second opinions, exploring alternatives, and carefully weighing risks and benefits is the opposite of negligence, even if others view a particular treatment as obviously superior. Claims of negligence severe enough to violate a child's rights must be proven before an impartial third party. Simply refusing a recommended treatment does not automatically constitute neglect. Kerry Baldwin's framework of fetal self-ownership (see Chapter 14) helpfully resolves Rothbard's error by grounding parental duties in the child's inherent rights from conception, establishing enforceable obligations without positive rights violations.

Parents retain the fundamental right to make informed choices about their child's care, including opting for non-standard approaches when they deem them appropriate.

170. How should libertarians approach emerging and risky medical technologies like gene editing, mRNA treatments, neurotechnology, or AI-driven diagnostics?

The libertarian position is that all peaceful activity in medical practice ought to be legal. Thus, libertarians default to encouraging innovation with clear ethical guidelines of consent and clear responsibility for harms. Patients deserve informed consent, honest disclosure of risks, and the freedom to seek second opinions. Governments, however, have routinely misinterpreted or even misrepresented risks to citizens, slowing innovation or sometimes squelching it entirely. We have enough data now to demonstrate that burdensome regulations slowing technological progress are responsible for preventable deaths—all caused by preventing treatments and technologies from coming to market.

Absent government interference, structures already exist in the marketplace to ensure new technology works as intended. Independent testing labs and professional societies can evaluate safety and efficacy without political gatekeeping that freezes progress. Post-treatment monitoring by watchdog organizations, medical device registries analogous to UL listings, and rapid recall pathways will help to alert the public and doctors to problems and correct mistakes quickly.

Different risk classes call for different guardrails, but markets manage risk far better than governments. Accountability in the marketplace works, since the incentives are aligned between suppliers of new products and the patients who are demanding them. By separating the state from healthcare, innovation will be unleashed in ways we can only imagine.

171. How does the medical freedom movement align with core libertarian principles such personal choice and limited government?

Medical freedom is a natural extension of libertarian principles. Patients should be free to accept or refuse treatment, seek second opinions, choose among different treatment options, and pursue off-label uses with their doctor. Clinicians should be free to practice according to conscience and evidence as opposed to following political dictates. Open debate and access to information are important to maintaining robust medical practices, whereas censorship, whether directly by government or prompted by government on public platforms, erodes trust.

Current medical and insurance practices, including licensing laws, burdensome regulations, and one-size mandates contradict these principles by narrowing options and protecting large incumbents from competition. A free system encourages reducing government involvement and increasing transparency so people can judge quality for themselves. Limited government means protecting against force and fraud, adjudicating genuine harms, and otherwise letting people contract for care as they see fit.

Government force in medical practice is antithetical to the goal of proper patient care. Compassion is not coercion. A society that practices non-aggression in all aspects of medicine will be safer, kinder, more creative, and ultimately have better health outcomes.

Additional Resources

Death by Regulation: How We Were Robbed of a Golden Age of Health How We Can Reclaim It by Mary J. Ruwart (Sunstar Press, 2018).

18

Public Health and Pandemics

"My contention is that good men (not bad men) consistently acting upon that position would act as cruelly and unjustly as the greatest tyrants. They might in some respects act even worse. Of all tyrannies, a tyranny sincerely exercised for the good of its victims may be the most oppressive. It would be better to live under robber barons than under omnipotent moral busybodies. The robber baron's cruelty may sometimes sleep, his cupidity may at some point be satiated; but those who torment us for our own good will torment us without end for they do so with the approval of their own conscience."

—C.S. Lewis

172. Can a society without a centralized public health agency guarantee health and safety for everyone?

No system or agency can guarantee perfect safety, and the promise of "guarantee" invites overreach. An achievable, realistic goal is to reduce risk while respecting rights. A decentralized approach does this better by aligning incentives of those responsible with healthcare provisioning with their customers—communities and patients. Local health departments, hospitals, universities, private labs, insurers, and employer consortia can all gather data, publish risk data, and adapt faster than a central planning government. When information is open and practice is not centrally managed, reputation and the redundancy of multiple overlapping marketplace actors is an added protection against errors, and those errors that are made are generally small in scope. But as we have distinctly observed with the COVID-19 pandemic, errors made from centrally-planned government agencies have much wider harms.

Nobody can abolish risk entirely, but we can provide transparency, options, and accountability. Decentralization provides many paths to the same goal: fewer deaths, less disruption, and fewer rights violations.

173. How should a government balance the need for public health with respect for personal freedoms?

If rights can be revoked when officials say "public health is at stake," then they are not rights in the first place. Government, if involved at all, should primarily be available to inform, help coordinate in acute emergencies, and punish aggression and fraud. Essential principles should serve as the test for all powers used. Necessity, proportionality, least restrictive means, and due process all limit the ability of government to overstep its bounds.

Respecting freedom also means being sensitive to the different situations that emerge in public health crises. Prioritize resources to nursing homes and high-risk facilities rather than closing parks, businesses, churches, and civic centers. Publish research on risk for different settings so people can self-sort and judge activities themselves. Safeguard freedom of movement and association unless a narrow, evidence-based measure is justified and time-limited.

Scientific humility matters. The COVID-19 pandemic era was a difficult and uncertain time. That suggests we should be exercising caution around restrictions, disclosing trade-offs with honesty, and willing to revise guidance in public. People can effectively cooperate when they are told the truth and are free to choose prudent measures for themselves and their families.

174. How does the concept of the Harm Principle apply to libertarian policies on public health and safety?

John Stuart Mill's Harm Principle allows restricting liberty only to prevent harm to others—a concept echoed in the Hippocratic Oath's prioritization of low-harm treatments. However, libertarianism's Non-Aggression Principle (NAP) differs fundamentally: it criminalizes only initiatory physical coercion, not any perceived harm. As Kerry Baldwin argues in "Harm or Aggression: How do Libertarians Establish What is Crime?," the NAP's objectivity makes it the superior rule.

Applied to public health, the COVID-19 pandemic lockdowns were implemented in the name of mitigating harm. If we applied the Harm Principle to Second Amendment rights, criminalizing their possession is arguably just. How about rape? Rape is a crime that, in our current legal code, is defined by harm. As Baldwin writes in her article,

> *"Rape occurs 'by the use of force or coercion that* ***results in*** *great bodily* ***harm or*** *great mental anguish* ***to the victim****.' (emphasis added). In other words, if a use of sexual force or coercion is not perceived to result in 'great bodily harm or mental anguish,' then it's not legally rape. Notice, rape is not simply sexual contact 'by use of force or coercion.' It must also 'result in great bodily harm or mental anguish.'"*

The Harm Principle's subjectivity risks tyranny by potentially criminalizing anything deemed "harmful" (e.g., gun ownership or speech) and inverts justice by burdening victims to prove sufficient harm. This appears in sexual assault cases requiring proof of "great bodily harm or mental anguish," often needing multiple accusers or granting perpetrator leniency.

Consequently, the Harm Principle plays no role in libertarian public health and safety policies. Individuals bear rights and responsibilities for personal safety (self-defense) and health (precautions and immunity). Government should act only to enforce the Non-Aggression Principle against actual initiatory aggression, not to preempt risks via mandates.

175. In a libertarian framework, who bears responsibility for harm caused by exposing others to infectious disease?

Exposure to infection, firstly, is a natural occurrence and just a fact of reality. A person, alone on a deserted island, is still exposed to infectious pathogens. Whether someone falls ill to the infection depends heavily on the strength of that individual's immune function. The mere fact that human beings have an entire physiological system dedicated to fending off infection, reinforces the reality that infectious disease is part of life, not a crime against you.

That said, it's indeed true that other people can contribute to contracting infections and while there may be some fact of which infected person passed it on to the next, that contraction—so long as it doesn't involve an action taken against the person of another—isn't a crime. What does this mean? Suppose you have a flu and you need some over-the-counter medicine to help relieve some of your symptoms. So you visit your local drug store, despite your fever and the runny nose you have. You try to keep to yourself as you can, grab your medicine and head to checkout. At checkout, you hand the cashier a $20 bill, and she touches it. She just came in contact with your flu. If she proceeds to touch her eyes, nose, or mouth, she's very likely to infect herself because of your $20 bill. This interaction does not constitute an act of aggression. So even if we could say the guy with the flu is ultimately responsible, it doesn't violate the rights of the cashier.

Many market innovations have helped and continue to help mitigate spread of infections where possible. But what we want to steer away from is the idea that every harm constitutes a need for a state-imposed policy.

176. In a public health crisis, does the Non-Aggression Principle permit the state to have emergency powers such as lockdowns and business restrictions?

The gravity of some urgent decisions does not negate an individual's right to make them. Nor does it necessitate action by the civil government. Economist F.A. Hayek warns that "Emergencies' have always been the pretext on which the safeguards of individual liberty have been eroded—and once they are suspended, it is not difficult for anyone who has assumed such emergency powers to see to it that the emergency will persist." Hayek recognized that crises like wars, rebellions, or natural disasters may necessitate temporary suspension of government restrictions for compulsory measures to preserve order, so he advocated separating the powers to declare an emergency from those who exercise them, ensuring mutual checks against abuse.

No one needs to deny the potential and real threat of some pandemics. If anything, the possibility of novel pathogens demand a free market fostering innovation, rapid adaptation, and personal freedom to act protectively. For some, this may involve temporarily closing their business or staying home from work. For others, they are providing the very services we need during such an event. Who gets to decide what action to take? Individuals are best positioned to assess their own circumstances and bear both the right and responsibility for such choices. Just because the weight of the decisions are heavier, doesn't mean the government has a right to usurp one's decision-making power.

Many assume that larger crises require more government action; but this is false. Governments exploit perceived crises to continually ratchet up their control over our daily lives. Civil government has one job! Adjudicate disputes of rights violations, and protect those rights through proper administration of civil justice.

The remaining things of vital importance to humanity are left to us, in our myriad capacities and free exchange in the market.

177. In the absence of federal mandates, how would coordination work across state or national borders during a pandemic?

Coordination does not require compulsion. It requires clear standards, reciprocal recognition, and open channels. Governments are poor standard setters already, and cooperation between private institutions always does better than government agencies that constantly find themselves behind bureaucratic red-tape. Of course, cooperation between governments internationally is far slower than what private institutions do to respond to emergencies.

Logistics firms already move goods globally and do so far better than governments; their real-time systems can prioritize scarce items where demand is spiking. Insurers and provider groups could coordinate alongside them to surge resources where they are needed most. For travel, information flowing freely and consent protocols are far better than blanket bans on the freedom of movement.

Like healthcare in general, one-size-fits-all mandates tend to fail. Instead, recognize that different places trying different approaches is a feature, not a bug. Let successful methods and results be published broadly, and copy what works. That is how learning spreads without placing the entire country under a single bet. Coordination by consent is more resilient, more respectful of liberty, and often faster than command.

178. How do libertarian principles apply during an infectious disease outbreak, and do those principles offer real protection for the most vulnerable?

Non-aggression, property rights, and voluntary association translate into practical protection. Property owners set risk rules for their spaces; customers and employees then choose accordingly. Information and guidance flowing freely enables people to assess risks for themselves and determine how they can personally respond. Centrally planned public health management will result in exactly the kinds of problems observed during the COVID-19 pandemic: shortages in personal protective equipment and drugs, mismanaged equipment distribution, and ineffective logistics to provide even the simplest of products like toilet paper.

Letting the market work even in these emergency situations enables resources to divert to places where the need is truly greatest. Instead of rationing, high-risk areas like hospitals and nursing homes will be properly prioritized when prices can modulate with demand. Insurance policies can ultimately account for price surges as well, mitigating the issue of price gouging in the short term. At local levels, churches and charities can still be a lifeline to those in need when the government gets out of the way.

Libertarian principles do not abandon the vulnerable; they channel attention and aid where it is most needed while preserving freedom for all.

179. But didn't the lockdowns help slow the spread of COVID-19?

The benefits of broad lockdowns were mixed and highly context-dependent, while the collateral damage was obvious: delayed medical care, learning loss, mental health crises, economic dislocation, community breakdowns, and the forced shuttering of churches. Freedom of assembly is fundamental, and doesn't get to be violated because a bureaucrat is concerned about public health. What might be defensible for a few days under extreme uncertainty cannot be justified for months, let alone years in some cases. Uncertainty calls for humility and restraint, not maximal force to keep people quarantined.

Better alternatives were available: prioritizing resources to high-risk facilities, improving indoor air, expanding testing where it matters, keeping outdoor activity open, and tailoring guidance by age and setting. Targeted, voluntary measures work with how people actually live and allow society to function.

Mandates not only failed to deliver results, they violated individual liberty and eroded what little trust was available to deliver truly useful information. Public health relies on cooperation, which grows when guidance is transparent but diminishes when questioning or dissent is met with force. We can acknowledge the difficulty of the moment without excusing rights violations that harmed millions.

180. Have decentralized approaches to pandemics worked in practice, and what are some examples?

Many decentralized responses during the COVID-19 pandemic adapted faster with fewer rights infringements. Businesses moved services outdoors, shifted to remote work, or improved their facilities to reduce risk of transmission. Manufacturers pivoted to produce sanitizers and PPE. Public venues upgraded filtration systems or added UV disinfection technology as safeguards. Neighborhood groups organized delivery networks and wellness checks for the elderly. Healthcare was dramatically affected, of course, but the growth of telehealth, direct primary care practices, and private surgery centers enabled care to be delivered in diffuse ways.

Churches reconfigured gatherings and kept support ministries running—or they bravely refused to comply with mandates at all. Even civil disobedience can be a decentralized approach.

Despite governments making life worse through lockdowns, many rose to the occasion with unique solutions to the problems their community faced. Then, word spread of successes and were replicated elsewhere. The creativity exhibited even in the face of government restriction should suggest that we can solve our problems even faster without those restrictions hampering us. Decentralization multiplies problem-solvers, speeds iteration, and respects liberty.

That combination proved more sustainable and successful than uniform mandates that treated every place and person the same.

181. What do personal responsibility and informed consent actually look like during a public health crisis?

Personal responsibility doesn't vanish in a crisis—it sharpens. It means deeply knowing your own body: how it functions generally and uniquely, what keeps it resilient, which remedies suit you, and what threats to watch for. You proactively strengthen your immune defenses now, so recovery is more likely if illness strikes. You also thoughtfully consider your potential impact on others and voluntarily take steps to reduce risks—out of care, not coercion. Crucially, none of these prudential actions can be forced by the state. True responsibility flourishes only when it remains voluntary.

Informed consent is the heart of responsible decision-making. When a health intervention is proposed—vaccine, treatment, or precaution—you pause to examine the problem fully, weigh the solution's benefits and risks, and match it to your body's specific strengths and vulnerabilities. This requires seeking information from diverse, credible sources, not relying on a single narrative or limited data. Only then can you confidently accept or decline with genuine consent.

Choices naturally vary. Someone with robust immunity may skip certain measures that an immunocompromised person strictly needs. Your vulnerable loved one can rightfully ask you to mask during a visit; you can agree out of love—or decline, accepting that visits pause until the risk feels lower. What no one can justly demand is that you mask everywhere, indefinitely, just in case you might encounter another vulnerable stranger.

In a crisis, personal responsibility and informed consent mean acting wisely, respecting real differences, and preserving freedom—because coercion undermines both health and humanity (see Question 167).

182. How can accurate health information be shared during a crisis without resorting to censorship or restricting free speech?

Trust in information distributed during a health crisis relies on transparency and reputation. Publish open data with documented methods, uncertainty ranges, and version histories. Reputations, whether individual or institutional, are built around track records, not titles. When officials look to squelch discussion, that promulgates confusion, compounds potential errors, and erodes trust in expertise. Honesty and transparency are always better policies.

Communicate risk by setting and audience: hospitals, nursing homes, schools, workplaces, and churches need different guidance. When recommendations are applied to all activity indiscriminately, that suggests that the recommending parties are not treating people as individuals and will continue to erode trust.

Distinguish fraud from dissent. Fraud is a form of aggression and should be treated as such, but good-faith debate and minority hypotheses ought never be punished. Scientific humility means admitting what we don't know, revising when evidence changes, and resisting the illusion of consensus created by censorship.

Churches and community groups can help by teaching source evaluation, sharing updates through their own channels, and modeling calm, truthful speech. People will make better choices when they can see the evidence, hear competing views, and understand implications of different courses of action.

183. How do we uphold freedom of assembly and religion when public health crises put pressure on civil liberties?

By now, you can see where we place the emphasis of right and responsibility over decisions concerning health and wellness. The freedom of assembly, whether for religious or non-religious reasons, is up to the individuals considering assembling. This falls completely outside the jurisdiction of civil governance so long as initiatory physical coercion is not involved. This may involve some choosing to adopt certain measures, close down entirely, or do absolutely nothing. And the individuals considering assembling must take those things into account when they are deciding whether or not to assemble.

This means lots of people choosing to do things you might not agree with. Some will be based on establishment ideas; some on alternative ideas; some based in ignorance; some based in mysticism; some based in fear, and so on. Pandemics are not reasons for the government to expand; they are reasons why they need to maximize free market innovations.

Additional Resources

"Harm or Aggression: How do Libertarians Establish What is Crime?" by Kerry Baldwin. *Libertarian Christian Institute*, 20 February 2020. https://libertarianchristians.com/2020/02/20/harm-or-aggression/.

A House Divided by Benjamin D. Giffone (Christians for Liberty Press, 2025).

Diary of a Psychosis: How Public Health Disgraced Itself During COVID Mania by Thomas E. Woods Jr. (Libertarian Institute, 2023).

19

The Culture Wars

"The first political task of the Church is to be the Church."
—Richard John Neuhaus

184. What are the culture wars, and how do they relate to political and social conflicts?

The term "culture wars" describes the ongoing clashes over certain moral, social, and religious issues that divide people into opposing camps. These battles often center on topics such as marriage, sexuality, education, and the role of religion in public life. What makes them "wars" is not the disagreements themselves but the way each side seeks to use state power to enforce its vision of society. In other words, the culture war is the use of legal violence to settle disputes that fall outside the non-aggression principle. Conflicts in society can only be resolved in one of three ways: persuasion, peaceful separation, or physical coercion (violence). Culture wars erupt when the first two are taken off the table, leaving only coercion.

Scripture reminds us that Christians "do not belong to the world" (John 17:14–16), so tension with prevailing norms should be expected. The real problem arises when those disagreements are fought through political coercion, turning them into battles to impose one side's beliefs on the other. This is an inherently collectivist and fear-mongering activity. Progressives and conservatives think they must fight the culture war to avoid being ruled by the other, but libertarian Christians can offer a unique perspective that avoids this struggle for power.

185. How do libertarian Christians engage in the culture wars in contrast to both progressives and conservatives?

While progressives and conservatives see culture as a tool to impose their moral visions on society, this mindset heavily influences their voting and policy preferences—leading to "culture wars" as socio-political battles. Often, both sides endorse similar policies in principle, differing only in the morals they seek to enforce.

In contrast, libertarian Christians regard culture as the essential product of human interactions, reflecting our creation in God's image. It manifests through interconnected layers: objects, behaviors, social relations, values, and beliefs. People's moral frameworks may align with or violate God's natural order. Through redemptive grace in Christ, Christians can increasingly conform to these God-given norms, while non-Christians may achieve some external alignment through common grace.

As noted in the previous question, most culture war issues concern non-violent behaviors and vices—practices that may be immoral but don't constitute aggression. As libertarians adhering to the Non-Aggression Principle and as Christians recognizing that gospel reception and faith cannot be coerced (especially by the church), we address these through persuasion to win hearts and minds, rather than political force.

It's worth noting that libertarian Christians may seem to take sides in culture war debates, sometimes appearing aligning with the left or right. However, our reasons differ fundamentally from those of progressives or conservatives, and our positions are typically more nuanced.

186. What is the libertarian Christian approach to addressing the increase in identity politics and cultural tribalism?

Free speech exists precisely for this purpose: to foster interaction among people, even amid peaceful disagreement, preventing culture from descending into identity politics and tribalism. When dialogue ceases, culture wars worsen through collectivist mindsets and fear-mongering tactics.

We believe each individual's identity is primarily rooted in Christ. They are also self-owners, endowed with God-given rights to steward their own lives (see Questions 14–16). It's crucial to discern what falls under their responsibility before God versus ours. While we are called to engage neighbors and communities with God's truth in love, we must avoid succumbing to the mob mentality that accompanies cultural tribalism.

We resist progressivism's fixation on identity politics as well as conservatism's elevation of national or cultural identity. Instead, our approach prioritizes self-ownership, equal dignity, and voluntary association over state favoritism or group privileges.

We approach communities with humility, recognizing that common grace enables shared cooperation without necessitating spiritual regeneration. Rather than fueling tribal divisions, we cultivate peaceful coalitions that uphold individual rights and promote human flourishing for all.

187. If freedom is meant for doing what is right, not just what is permitted, how should libertarian Christians think about the limits of moral liberty?

If freedom is intended solely for doing what we ought, why didn't God restrict moral liberty in the Garden of Eden to only righteous choices? True moral actions require genuine choice; without it, they lack ethical weight. To argue otherwise is to impugn God's own design.

We do impose limits on moral liberty when aggression is involved, using civil governance to address such violations. However, non-aggressive immorality must be confronted through non-aggressive means, like persuasion.

Who decides what "ought" means in every situation? Scripture offers specific commands and prohibitions, but most decisions rely on individual conscience. No human group can dictate these, especially since God does not prescribe them exhaustively. Christians must resist adding to God's law. The God-ordained "sword" of authority is limited to enforcing against aggressive acts; for non-aggressive ones, we turn to persuasion and influence.

God's design for creation, including marriage, family, and stewardship, establishes natural boundaries for human flourishing. Civil governance should only intervene in violations of the non-aggression principle, such as abortion, child exploitation, or coercion. The church and families, not the state, bear responsibility for moral formation and discipleship. Libertarian Christians honor freedom of conscience, refusing to impose beyond God's revelations in matters of Christian liberty. We distinguish divine justice—God's perfect standard—from civil justice, which focuses solely on protecting against aggression.

188. How is the "live and let live" mentality of libertarianism compatible with a Christian view of sexuality?

The phrase "live and let live" can be misleading if taken to mean indifference. A Christian who accepts libertarianism is not apathetic toward sin. Scripture teaches clear truths about sexuality, and Christians must faithfully uphold them. What libertarianism rejects is the use of state aggression to enforce those truths.

Libertarianism is often called a "thin" philosophy because it builds outward from one central question: when is force justified? The answer is in defense against aggression—not to impose religious doctrine, cultural preferences, or particular moral doctrines unrelated to aggression. Even when society normalizes sinful views of sexuality, Christians are not authorized to use government coercion to correct it. The only proper role for civil governance in matters of sexuality is to punish acts of aggression—such as rape, sexual assault, or sexual activity with a minor. Beyond that, it is the responsibility of believers to contend for the faith through proclamation, discipleship, and example.

One practical benefit is that libertarianism opposes using state power or tax-funded institutions to impose ideology—whether progressive or conservative. It affirms the role of parents to instruct their children according to God's design rather than outsourcing that role to political authorities. In this sense, libertarianism protects space for Christian conviction while keeping civil governance within its proper bounds: addressing rights violations, not engineering culture.

189. How should libertarian Christians respond to a culture that seeks to normalize sexual immorality?

Christians contend for the faith and against falsehood with the tools God has given us. Since government force is off the table for libertarian Christians, our response is persuasion—bearing witness in personal relationships and engaging the marketplace of ideas in ways that testify to the gospel and to Christian libertarian principles. Christians should not retreat from the public square but answer activism for immorality with activism for truth—peacefully promoting God's design for sexuality and liberty.

This does not mean we expect everyone to be persuaded or to abandon sinful lifestyles. Yet libertarianism allows for a social order where people freely choose their associations. Christians can, according to conscience, associate or disassociate with those practicing immorality (cf. 1 Cor 5:9–10; Rom 12:18).

Scripture does not prescribe a rigid formula for this balance. We must not call good what God has called sinful, yet neither should we isolate ourselves from sinners entirely. Libertarian Christians are called to navigate work, social, and family life faithfully, living peaceably with all as far as it depends on them, praying for those who do not yet know Christ, and bearing witness in word and deed. Even when persuasion fails, we trust God to work through our faithfulness rather than through coercion.

190. How do libertarian principles guide public policy on gender identity education in schools?

Libertarianism opposes any public policy on education or gender identity, but the issue is now unavoidable in the culture. Regardless of your views, if you have school-aged kids, they'll encounter peers who disagree with you on gender. Here's a libertarian approach:

First, where the NAP has not been violated, no use of coercion is appropriate when dealing with whom you disagree. That said, where the NAP is violated, responsive proportional coercion is appropriate. This addresses typical schoolyard problems, such as bullying.

Second, the principle of self-ownership aids in understanding where responsibilities (and corresponding rights) lie (see Questions 14–16). Preferences do not create obligations on others to validate that preference. This applies as much to the affirmation of preferred pronouns, to the exercise of a preferred religious belief. These boundaries are the sort of thing that should create the framework for peaceable relations between differing views in a free society.

Third, free thought and free speech are the means by which we educate ourselves. The purpose for these two particular freedoms are not merely to be antagonistic, air grievances, speak against the government, or even say things deemed "hateful." We don't have these freedoms because all ideas are valid. We have them because most ideas are invalid to various degrees. We have the freedom to think and speak so we may sort through the errors and arrive at the truth.

Our kids will and must understand they have a developing responsibility for themselves, and they may not initiate aggression against others. While they're free to hold the ideas they do, their education is fundamentally a lifelong pursuit of truth.

191. Should the government define what it means to be male or female, or should that be left to individuals and private institutions?

What does it mean to define something? Definitions—in common parlance, logic, philosophy, mathematics, science, and beyond—provide clear, precise explanations of meaning, boundaries, or essential traits to distinguish one thing from others. Governments should not create these language boundaries but instead recognize those definitions that accurately reflect objective reality. This isn't always simple (e.g., debates on personhood), yet governments shouldn't serve as the ultimate arbiter. Putting any institution in charge of "official truth" almost inevitably leads to propaganda and power struggles.

Hayek showed that societal knowledge is dispersed, tacit, localized among individuals, and impossible for central authorities to aggregate without distortion. Similarly, language and meanings evolve decentrally, like economies. Governments imposing definitions ignore personal, historical, cultural, and contextual insights. Impositions cause errors, rigidity, and unintended effects like suppressing universal application of human rights, disrupting consensus, or stifling adaptation. It's better to let terms emerge via free expression, enabling self-organization of common language. This issue arises because governments enact laws protecting rights or banning discrimination, in this case based on gender and now gender identity; a major flaw.

Legal definitions must mirror the best from religion, science, philosophy, and common usage; recognizing, not recreating, reality. Disputes, like the claims that science supports a multitude of genders, belong to those fields, not government fiat. Definitions shouldn't shift with political whims or be drivers of social change; if experts can't convince peers, governments have no role in deciding for them.

192. How should libertarian Christians approach the issue of transgender women participating in women's sports and entering female-only spaces?

Libertarian philosophy doesn't take an absolute position on these questions. These are matters left up to individuals and how they wish to use their own property. That means it may be possible that two businesses operating side-by-side, offering essentially the same service can have different policies. One caters more to a demographic that recognizes gender fluidity and the other recognizes only binary gender, or even operates on gender segregation entirely.

All are permissible in a libertarian free market, because their success is determined by market needs. If the market responds such that one must shut down for failing to be economically viable, no government policy is going to swoop in and rescue the failing model in the name of diversity, tradition, or whatever. Nothing in a free market is too big to fail, and nothing is so socially important that it requires legal coercion to operate.

This way of viewing society comports with a Christian view as well, where we're called to live at peace (so far as it is possible) with others, while maintaining Christian morality through our own life and practice. How this looks in practice is left up to the conscience of the individual, with communities of Christians (i.e. churches) holding each other accountable, through persuasion and not force, both to the moral will of God and to the grace and mercy of Christ offered through the gospel to a dying world.

Would a libertarian free market society necessarily be pro- or anti- trans, or pro- or anti- binary gender? In all likelihood, there would be spaces for both until market demand says otherwise. However, it wouldn't be civil governance dictating it.

193. Are you arguing that the public square can be neutral?

Neutrality in the public square must be carefully defined. At the level of political institutions and civil law, neutrality is both possible and desirable. Civil governance must not enforce or privilege one creed over another; its jurisdiction is limited to protecting life, liberty, and property, and in that sphere it ought to be impartial. This civic neutrality results in civil religious pluralism, allowing people of differing convictions to live together peaceably under equal protection of the law.

At the level of cultural life, however, neutrality is a myth. Every person acts from ultimate commitments, whether or not they are recognized as "religious." In this sense, religious neutrality is impossible. The public square will always be filled with competing visions of the good. The question, then, is not whether religion will shape society, but whether the state should wield coercion to enforce one of those visions.

Some Christians worry that without grasping for power, they will be ruled by non-Christians. But if civil governance is properly ordered, it has no authority to impose sinful practices or teachings upon believers. The greater danger is when Christians pursue cultural control through political means, becoming trapped in endless battles over power and neglecting the mission Christ gave his church. Civil governance ordered toward justice creates space for persuasion and witness; civil governance ordered toward cultural dominance only breeds endless conflict (see Question 89).

194. If cultural decline threatens moral and social order, shouldn't Christians support a state that enforces biblical values?

Christians may lament cultural decline, but the solution is not to hand the state authority to enforce biblical values. Culture refers to the shared practices, institutions, and beliefs that shape how we live together. It is not engineered from the top down. Rather, it emerges through families, churches, and communities. Scripture never promises us a Christian majority or the ability to secure one by coercion. Christ even indicates the opposite is true (John 15:18–21). Our hope rests in him, who fulfills the original mandate to bring God's glory to the nations.

Some Christians believe that Scripture provides a "blueprint" for civil government in the Mosaic law. However, the Mosaic covenant was temporary; its laws and statutes pointed ahead to the Kingdom of God and final judgment but are now fulfilled in Christ and made obsolete (Heb 8:13). Since the Mosaic Covenant and theocracy are obsolete, attempts to make the state punish non-aggressive immorality run contrary to the New Covenant. Christians bear faithful witness by conforming to Christ, serving neighbors, and submitting to civil governance as instructed in Romans 13.

Scripture teaches civil governance is the administration of civil justice through the use of proportional force. When theocrats claim the state should criminalize sins that are not acts of aggression, they are misapplying the Mosaic framework Christ fulfilled—what Hebrews chapters 8 and 10 declare has passed away. Civil governance that goes beyond civil justice is not enforcing biblical values at all, but contradicting them.

195. Don't we need a Christian culture in order to save sinners through the sharing of the gospel?

Salvation comes by the Spirit working through the proclamation of Christ's gospel, not through the establishment of a "Christian culture." While cultural norms shape how people hear the message, outward conformity to cultural morality doesn't produce saving faith. If it did, then America's past "Christian culture" should have prevented moral decline.

History also refutes this claim. The early church grew under the hostile Roman Empire. Far from needing cultural dominance, the gospel flourished under persecution. The same is true today: in places like China, North Korea, and parts of the Middle East where Christianity is outlawed or violently opposed, the church continues to grow. Christ's kingdom cannot be stopped by man.

Confusing evangelism with cultural dominance distorts the Gospel message. God's power is made perfect in our weakness (2 Cor 12:9–10) and human strength can become a liability (1 Cor 1:25–29). When Christianity is tied to political or social control, it presents a false gospel of salvation through culture and power. Those drawn are not conformed to Christ but to external rituals (legalism), producing nominalism—Christianity in name only. Nominalism cannot transform societies. The cultural regression in the West traces to generations of nominal Christianity mistaking cultural conformity for discipleship. As Nancy Pearcey notes, nominalism has fueled abuse within the church (see "Nancy Pearcey Explains" in Additional Resources below).

Sinners need the Gospel, not a Christianized environment. The task of believers is to proclaim Christ faithfully, trusting God to draw people to himself. As hearts are changed, cultural improvement may follow, but as the fruit of evangelism—not its foundation.

196. If we expect to be blessed with a free and flourishing society, don't we need to use the state to force moral conformity?

No, and Scripture actually teaches the opposite: lasting moral change and true human flourishing flow solely from the Spirit's regenerating work in the hearts of believers, producing voluntary obedience to Christ, not from coercive power.

A lot of sincere Christians—whether theonomists and Christian nationalists on the right, or liberation theology and social gospel advocates on the left—make the same basic mistake: they read the sanctions of the Mosaic theocracy (Deut 28) or the judgment scene of Matthew 25 and assume that modern civil governments must legally compel either love of God, or love of neighbor (or both). That entire approach is unbiblical. The Mosaic covenant has been fulfilled and rendered obsolete by the death and resurrection of Christ in the new covenant (Heb 8:6–13; Gal 3:23–25; Col 2:16–17). No modern nation-state, America included, is heir to ancient Israel's theocratic charter or its land-linked sanctions.

Furthermore, New Testament "nations" (*ethnē*) means ethnic peoples, not nation-states. Matthew 25 and Revelation 5–7 describe individuals from every ethnicity judged by their union with Christ, not the laws of their geo-political territories. God's only holy nation now is the transnational church (1 Pet 2:9), whose citizenship is heavenly (Phil 3:20) and whose every blessing is already secured in Christ (Eph 1:3). Obedience therefore flows from gratitude, never compulsion.

New-covenant ethics are always voluntary: "Each one must give as he has decided in his heart, not reluctantly or under compulsion" (2 Cor 9:7, ESV). History bears witness: whenever the church has seized Caesar's sword—medieval, Puritan, or socialist, nationalist—the result has been hypocrisy, persecution of the saints, and a gospel obscured by political power.

A free and flourishing society arises only as the Spirit sovereignly regenerates hearts through the preached gospel, producing voluntary obedience—one converted life at a time, never by the sword. Christ's kingdom advances solely by grace freely received, not by legislation. That alone is the biblical path.

197. How should libertarian Christians think about compassion and empathy when the right often sees it as excessive and the left sees it as insufficient?

Empathy and compassion are fruits of the Spirit and expressions of Christian virtue. Yet like all virtues, they must be guided by wisdom. Compassion that ignores truth or economic reality can easily become sentimentality, and empathy that lacks discernment may support destructive choices rather than healing them.

Libertarian Christians recognize that caring for others involves both moral intention and correct means. Economics helps us understand how scarce resources can best serve human needs, while the non-aggression principle reminds us that love cannot be coerced. The left is right to care for the poor, but wrong to entrust that care to the state, whose redistribution of wealth depends on force and ultimately impoverishes society. It is not compassionate to subsidize sin, or to punish productivity.

Likewise, the right often appeals to moral order but neglects the biblical calls to mercy and justice. The prophets condemned rulers who "trampled the poor" and ignored widows and orphans. A society truly shaped by Christ's Spirit cannot separate moral responsibility from compassion, nor confuse justice with mere punishment. Properly ordered compassion does not replace law or economics—it strengthens them, grounding both in love that seeks genuine human flourishing.

Additional Resources

"Nancy Pearcey Explains The Toxic War on Masculinity plus a Review." *Dare to Think*, 04 Mar. 2024. https://www.mereliberty.com/041.

The Toxic War on Masculinity: How Christianity Reconciles the Sexes by Nancy Pearcey. (Baker Books, 2023).

Total Truth: Liberating Christianity from Its Cultural Captivity by Nancy Pearcey (Crossway, 2004).

"The Use of Knowledge in Society" by F. A. Hayek. *American Economic Review*. XXXV, No. 4, pp. 519–30. 1945. https://www.econlib.org/library/Essays/hykKnw.html

20

Family and Education

"God has instituted different spheres... The family is a sphere of its own, with its own authority directly from God, not derived from the state... The state may never encroach upon the sovereignty of the family in its own domain."

—Abraham Kuyper

198. How do libertarian Christians prioritize the importance of the family as it relates to society as a whole?

Christianity sees the family as society's foundational sphere—the primary community for bearing and raising children, through which culture is built. Libertarianism, lacking a full worldview, views the family mainly through rights (parental self-ownership over children) and economics.

It is in raising families that needs for sufficiency and efficiency are made most plain. We find that we need innovative answers to storing food, building shelter, finding suitable transportation, and so on. The raising of families is what creates needs within the market for innovators and entrepreneurs to respond to. Often, parents themselves become the entrepreneurs who solve the problem and then offer it for sale. And this pattern continues as families come across new problems, new solutions, new innovations, and new goods and services.

Those who are unmarried benefit from having the economic needs of families met. Take the production of food, for example. Roughly a century ago, many families—particularly in rural areas—produced much of their own food. That task was far easier when the work was spread among the family, rather than by a single individual living alone. When people started producing more than they themselves needed and traded and sold their surpluses, that benefited those without families.

The state repeatedly invades this sphere because the family is so vital. Libertarian Christians affirm not only its practical and economic importance but its spiritual, relational, emotional, and psychological primacy. Many libertarians do not. This gives libertarian Christians a unique opportunity to persuade the broader libertarian movement that the family—prior to the state—is the true foundation of a free and flourishing society.

199. What are the key cultural debates surrounding the role and structure of the family in society?

Related to the questions about abortion in Chapter 14, the key debates about the role and structure of the family in society begin with reproductive rights—namely, to what degree bodily autonomy liberates women from the role of "mother" if/when they become pregnant. From there, the debates over parental and children's rights ensue—not only pertaining to rights, but also to responsibilities. The phrase "best interests of the child" has been both properly and improperly invoked in debating tangential issues indirectly related to the family (e.g., climate change).

Nearly every aspect of family life has been put up for debate, especially in recent years. Do parents have the right to refuse vaccines? Or to educate their children themselves at home? Or to allow their children to eat only a vegan diet? Or to allow them to get jobs at a young age? Or to try an experimental treatment? Or to teach them to follow a religious belief? Or not to affirm their kids' preferred pronouns? Everything seems to be at stake! And this fuels ongoing culture wars.

When we understand the foundational nature of the family to society, and that the state is the legal violence most often leveraged to intervene in family activities, it becomes much clearer why and how these cultural debates arise. The irony is that, without the legal violence of the state and its monopoly control over civil governance, these culture wars would be largely diffused. The disagreements would persist, but the incentive to leverage legal violence against one's neighbor is reduced.

200. How does libertarianism inform the balance between parental rights and children's rights when cultural trends challenge parental authority over a child's well-being and identity?

Self-ownership and the NAP apply clearly to adults but require careful extension to children. Kerry Baldwin's fetal self-ownership framework (see Chapter 14) resolves this by establishing clear rights and duties from conception.

This approach creates a natural (not state-imposed) parental obligation to provide life support. Newborns lack all capacity for self-care (walking, feeding, bathing), so this duty is broader at birth. As children gradually develop these abilities, parental obligations naturally diminish, phasing out as the child develops his or her own ability to act on their self-ownership.

Civil governance is responsible for enforcing all negative rights for offspring derived from the non-aggression principle, plus the natural obligation of providing nutrition and shelter. The state is not positioned to determine the best diet, healthcare decisions, or education for children. Parents, both naturally and practically, are best suited to make these decisions. In a free market, the best knowledge on these things rise to the top.

Identity is distinct from basic care. Neither parents nor civil governance are positioned to determine a child's identity. However, an individual's identity isn't simply a blank slate for self-invention either. Each person possesses genetic predispositions to specific characteristics, natural abilities, temperaments, and potential health conditions, while also interacting with their environment (to include their parents) in unique ways.

Adolescence is when youth explore their identity and place in the world. Identity is shaped primarily by natural factors (genetics, temperament, abilities); cultural influences are secondary and changeable.

Kerry Baldwin's fetal self-ownership framework resolves child-rights dilemmas: it establishes natural parental duties that gradually diminish as children gain capacity. Parents cannot guarantee perfect outcomes but remain best positioned to guide well-being decisions, adjusting authority as their children mature.

201. Does the state have a role in regulating medical treatment for minors, given libertarian opposition to state control and minors' limited capacity for informed consent?

In a legal sense, civil governance may intervene when a child faces aggression. This includes medical treatments not required to preserve health or normal development. Parents may authorize treatments such as removing a tumor or treating asthma—treatments that remove a threat to the child's health or restore normal bodily functions and development. By contrast, treatments that are purely cosmetic or that intentionally diverge from normal development fall outside parental authority and constitute aggression because children lack the capacity for informed consent to such treatments.

This does not mean granting the state sweeping authority to regulate health care through broad legislation. Protecting children requires restraint. The possibility of abuse should not be used as a pretext for expanding the role of civil governance from adjudicating aggression into usurping parental authority in all medical decisions for their children. That is a quick path to medical totalitarianism.

Recent controversies highlight both dangers. The "trans-kids" debate illustrates how life-altering procedures can be carried out without genuine informed consent or exaggerated threats to a child's health. Meanwhile, the COVID-19 pandemic showed how quickly the state's role in health can expand into coercive mandates over masks, closures, and vaccinations. Both demonstrate that centralized control erodes liberty without solving underlying problems.

Practically, given these dangers and the complexity of medical decisions, the better path is decentralization—limiting civil governance to its narrow role of addressing acts of aggression. By keeping its focus there, families and communities remain free to make their own health care choices.

202. How do libertarian principles apply when parents, children, and the state clash over what's best for a child?

Civil governance should only intervene in parent-child conflicts when there are violations of the NAP or when basic necessities like food and shelter are withheld. When government extends beyond these fundamental protections, it infringes upon parental rights.

Non-violent conflicts between parents and children can be resolved through market solutions and community support—one of the key functions of communities. Anyone raising children understands the numerous disagreements that can arise. Parents disagree with their children, with each other, and with other adults about the best approaches to various situations.

These regular disagreements don't signal a problem requiring state intervention. Rather, they reflect the challenges of a free society, which needs both a dynamic market offering multiple solutions and a recognition that certain truths about raising children exist.

The fact that better ways to raise children might exist suggests there are truths worth pursuing.

Consider the age of consent debate. This involves complex questions: What constitutes consent? How do we determine someone's capacity to give authentic consent? What does coerced consent look like? How can one resist such coercion? How do these issues manifest in close relationships? Unless violence is involved, civil governance isn't equipped to address these questions.

Regarding transgender policies for minors, we must first apply principles of self-ownership and the NAP before discussing policy. Governance should intervene where NAP violations exist. In non-violent conflicts, persuasion becomes essential. Throughout these discussions, everyone is ultimately seeking truth.

203. How can the rights of parents be reinforced to protect their children from premature decisions about gender or sex without relying on government overreach?

Children are entrusted to parents by God. Children bear God's image and possess inherent dignity, but their capacity to exercise agency develops gradually. Until then, parents act as trustees. Parents must discern what best serves a child's well-being and protect them from premature, life-altering decisions—including (and perhaps especially) regarding sex and gender.

This protection is best reinforced through decentralized and voluntary mechanisms. Schools, camps, and clinics should operate with contractual transparency, requiring explicit parental consent for any counseling, data collection, or medical referrals related to sex and gender. Professional accountability also plays a role. Medical boards, hospital ethics committees, and malpractice law create civil liability for providers who bypass parents or pressure minors into experimental interventions. In a free market of education, competitive accreditation and insurer standards raise expectations. Expanding educational freedom through private schooling, homeschooling, and other market innovations allows families to choose environments that align with their convictions, rather than being bound to centralized curricula.

Civil society and innovation further strengthen these safeguards. Churches, mutual-aid groups, and legal defense organizations can publish model policies, provide counsel, and defend families when institutions overreach. The market also develops tools—family accounts, parental controls, verification systems—that enable oversight without government surveillance. Together, these mechanisms preserve liberty and empower parental rights, reserving coercion only for clear instances of aggression.

204. How should libertarians respond to concerns that an unregulated internet exposes children to dangers like exploitation, trafficking, and mental health issues?

Libertarians recognize that the internet poses real risks to children. The question is not whether these problems exist, but whether government regulation is the best solution. Libertarians argue it is not. Heavy-handed regulation often punishes ordinary users and innovators, erodes privacy, and threatens free speech—while doing little to stop determined bad actors.

Instead, libertarians emphasize voluntary, decentralized solutions. Families, churches, schools, and local communities are best positioned to guide children and build resilience. Parents should have access to effective tools—such as filters, monitoring software, and educational programs—developed by private companies and nonprofits that can adapt faster than government mandates. Civil society can also provide victim support, raise awareness, and foster digital literacy to equip young people to navigate online spaces wisely.

Children need education as much as they need protection. While the internet carries risks, it is also a tool that parents can use—and teach their children to use responsibly. Decisions about what children should or should not see belong with parents, not the state.

Where crimes like exploitation or trafficking occur, they should be addressed through targeted law enforcement with due process, not blanket restrictions on the entire internet.

205. How should libertarian Christians respond to the cultural normalization of non-traditional sexual and family relationships?

As libertarian Christians, we recognize that the cultural normalization of non-traditional sexual and family relationships deviates from God-given norms ordering creation—norms calling for sexual relations and family structures to reflect divine design. This includes lifelong monogamous unions between one man and one woman for procreation, nurture, and mutual support, as revealed in Scripture, as well as the valid calling to faithful singleness and celibacy exemplified by the Apostle Paul in 1 Corinthians 7, where he presents singleness as a gift that allows undivided devotion to the Lord.

Through redeeming grace in Christ, we are enabled to align our lives with these norms amid cultural shifts, while common grace allows even the unregenerate to conform externally to some degree. Our primary duty, therefore, is personal and communal faithfulness: modeling biblical sexuality, marriage, and faithful singleness in our households and churches, teaching and discipling others, and engaging in gracious evangelism that turns hearts to the true God rather than idols.

We view society as a network of diverse relations with distinct jurisdictions (families, churches, voluntary associations) that should coordinate through self-government, not as a monolithic whole. Thus, we oppose using civil governance—limited to punishing aggression (initiated coercion against persons or property)—to enforce conformity on non-aggressive moral issues.

Rather than pursuing legal prohibitions or mandates, we advocate liberty, allowing individuals to choose freely while bearing natural consequences, and we resist state violations of property rights or the non-aggression principle.

Our ultimate response is the persuasive power of the gospel: speaking truth in love, building voluntary communities that uphold God's norms, and trusting his sovereignty to renew culture through transformed lives—never through force or monopoly power.

206. Should public funds be used to support pro-family and pro-natalist policies?

Libertarians would say no to this question solely based on the premise of using public funds to fund anything at all. Supporting families and encouraging childbearing are worthy goals. Yet just as libertarian Christians reject caring for the poor or sick with stolen taxpayer money—or with borrowed or inflated currency—they also reject funding pro-family programs by such means.

Beyond this ethical concern, pro-natalist subsidies create moral and economic hazards. When government redistributes wealth, it distorts the natural market signals families and communities rely on to make sustainable decisions. Subsidies may encourage people to become parents before they are ready, or even incentivize single parenthood, trapping households in cycles of poverty. Financial incentives may also attract individuals lacking the maturity or resources to raise children well, undermining rather than strengthening family life. Free money comes without accountability: it does not ensure that resources are used responsibly or in ways that genuinely nurture children.

By contrast, private charity and church support are embedded in real community. These contexts provide not only material help but also mentorship, accountability, and relational structures that build families up in ways government programs cannot replicate.

Christians are called to bear one another's burdens—but doing so through coercive taxation undermines both liberty and the integrity of family life.

207. Haven't government policies such as no-fault divorce already weakened marriage and the family, and wouldn't a libertarian society risk accelerating that decline by eliminating legal constraints on divorce?

This really is a question of causes. Did no-fault divorce cause the weakening of marriage and family ties? Or does no-fault divorce expose an inconvenient truth hidden by strictly enforced marriage arrangements? Critics of no-fault divorce often blame women and feminism, since women file most divorces. Yet research suggests men are often decisive factors in attempts to salvage troubled marriages. To claim no-fault divorce itself caused the destruction of the family ignores deeper problems that created the demand for legal change in the first place.

Moreover, a libertarian society doesn't have zero constraints on marriage and divorce. Aside from social norms developing away from authoritarian views of marriage and toward individual choice—i.e., parent-arranged marriages would likely decrease, and child marriage could stand a chance of being legally prohibited (because free religious practice cannot violate self-ownership and the NAP)—prenuptial agreements would likely increase dramatically. Prenuptial agreements are a longstanding practice, including in ancient Israel. A marriage contract known as a *ketubah*, which involved a bride price, dowry, etc., was set aside along with conditions. In the case of a husband's death or unjust divorce, the woman would receive that money as a financial safety net. If she initiated an unjust divorce, the man would receive it.

As usual, this objection boils down to a failure to imagine legal and social orders outside the authoritarian state apparatus. And that's no objection.

208. Without government oversight of education, what practical alternatives to accreditation can ensure academic rigor and intellectual integrity in schools?

Accreditation is voluntary, though states may endorse certain agencies aligned with their policies while ignoring others. Tax-funded schools are typically required to be accredited, while private schools choose agencies that best fit their model and curriculum. These agencies act as third-party certifiers, signaling oversight to parents. The quality of that oversight varies—some are mere rubber stamps, while others maintain high standards. And just because a government education department has endorsed a particular accrediting agency, doesn't mean that agency is even worth its salt. In a free market, competition among agencies creates the incentive to uphold diligent and trustworthy standards.

Furthermore, accreditation is not required for college entrance or for achieving valid diplomas. Those interested in the academic acumen of an applicant will take into consideration a variety of factors, including standardized test scores like the SAT or ACT, application essays and interviews, personal recommendations, portfolios of work, and so on. In recent years, the conventional Carnegie unit and GPA system is becoming meaningless, as public schools have reoriented their programs to "teach to the test."

Education in a free society would benefit both from innovation and a variety of models, programs, curricula, and so forth. Eliminate compulsory education requirements, and more experiences can count as learning. Will there be a need for some oversight over educational institutions claiming they have a sound education model? Sure. But that's already provided for by the market.

209. How can parental concerns about ideological indoctrination be addressed without government oversight of education?

Government oversight of education is arguably what drives ideological indoctrination in K-12 education options—including private and homeschooling ones. Ideological indoctrination can look like any variety of things including compelling national patriotism, teaching only one perspective of history, teachers waxing eloquent (or ranting and raving) about their various political pet peeves or agendas, to more expansive meta-ethical ideologies including religious beliefs, transgender and sexual agendas, and so on.

The classical liberal, or liberal arts, approach was quite different. It entailed reading and discussing a variety of viewpoints and perspectives to understand, evaluate, analyze, and synthesize those ideas. It respected learners as individuals with their own agency, reasoning capacity, and ability to form conclusions, and those conclusions weren't threatening to any sort of agenda by the school administration. This was of course with reason. Liberal arts eventually became the intellectual free-for-all we see, with a deep and abiding skepticism for the truth, or even being able to discover it.

Christian evangelicals who opt for homeschooling think they know the answer to public school indoctrination: indoctrination by private instruction. (They aren't shy about the reality that they too are indoctrinating). So, in one sense of the term, you can't avoid indoctrination! And a free market education would no doubt allow for this from a supply perspective. The more relevant point is that classical liberal models, upholding principles of academic freedom, would also be available in free market education. The effectiveness of these models would be tested by market forces, not monopolistic government (or religious) ones.

210. How can educational freedom help preserve shared moral and cultural values while preventing society from fragmenting into isolated or ideological groups?

The first thing to remember is that society is not a single whole. So, it's already fragmented, so-to-speak, into groups and those are often differentiated by various ideologies. That's sort of the point of living in a free society—freedom to associate with those of your choosing, and of course to not associate with others.

This question often comes from people who promote ideas of multiculturalism, diversity, equity, and inclusion. The rationale is that "inclusive" societies are the most peaceful. Not only is this claim dubious, but even advocates for these ideas would not want to be forced to associate with groups with whom they have vehement disagreement. These might include fundamentalist religious groups, for example.

Education freedom isn't about ensuring society conforms to the ideas you've concluded are the best ideas. It's about continually critiquing the ideas that predominate our society in pursuit of the truth. Proverbs 18:17 is apt here: "The one who states his case first seems right, until the other comes and examines him" (ESV).

Not only do we need to be free to challenge ideas that might be wrong, but we must be free to understand why right ideas are right. We can't be confident in what we know as being right, or in our ability to defend the truth, if we have forced conformity to ideas. This only comes from the freedom to disagree, be wrong, and the freedom to arrive at the truth in our own ways in our own timing. In other words, the goal of a free society is not to prevent siloing into differentiated groups. It's about the freedom to leave those silos when you want to.

211. How is educational quality preserved if anyone is allowed to start a school, even without formal training or credentials?

Before the Department of Education was established in the U.S., we were number one in the world in education. Now we are 34th. This begs the question. Public school teachers receive training and credentials and our quality of education has only plummeted.

Free market education is subject to market forces. We realize this is a bit like beating a dead horse at this moment, but it's one of the main features that make the free market so desirable. Those education institutions that provide poor quality education are not likely to stay in business for long. And there are plenty of market regulatory factors that will test these institutions: colleges, trade schools, employers, mentors, coaches, parents, and even students won't tolerate bad models. A free market is the best way to ensure the best models rise to the top.

Contrast this with the public education model, where education is effectively monopolized by the state. For whatever reason, people have been persuaded that government oversight is the key to high quality. Even parents who homeschool or send their kids to private school because of complaints of the public schools, still look to state standards as the necessary benchmarks for a quality education. Before the Department of Education was established in the U.S., we were number one in the world in education. Now we are 34th. This begs the question. Public school teachers receive training and credentials and our quality of education has only plummeted.

Formal training will still be a highly-sought after feature of free market education. But what qualifies as formal training will likely expand given the need for not just academic training, but trade and vocational, entrepreneurial, and technical training and expertise as well.

Additional Resources

"The Cultural Context Of Politics", hosts. Gregory Baus and Kerry Baldwin. *Reformed Libertarians, episode 22, Feb 18*, 2025. https://libertarianchristians.com/episode/cultural-context-of-politics/.

Dumbing Us Down by John Taylor Gatto (New Society Publishers, 2002).

Free to Learn by Peter Gray (Basic Books, 2015).

National Center for Education Statistics. "International Comparisons of Achievement." Fast Facts, U.S. Department of Education, Institute of Education Sciences, 2024, nces.ed.gov/fastfacts/display.asp?id=1.

"An Open Letter to Christian Singles" by Gregory Baus. *The Laymen's Lounge, thelaymenslounge.com/an-open-letter-to-christian-singles/.*

"Reformed Libertarianism Statement & Principles." Reformed Libertarians. reformedlibertarians.com/reformed-libertarianism-statement/.

"Two Kingdoms And Christian Cultural Activity", hosts. Gregory Baus and Kerry Baldwin. https://libertarianchristians.com/episode/ep-21-two-kingdoms-and-christian-cultural-activity/.

Woke and Weaponized: How Karl Marx Won the Battle for American Education, and How We Can Win it Back by Robert Bortins and Alex Newman (Classical Conversations MultiMedia, Inc., 2025).

21

Christian Nationalism

"Enforced uniformity of religion throughout a nation breeds hypocrisy and persecutes Christ Himself."

—Roger Williams

"Religion is a good thing when it goes to church, but it is a bad thing when it goes to the state."

—Reinhold Niebuhr

212. What is Christian nationalism, and how do its proponents defend it?

Christian nationalists begin with the belief that a nation's identity and government should be explicitly aligned with Christian principles. They argue that political and cultural life should be shaped by what they regard as Christian values rather than by secular or pluralistic ideals. Christian nationalists also embrace nationalism more broadly, emphasizing strong borders, cultural preservation, and the defense of national identity. They see religious neutrality as a myth, since every law reflects some moral framework. Therefore, they contend it is better for the state to impose—or at least promote—Christian morality than to permit what they view as sinful patterns to dominate society.

Writers such as Andrew Torba and Andrew Isker describe Christian nationalism as loving one's neighbor by shielding citizens from foreign ideologies or influences. Stephen Wolfe argues that a Christian nation will act to "procure for itself both earthly and heavenly good in Christ." Proponents also attempt to ground their views in Scripture. The Great Commission, they say, calls not only for individual discipleship but for nations to be Christian, with leaders discipled to govern in line with God's law. From Romans 13, they argue that rulers cannot punish evil or promote good apart from divine revelation, so governments must enforce Christian morality. Because people naturally separate into distinct cultures, they conclude that national identity is part of God's providential design and should be politically maintained.

213. What are the main biblical and theological arguments against Christian Nationalism?

The New Testament never calls for the state to enforce Christian imperatives on non-Christians. Its civil ethic is grounded in natural law, not covenant law. Jesus explicitly rejected the idea of an earthly kingdom (John 18:36). His apostles, following his lead, made disciples of all nations by baptizing and teaching willing converts, not by coercing outward conformity through law. Christian nationalism often conflates the present spiritual reign of Christ with a visible political expression of his kingdom through the state.

The Law of Moses has been fulfilled in Christ and his new covenant of grace, and God's people are no longer under a theocratic system. In this new covenant era, civil governance is ordained only to deal with civil justice and disputes. It has no role in teaching society to be righteous, adjudicating doctrine, or administering divine punishment for sin. Such governance is not morally neutral, but fulfills God's purpose when it limits itself to its divinely ordained functions of protecting life, liberty, and property—upholding justice without claiming spiritual authority.

Most importantly, in Christ, the dividing walls between nations and peoples have been broken down. Our loyalty is to him first, not to earthly kingdoms, political projects, national identities, or ethnic divisions (Gal 3:28–29; Eph 2:14).

214. How does Christian nationalism align or conflict with libertarian principles?

Christian nationalists and libertarians both desire a society where people worship God and live by Christian principles. Both are skeptical of the bipartisan political establishment and the expanding influence of federal bureaucracies and international bodies. Both tend to oppose military interventionism, and push back against cultural trends that erode Christian sexual ethics and the family. On many issues, Christian nationalists and libertarians find common ground in diagnosis, but not in the cure.

The conflict hinges on the role of civil governance. Libertarianism sees civil government as limited to protecting individual rights and enforcing natural law. Christian nationalism, by contrast, tends to sacralize government—treating it as a tool to advance Christian imperatives in civil society. It assumes that because Christianity is true, the state should prosecute public dissent, effectively turning the government into a theological enforcement agency. This violates both the libertarian principle of individual conscience and the biblical teaching on the distinct roles of church and state. Under this framework, religious freedom becomes a conditional privilege instead of an inalienable right.

At first glance, the premise of Christian nationalism sounds uncontroversial. What Christian wouldn't want to live in a nation composed largely of believers? The problem is not only its contradictory aim of imposing biblical values through force (see Questions

194 and 213), but the simple fact that a Christian nation cannot be engineered by legislation. Faith cannot be compelled. A Christian nation, or a society shaped by Christian values, can only come about from the transformation of people's hearts.

215. Is it better to have Christian leaders in government than to have leaders indifferent or hostile to Christianity?

This question makes certain assumptions about governance. The first is that its functions cannot be adequately performed by those who don't believe in Jesus. The second is that governance must necessarily be detrimental to some section of society or another, and if Christians don't take it over for ourselves, it will certainly be used against us.

While none of us would argue that someone must believe in Jesus to be a good architect, sushi chef, or motorcycle mechanic, Christian nationalists believe that for governance to perform its function properly, those who write and enforce the laws must borrow liberally from the Bible. However, one does not have to be a Christian to understand that the legitimate (and biblical) function of government is limited to dealing with aggressors like murderers, thieves, and assailants. On the other hand, Christians do serve an important prophetic function in speaking truth to power and holding it accountable; and may even have a legitimate role to play within government itself.

The second concern has more weight behind it. Government as we have often experienced it has been a bludgeon which one class of people uses against another. Certainly Christians don't want it used against us, so does that mean our only recourse is to use it against everyone else? Is our only choice to either kill or be killed?

Libertarians argue that we have a third option. We can work alongside those who love liberty to create a society where government is not a terror to those who live at peace with their neighbors, and we choose to adopt practical approaches to working toward such a society (see Questions 222, 224–227, and 230).

216. How has the rise of Christian nationalism affected various denominations within Christianity in the United States?

You can find both libertarians and Christian nationalists in most denominations and Christian traditions. Among Roman Catholics, there is an appreciation for the classical liberal tradition, but also a call from some to return to integralism—the union of church and state which marked medieval Europe. Pentecostalism has a suspicion of statism at its foundation through leaders like Charles Parham and A. J. Tomlinson, but it has also sparked a unique form of Christian nationalism called dominionism that has been closely tied to religious right politics. Reformed theology gave us Kuyper's sphere sovereignty, but also Rushdoony's reconstructionism. Indeed, even among mainline and Anabaptist denominations which have rejected the Christian right, you will find many promoting a left wing Christian statism in its place.

The primary question is not whether one can find examples of Christian nationalist thought within one's tradition or denomination–Jesus himself had disciples who utterly failed to understand his mission (see Matt 20:25–28). The real question is this–what is the best and most biblical thought within one's tradition which ought to be emulated and built upon? As libertarian Christians, we would urge you to seek out the best thought within your own Christian community and build on it to further a theology that looks more like Jesus.

217. Can well-meaning Christians unintentionally support Christian Nationalism by confusing cultural influence with political power?

Yes, this is always a potential danger. We are often taught to think of voting and political activism within a democratic system as the moral duty of every American citizen, and that any kind of violence we unleash on our neighbors through the political process is inherently clean because of that process. As a result of this mindset, we can think of political force as just another way in which we can impact our community or country for the better. Former congressman Barney Frank said it this way: "government is simply the name we give to the things we choose to do together."

Christian nationalists embrace a version of this myth as strongly as any progressive does. They charge Christians who reject political violence of being cultural isolationists and "pietists." But Jesus and the apostles never saw separation from empire as opting out of the culture–they traveled from place to place spreading the gospel message and changing lives. The one thing they did not do was promote or defend Christian ideas with the sword. Christian Nationalists see contemporary Christians who emulate this approach as handicapping themselves and being derelict in their duty to make disciples of all nations. Libertarian Christians respond that faithfulness to Christ's commands to love our neighbors, remember that Christ's kingdom is not of this world, and to put the sword back in its place is never a dereliction of Christian duty.

218. How viable is Christian Nationalism in today's political landscape, and does it pose a real threat to the well-being of society?

It remains to be seen whether Christian nationalism will be largely relegated to a handful of Christian pastors and online activists or if it will be a significant force in American politics. Christian nationalists have certainly made efforts to create political alliances within the Republican Party, but the most effective coalition builders have not generally been the most radical elements within the Christian nationalist movement. The underdog status of the Christian nationalist movement will likely continue, but considering the growing turbulence of western politics only time will tell. If the progressive movement continues its move leftward, this could certainly create a reciprocal backlash on the right toward Christian nationalism.

In the final analysis, the greatest danger of Christian nationalism might not be political, but spiritual. It encourages us to yoke Jesus with the violence of the state and to attempt to maintain dual allegiances which contradict each other. This not only hurts our discipleship, it hurts our witness. Many who would otherwise be drawn to Jesus will be turned off by those who try to align him with extremist politics and state violence. A church which does not faithfully follow its Lord has much less to offer the world, so the world will take very little notice of it.

219. How should libertarian Christians respond to the rise of Christian Nationalism?

Christian nationalism urges that there is no such thing as neutrality—that if we oppose the left forcing its values onto our country, the only alternative we have is to force Christian nationalism upon our neighbors instead. But libertarian Christians are suggesting a third way. We don't believe that every aspect of Christian ethics should be forced onto others. God has circumscribed the role of governance to the performance of only the functions which it is suited and ordained for. Beyond the edge of those functions, freedom must flourish. If it does not, force will replace discipleship and our ability to evangelize for Christ with sincerity and integrity will be undermined.

Libertarian Christians promote these values by encouraging engagement in traditional forms of advocacy—like voting and activism—as conscience allows. But we must also speak clearly about a better way: one modeled by Jesus who chose persuasion, service, and sacrifice over coercion. Following the insight of economist Ludwig von Mises that every action we take comes at the expense of another that we didn't, we must recognize that seeking political power displaces more faithful approaches like preaching, discipling, and persuasion. The early church transformed the world not through law or empire, but through radical love, servant leadership and bold proclamation of the gospel. Choosing force over freedom doesn't just distort our politics—it reshapes our hearts. It trains us to see our neighbors as threats to overcome rather than souls to love. We must not only refute the theology of Christian nationalism, but expose the high spiritual and societal costs of its methods (Mark 10:42, 2 Cor 10:3–5, 1 Pet 1:17).

220. How can libertarian Christians expose the theocratic agenda hidden behind Christian nationalist rhetoric that borrows libertarian language?

Christian nationalists often borrow libertarian-sounding words and phrases like liberty, freedom of religion, natural law, and general equity. On the surface, this makes their vision appear compatible with Christian libertarianism, but closer inspection shows these terms are being redefined to justify state coercion.

Take the phrase, "freedom of religion." Christian nationalists claim it is a uniquely Christian idea, but they restrict it to mean only that the state cannot compel belief and that different Christian denominations may coexist. They deny that historic Christianity ever envisioned legal protection for non-Christian faiths. This lets them sound like defenders of liberty while actually advocating a theocratic order.

Their definition of liberty itself is also misleading. Rather than understanding liberty as freedom from coercion, they insist liberty includes a supposed right to avoid exposure to sinful lifestyles or to raise children in a Christian society—"rights" that can only be created through government enforcement In this way, liberty becomes a tool for cultural control.

Christian nationalists likewise use terms like general equity and natural law, but argue these mean civil governments must apply biblical law or enforce their interpretation of morality, obscuring the libertarian Christian understanding that natural law protects against aggression and secures liberty of conscience for all.

Libertarian Christians can expose this bait-and-switch by showing how Christian nationalist rhetoric invokes liberty only as a mask for coercion.

Additional Resources

The Air We Breathe by Glen Scrivener (The Good Book Company, 2022).

The Believers' Church: The History and Character of Radical Protestantism by Donald F. Durnbaugh (Wipf and Stock Publishers, 2003).

Christian Nationalism: A Biblical Response by Cody Cook (2024).

The Global Politics of Jesus by Nilay Saiya (Oxford University Press, 2022).

The Religion of American Greatness by Paul D. Miller (IVP Academic, 2024).

Why Do the Nations Rage?: The Demonic Origin of Nationalism by David A. Ritchie (Wipf & Stock, 2021).

A World after Liberalism: Philosophers of the Radical Right by Matthew Rose (Yale University Press, 2022).

22

How Do We Get to a Free(r) Society?

> *"I do not ask that you place hands upon the tyrant to topple him over, but simply that you support him no longer; then you will behold him, like a great Colossus whose pedestal has been pulled away, fall of his own weight and break into pieces."*
>
> —*Étienne de La Boétie*

221. How should we work to promote a freer society and persuade others to embrace the values of liberty?

In some sense, we could sum up this question and perhaps this entire chapter with five words: Be Christian. Produce. Learn. Communicate.

First, we need to live out our Christian faith meaningfully day in and day out. The more we imitate Jesus, the less we will imitate the worldliness around us. We should seek first the Kingdom of God. However, this is not a means by which to exit the world, become hermits, or turn insular against all others outside our immediate church community. Rather, our orientation toward Christ becomes the lens through which we see the world as it is and as it should be. This is how we build the character in ourselves to support a free society.

Second, we need to be productive. If we believe that, beyond the church itself, God's main way of providing for human flourishing is through free markets and commerce, then we need to participate in the marketplace in some way so that we can provide for ourselves and be of service to others. In remembering this, we recognize that all worthy work is done to the glory of God.

Third, we need to educate ourselves about the principles of a free society. While the basics may be obvious, not all of it can come without some form of training. The broader culture, decaying as it is, will not transmit these important values in the future. It's up to us to learn about philosophy, economics, ethics, and history so that we understand the importance of individual liberty.

Fourth, actively communicate our values to others. Call out the evils of statism for what they are. Defend capitalism. Practice explaining these ideas to liberty-loving friends, and look for opportunities to share. As Christians, we're used to evangelism, and one could say we are evangelizing liberty in an analogous manner.

Finally, finding like-minded people to work with and learn from is crucial. Don't be an island, get out there and make friends with fellow libertarians, and join the cause in some small way. Not everybody can be a Ron Paul, but when we're all doing something to support promoting liberty, we will make an impact together. Do it locally, do it online, but be sure to do something!

222. What are the most effective ways to challenge the rise of anti-liberalism from both the left and the right?

Anti-liberalism exists on both ends of the political spectrum. The left often champions state control in the name of equality, while the right often embraces authoritarianism under the guise of order or nationalism. As Christians, we should reject both as expressions of statism and antithetical to the Christian way of life.

The false view of equality the left espouses is effectively countered by the proper understanding of equality through the Christian worldview. We are all equally responsible to the moral law, and no one receives special privileges of morality due to status, whether they are a state actor, have political or economic or religious authority, or are part of any other particular class of people.

On the right, we make the case that proper order happens when liberty is the rule, and not the other way around. Impositions of order at the expense of individual liberty is against the vision of America's founding fathers, natural law, and biblical witness. Furthermore, we can oppose nationalism (as discussed in previous chapters) by appealing to shared values. Yes, you can love your country, but that does not give you the right to commit aggression against others.

Libertarian Christians can model a better way by living out liberty, showing humility, serving cheerfully, and telling the truth about statism. We fight back not with weapons but with better ideas, appealing to what is true, just, and rooted in a Christian worldview. That means calling out the failures of government coercion, regardless of whether the rhetoric sounds "conservative" or "progressive." The beauty of this position is that it is non-partisan, as individual liberty is grounded in moral principles rather than party loyalty.

223. How can we persuasively explain libertarian principles to people who may be skeptical or unfamiliar with them?

The first step is to establish common ground. It is easiest to persuade a person of an idea if they conclude that idea is congruent with foundational values to which they already subscribe. Assume good faith, and proceed as though the person is sincerely seeking the right answer and will be open to evidence and persuasion.

If a person is concerned about compassionate treatment of homeless people, talk about how libertarianism can address housing shortages, drug abuse, access to mental health services, and other related concerns. If a person is concerned about the environment, they might be shown examples of how government management of natural resources has resulted in major environmental catastrophes like the Aral Sea Devastation in the Soviet Union during the 1960s or the deadly air pollution in the Black Triangle created by Soviet industrial planners. If a person is concerned about religious liberty, point out the widespread restriction on religious liberty in communist regimes, and also point out the curtailment of such liberties even in countries like the United States during the COVID-19 pandemic.

Don't fall into the trap of taking responsibility for how every aspect of the structure of production would work for every good or service imaginable. While it is possible to postulate how even quintessential government services like defense services and courts could be performed in a voluntary market, it is not possible to definitively answer the question of which specific business model will be successful. At the crux of the libertarian position is the idea that the process of market discovery is not something that can be simulated by bureaucrats or political activists. Libertarians can point to past examples and new proposals, when available, but we cannot and should not attempt to provide a "libertarian central plan" to replace the statist ones.

224. Given libertarianism's limited influence in national politics, should Christians who value liberty consider partnering with other political movements to advance meaningful change?

Yes, but proceed with extreme caution! It's possible for a libertarian to work with non-libertarians toward a specific libertarian goal or policy, but when "bad company corrupts good character" (1 Cor 15:33, NIV) the result can be ethical compromise. Libertarianism, first and foremost, is a theory of justice that instructs us on how to avoid violating the rights of other people. It is not a utopian scheme, and it does not promise the total abolition of injustice in the world

If a Christian believes that libertarianism is the best expression of Christian political thought, deviating from that standard would be wrong, even in an attempt to gain political advantage. Christians are instructed not to be unequally yoked with unbelievers (2 Cor 6:14), and we are also told to avoid keeping company with those who are quick to anger (Prov 22:24–25) or who set out to victimize others (Prov 1:10–15). Furthermore, we should never envy the violent or adopt their wicked ways (Prov 3:31–32). But it is also a mistake to think that this means that all engagement with the politics and rulers of this world is strictly forbidden.

Christians are called to pray for those in authority over us, that they would make decisions that allow us to live in peace (1 Tim 2:1–2). Wise rulers seek out the counsel of many (Prov 11:14), and even a non-believer may recognize the wisdom that a faithful person possesses (Gen 41:37–38). A Christian who is asked to provide guidance should provide it conscientiously, with wisdom founded on the words of Christ (Col 3:16). Sometimes that may look more Nathan rebuking King David, and other times it might look more like Daniel calling Nebuchadnezzar to rule with justice and mercy, to "renounce your sins by doing what is right, and your wickedness by being kind to the oppressed" (Dan 4:27).

We are called to be salt and light, preaching repentance and teaching about a kingdom unlike the world's kingdoms. We should not introduce leaven and adulterate that message.

225. Is lasting change more likely to come through local action, or should we focus on national and global efforts to advance liberty?

There is a political aphorism attributed to former Massachusetts congressman and Speaker of the House Tip O'Neill: "All politics is local."

Understanding the needs and concerns of everyday people is essential to any successful political movement. Whether a policy is a local one of limited scope, or a national one impacting hundreds of millions of people, the common man analyzes most policies based on how he thinks they will affect him, in his town, at his house, with his family. No matter the scale of the project, it is likely doomed to failure if it fails to relate to the needs and desires of normal people.

Local policy issues often involve smaller stakes, but the human impact is often easier to understand. Working on local issues also typically means that fewer people have to be persuaded in order to make a difference in the outcome, whether it is in a local election or a local issue campaign.

National policy changes can have a very broad impact on a great many people, but electoral campaigns and lobbying efforts at the national level are tremendously expensive and difficult to undertake, involving the coordination of networks of activists and cultivation of relationships with the transient population of officeholders who have the actual policymaking authority.

But as Tip O'Neill said, the difference in scale does not represent a difference in kind. Local action can help equip and prepare an activist for action at a larger scale later. And local activism need not be viewed as less important than national activism. In the United States, only about half of the tax burden is from the federal government. The other half is imposed by state and local governments.

226. How do approaches such as decentralization, privatization, and peaceful secession contribute to the pursuit of liberty—and how should they be prioritized?

Each of these strategies tends to limit centralized coercion and promote consent-based order. Decentralization brings governance closer to people, increasing accountability and cultural relevance. Privatization places resources into voluntary and efficient hands, reducing bureaucratic waste. Secession asserts the right for communities (and individuals) to be self-determining, affirming that political unions should be voluntary, not forced.

These are not libertarian silver bullets, but they are valuable tools. They work best when rooted in the principle of non-aggression, practiced peacefully, and aimed at reducing further conflicts rather than fomenting them. Prioritization generally depends on context. Decentralization is often the most feasible, scalable, and fastest solution to problems. Privatization is often a logical next step to services already decentralized from a federal power. Secession, while perhaps sounding extreme, is the most final of solutions when it can be accomplished peacefully.

Scripture affirms the principle of limited authority and local responsibility. From Jethro's advice to Moses to the early church's decentralized order, subsidiarity is biblical. Christians should see these mechanisms not as scary concepts but as means to foster peace, virtue, and human flourishing.

227. If decentralization, privatization, and secession offer paths to greater liberty, how can they be pursued seriously while still accounting for their potential risks?

These approaches are not inherently virtuous, even though on a marginal basis they will often enhance liberty compared to statism. Nonetheless, the method used is only as good as the moral principles behind it. Local governments can still be tyrannical. A privatization effort could turn into a state-created monopoly and end up just as coercive as before. Secession can devolve into tribalism or violence if not handled wisely.

Libertarian Christians should pursue these policy strategies with discernment. "Be wise as serpents, but innocent as doves" (Matt 10:16). We need to ground our goals in love for neighbor, justice, and peaceful cooperation. We must never pursue liberty by authoritarian means. Shall we do evil that good may result (Rom 3:8)? By no means!

Prudence and humility should be guiding principles as well. We need to be self-critical of our plans in action, ensuring that our efforts don't get compromised and turned against our core values.

The early church's example shows us how to flourish in hostile conditions through faithful practice of principles. Likewise, we should build resilient communities that model liberty, educate others, and press for change through peace and persuasion.

228. Beyond education and politics, what meaningful contributions can individuals make to help build a free and flourishing society?

Your daily life is the ultimate front line of liberty, as we are only able to affect that which is within our own circle of influence. As our circle grows, the more impact we can have around us. Being a productive worker, loving parent, faithful church member, and ethical businessperson is more powerful than a hundred social media political rants.

Christians are called to be salt and light, meaning our example matters. When you create value for others, keep your promises, teach your children well, and help your neighbors, you are building a free society because you are living the way God intended for his creation.

Start a business. Join a mutual aid group. Create culture. Practice hospitality. Model peacemaking. These are real contributions that build trust, strengthen civil society, and reduce dependence on coercive institutions.

Our present age may not be ideal for liberty, but that should not stop us from putting our principles into practice. Liberty grows in environments of responsibility and voluntary cooperation. The more people act in accordance with liberty values and ethics, the more free we all become. So become the kind of person a free society needs. We like to say that's becoming the "one improved unit" of society, and that is no small thing.

229. How can Christians fulfill their duty to God's Kingdom while residing in a state system in rebellion to God?

Christians are never called to seize the state (a beastly, satanic temptation, according to Revelation 13), nor to submit to tyranny as though it were God-ordained authority. Scripture and the ancient church (including Chrysostom's exposition of Romans 13) teaches that God ordains the civil magistrate solely for the administration of public justice. When a regime abandons justice and becomes the oppressor, it forfeits divine authority. Christians therefore owe it no obedience, only lawful resistance.

In such a state we advance Christ's Kingdom by refusing to render to Caesar what belongs only to Christ, obeying God rather than men (Acts 5:29) in every sphere where the magistrate oversteps or perverts its narrow, God-given mandate. We bear public witness against evil, disobey or ignore every command that lies outside the sphere of civil justice or that subverts justice itself, build parallel Christian institutions of family, church, school, and mutual aid that embody the justice and mercy of Christ, and, when necessary, defend the innocent by whatever means God's Word permits.

All the while we live quiet, diligent, and peaceable lives so far as it depends on us (1 Thess 4:11; Rom 12:18), never mistaking quietness for complicity or peaceableness for surrender. Joyful, Spirit-filled obedience that includes the biblical right—and sometimes duty—of resistance to tyranny is how the confessing church has always lived under the Beast, and how we are called to live today.

230. How can Christians integrate their faith and daily work in ways that support and sustain a free society?

Christians should see their work as a holy calling. When we serve others through our work—whether as business owners, employees, parents, or volunteers—we glorify God and strengthen the fabric of a free society.

The Christian doctrine of vocation teaches that all honest work has dignity. It's not just pastors and missionaries doing kingdom work, but also teachers, baristas, mechanics, scientists, and entrepreneurs. This perspective combats the elitist idea that value comes only from status, the most high-paid job, or state-approved professions.

In free markets, our work blesses others through voluntary exchange. We serve our neighbor not just in charity, but in commerce—delivering real goods, services, and solutions. This fosters peace, prosperity, and mutual respect.

When Christians work diligently, with integrity and love for neighbor, they reflect God's character and uphold the moral conditions necessary for liberty to flourish. A free society needs moral people—and that starts with us.

Additional Resources

How I found Freedom in an Unfree World by Harry Browne (1973).

Left and Right: the Prospects for Liberty by Murray Rothbard (Ludwig von Mises Institute, 2010).

But What About...?

The question above could be asked forever. In the first edition of the book, we set out to provide succinct and clear answers to the most common questions we are asked as libertarian Christians. Even after more than doubling the content in this second edition of the book, we are under no illusions that we have said everything that needs to be said. There will always be more questions, and there will always be fresh ways to articulate answers to reach more people. New political circumstances, scientific discoveries, and technological advancements often require us to speak differently about timeless truths, and we are prepared to adapt to reach more people.

In other words, this book is just the beginning of an ongoing conversation. We invite you to keep that conversation going by continuing to ask more questions and by inviting more people into it. That's why we've created a website as a place to share this work with others, ask new questions, and dive into more resources to satisfy your curiosity. We welcome and appreciate all polite and civil responses, whether they are positive, negative, or a mixture of the two.

Welcome to the conversation! Please keep it going by joining us at faithseekingfreedom.com.

Discussion Guide

Before you start...

This study guide is intended either for individual readers who want to interact more with the text or small groups that want a starting point for their regular discussions about their readings.

For a small group, you'll want to keep in mind that each person is going to come at the reading with a different point of view, and sometimes taking in information like this can be very challenging. Always remind your participants to be gracious and kind to one another, being quick to listen, slow to speak, seeking to understand first rather than be understood. Play with the ideas and learn together, rather than try to answer everything definitively the first time around. Enjoy the thinking and discussion process.

In addition, you may find through the readings that you have additional questions that we did not address in the book. We encourage you not to let those go, and instead let us know what's on your mind. Reach out to us at LCI at our website, libertarianchristians.com.

Finally, we included Additional Resources at the end of every chapter, and we encourage you to seek out more from those lists for any subject that sparks your curiosity. You can find the full list at faithseekingfreedom.com

Enjoy the journey!

Chapter 1

Why Should I Care about Politics?

General Understanding Questions

These questions help readers identify the chapter's main goal, the issues it addresses, the key details shared, and the main ideas it concludes with. They encourage basic comprehension of how politics relates to Christian faith without assuming advanced knowledge.

1. What is the main reason this chapter says Christians should think about politics?
2. What problems do people face when they mix faith with government rules?
3. What Bible stories and ideas does the chapter use to show God's view on rulers, and what does it say we should do about them?

Deep Dive Questions

These questions prompt readers to explore the big ideas like God's kingdom, hidden beliefs about power, what happens if we follow or ignore these views, and different ways people see faith and government. They push for deeper thinking about how these ideas affect life and society.

1. What does the idea of "kingdom of God" really mean in this chapter?
2. What things does the chapter take for granted about how governments start and work?
3. How might following these views on politics change the way Christians live with others?
4. What one idea from this chapter most caught your attention or helped to clarify your thinking?

Chapter 2
Libertarian Basics

General Understanding Questions

These questions guide readers to grasp the chapter's aim in defining libertarianism, the challenges it solves like aggression, the facts on principles like NAP, and its wrap-up on rights and justice. They build a simple overview of libertarian basics.

1. What does the chapter aim to explain about being a libertarian?
2. What big issue does the non-aggression principle try to fix?
3. What details from the Bible and ideas like rights does the chapter give, and what does it end by saying about justice?

Deep Dive Questions

These questions help readers dig into key terms like non-aggression, beliefs about force, what could happen from following these rules, and how Christians see them. They spark thought on how these fit with faith and life.

1. What is the non-aggression principle all about?
2. What does the chapter assume about how people should use force?
3. How could living by these ideas affect how people get along?
4. What one idea from this chapter most caught your attention or helped to clarify your thinking?

Chapter 3

Christian Misconceptions of Libertarianism

General Understanding Questions

These questions focus on the chapter's goal to clear up wrong ideas about libertarianism for Christians, the mix-ups it fixes, the proofs from Bible and logic it shares, and its final points on matching faith. They offer a clear path to understanding common errors.

1. Why does the chapter talk about wrong ideas Christians have on libertarianism?
2. What mix-ups about greed and morals does it try to sort out?
3. What Bible parts and reasons does it use, and what does it say is true in the end?

Deep Dive Questions

These questions lead to examining ideas like selfishness, guesses about people being good, results like no rules, and Christian views on them. They encourage weighing how these match God's ways.

1. What does the chapter mean by selfishness in libertarian views?
2. What does it take as true about why people need rules?
3. How might these ideas change how Christians see right and wrong?
4. What one idea from this chapter most caught your attention or helped to clarify your thinking?

Chapter 4
Government

General Understanding Questions

These questions help see the chapter's purpose in questioning government, problems like its power, Bible info on it, and ends with ideas on true rule. They make the topic easy to understand.

1. What does the chapter want us to think about government?
2. What troubles does it say come from how governments act?
3. What Bible tales and thoughts does it share, and what does it decide about them?

Deep Dive Questions

These questions dive into terms like state vs rule, beliefs on God's plan, effects like bad power, and Bible angles. They prompt looking at government through faith.

1. What is the difference between government and rule here?
2. What does the chapter believe about God's part in government?
3. How could these views on government change our world?
4. What one idea from this chapter most caught your attention or helped to clarify your thinking?

Chapter 5

The Limits of a Free Society

General Understanding Questions

These questions cover the chapter's aim on free society bounds, issues like no rules, facts on choices and results, and wrap-up on true freedom. They keep it straightforward for grasping limits.

1. Why does the chapter ask if free places need rules?
2. What worries does it fix about people doing anything?
3. What Bible wisdom and life facts does it give, and what does it say is best?

Deep Dive Questions

These questions explore ideas like own choices, guesses on sin, outcomes like right acts, and faith takes. They push thinking on freedom with God.

1. What does freedom mean for what we can do?
2. What does it assume about why people pick bad things?
3. How might these limits help or hurt how we live?
4. What one idea from this chapter most caught your attention or helped to clarify your thinking?

Chapter 6

Economics and the Christian

General Understanding Questions

These questions highlight the chapter's goal linking money to faith, problems like bad choices, Bible and money info, and ends on wise use. They aid basic grasp of economics in faith.

1. Why should Christians learn about money ways?
2. What troubles come from not knowing money rules?
3. What Bible lessons and key ideas does it share, and what does it end with?

Deep Dive Questions

These questions go into terms like scarce things, beliefs on work, effects like better life, and Christian sights. They encourage deep look at money through God.

1. What does scarce mean for our choices?
2. What does the chapter think about God's plan for work?
3. How could these money ideas change our faith life?
4. What one idea from this chapter most caught your attention or helped to clarify your thinking?

Chapter 7

Capitalism and the Christian

General Understanding Questions

These questions focus on the chapter's purpose of tying capitalism to faith, fixes wrong views on profit, shares Bible and market facts, and concludes on good ways. They simplify capitalism for Christians.

1. What does the chapter say about capitalism and faith?
2. What bad ideas about profit does it sort out?
3. What Bible parts and market truths does it use, and what is its main point?

Deep Dive Questions

These questions probe concepts like gain chase, assumptions on greed, consequences like uneven wealth, and faith views. They spark thoughts on capitalism ethics.

1. What is the role of profit in markets?
2. What does it assume about why people get rich?
3. How might capitalism affect who has more or less?
4. What one idea from this chapter most caught your attention or helped to clarify your thinking?

Chapter 8
Libertarianism and Christian Ethics

General Understanding Questions

These questions guide to the chapter's aim on ethics in freedom, issues like guns and vices, Bible ethics info, and ends on right acts. They make ethics clear with liberty.

1. Why mix freedom views with Christian right and wrong?
2. What hard ethics questions does it answer?
3. What Bible rules and ideas does it give, and what does it say to do?

Deep Dive Questions

These questions delve into ideas like self-guard, beliefs on force, results like no rules, and Christian ethics. They prompt weighing liberty with morals.

1. What does owning guns mean for safety?
2. What does the chapter believe about bad habits?
3. How could these ethics change how we treat others?
4. What one idea from this chapter most caught your attention or helped to clarify your thinking?

Chapter 9

Public Goods and Services

General Understanding Questions

These questions cover the chapter's goal questioning state help, problems like who does jobs, facts on private ways, and conclusions on better options. They help see no need for state in all.

1. Why ask who does public jobs without state?
2. What worries does it fix about no government help?
3. What past and idea proofs does it share, and what does it decide?

Deep Dive Questions

These questions explore concepts like private jobs, assumptions on state need, implications like lower cost, and views on help. They encourage thinking on life without state.

1. What does public good mean here?
2. What does it assume about why the state does things?
3. How might private ways change our towns?
4. What one idea from this chapter most caught your attention or helped to clarify your thinking?

Chapter 10

Democracy, Voting, War, & Patriotism

General Understanding Questions

These questions focus on the chapter's purpose on rule by people and war, issues like vote and fight, Bible and history info, and ends on true love for land. They clarify Christian views on country.

1. What does the chapter want us to think about rule by vote and war?
2. What problems come from loving one's country too much?
3. What Bible stories and thoughts does it use, and what does it say is right?

Deep Dive Questions

These questions dig into terms like people rule, beliefs on war, consequences like no peace, and faith angles on land love. They push deep thoughts on voting and fighting.

1. What is democracy's real meaning?
2. What does the chapter assume about joining the army?
3. How could these views on country change our faith?
4. What one idea from this chapter most caught your attention or helped to clarify your thinking?

Chapter 11
Social Justice

General Understanding Questions

These questions are designed to help you quickly identify the chapter's purpose (why it was written), the problem it aims to solve (misunderstandings about social justice and government), the key information it provides, and the main conclusions it draws. They are relevant because they give you a clear, high-level summary of the document's core message before you dive deeper.

1. What is the main purpose of this chapter on social justice, and what problem does it try to solve by mixing Christian beliefs with libertarian ideas?
2. What information does the chapter provide about how governments and free markets affect poverty, and what conclusions does it draw about which one helps people more?
3. Based on the examples given (price gouging, racism, the early church in Acts), what problems with government rules does the chapter point out, and what conclusions does it offer about better ways to handle business, racism, and community?

Deep Dive Questions

These questions explore the concepts, assumptions, implications and consequences, and viewpoints/perspectives in the chapter. They are relevant because they push you to think critically about the hidden beliefs behind the arguments and what real-world effects those ideas could have.

1. What key concepts (human flourishing, social justice, stewardship) does the chapter explain, and what assumptions does it make about the proper role of government?
2. If we follow the chapter's ideas about free markets and limited government, what implications and consequences (good and bad) might there be for poor people, the environment, or society as a whole?
3. How does the chapter present libertarian Christian viewpoints on racism, immigration, and the early church, and what other perspectives (e.g., progressive or traditional Christian views) does it challenge or leave out?
4. What one idea from this chapter most caught your attention or helped to clarify your thinking?

Chapter 12
The War on Drugs

General Understanding Questions

These questions are designed to help you quickly identify the chapter's purpose (why it was written), the problem it aims to solve (issues with drug prohibition and the War on Drugs), the key information it provides, and the main conclusions it draws.

They are relevant because they give you a clear, high-level summary of the document's core message on blending libertarian and Christian views on drugs before you dive deeper.

1. What is the main purpose of this chapter on the War on Drugs, and what problem does it try to solve by explaining libertarian opposition to prohibition?
2. What information does the chapter provide about how drug prohibition affects things like overdoses and gang violence, and what conclusions does it draw about why legalization might help?
3. Based on examples like Portugal and Switzerland, what problems with current drug laws does the chapter point out, and what conclusions does it offer about better ways to handle addiction through personal responsibility and community support?

Deep Dive Questions

These questions explore the concepts, assumptions, implications and consequences, and viewpoints/perspectives in the chapter.

They are relevant because they push you to think critically about the hidden beliefs behind the arguments, like self-control and property rights, and what real-world effects those ideas could have on society and faith.

1. What key concepts (prohibition, personal responsibility, self-control) does the chapter explain, and what assumptions does it make about how laws should or shouldn't control people's bodies and choices?
2. If we follow the chapter's ideas about legalizing drugs and focusing on voluntary help, what implications and consequences (good and bad) might there be for communities, addiction rates, or crime?
3. How does the chapter present libertarian Christian viewpoints on drug abuse as a spiritual issue like idolatry, and what other perspectives (e.g., government-focused or prohibitionist views) does it challenge or leave out?
4. What one idea from this chapter most caught your attention or helped to clarify your thinking?

Chapter 13
Immigration

General Understanding Questions

These questions are designed to help you quickly identify the chapter's purpose (why it was written), the problem it aims to solve (common myths about immigration and borders from a Christian libertarian view), the key information it provides, and the main conclusions it draws. They are relevant because they give you a clear, high-level summary of the document's core message on blending faith, freedom, and migration before you dive deeper.

1. What is the main purpose of this chapter on immigration, and what problem does it try to solve by using Bible stories and libertarian ideas to talk about treating foreigners?
2. What information does the chapter provide about how immigration changes a country's economy, culture, and safety, and what conclusions does it draw about why open borders might help more than hurt?
3. Based on examples like borders as property or the welfare state, what problems with strict immigration rules does the chapter point out, and what conclusions does it offer about better ways to handle migration through markets and personal choice?

Deep Dive Questions

These questions explore the concepts, assumptions, implications and consequences, and viewpoints/perspectives in the chapter. They are relevant because they push you to think critically about the hidden beliefs behind the arguments, like non-aggression and justice, and what real-world effects those ideas could have on people and communities.

1. What key concepts (open borders, non-aggression, cultural change) does the chapter explain, and what assumptions does it make about how governments should or shouldn't control people's movement?
2. If we follow the chapter's ideas about lifting border restrictions and ending the drug war, what implications and consequences (good and bad) might there be for poor countries, jobs, or national security?
3. How does the chapter present libertarian Christian viewpoints on immigration as a way to show love and justice, and what other perspectives (e.g., strict border control or welfare-first views) does it challenge or leave out?

Chapter 14
Abortion

General Understanding Questions

These questions help you think about the big picture of the chapter. They focus on the purpose (why the chapter was written), the problem to be solved (what issue it's addressing), the information provided (facts and details given), and the conclusions (main ideas or decisions reached).

1. What is the main purpose of this chapter on abortion, and what big problem is it trying to solve for people who believe in libertarian ideas like not hurting others?
2. What key information does the chapter give about when human life starts, and how does it use science and history to explain if abortion breaks the rule against aggression?
3. What conclusions does the chapter reach about why abortion might be wrong under libertarian rules, and what solutions does it suggest for handling tough cases like rape?

Deep-Dive Questions

These questions help you dig deeper into the ideas. They focus on concepts (main ideas or terms), assumptions (things taken for granted), implications and consequences (what could happen as a result), and viewpoints and perspectives (different ways people see the issue).

1. What are the main concepts like self-ownership and the Non-Aggression Principle in this chapter, and what assumptions does the author make about how they apply to a baby before it's born?

2. If we follow the chapter's ideas about fetal rights, what implications and consequences might there be for moms, dads, and society, especially in cases where pregnancy happens by choice or not?
3. How does the chapter show different viewpoints, like pro-choice libertarians versus pro-life ones, and what perspectives does it give on ideas such as evictionism or personhood laws?

Chapter 15
Environmental Stewardship

General Understanding Questions

These questions are designed to help you quickly identify the chapter's **purpose** (why it was written), the **problem** it aims to solve (misunderstandings about environmental care and government roles), the **key information** it provides, and the **main conclusions** it draws. They are relevant because they give you a clear, high-level summary of the document's core message on combining Christian teachings with libertarian ideas for protecting the earth before you dive deeper.

1. What is the main purpose of this chapter on environmental stewardship, and what problem does it try to solve by using Bible verses and free market ideas to explain our role in caring for the earth?
2. What information does the chapter provide about how private property and free markets can help the environment, and what conclusions does it draw about why they work better than government rules?
3. Based on examples like pollution and climate change, what problems with government actions does the chapter point out, and what conclusions does it offer about better ways to handle these issues through personal responsibility and property rights?

Deep Dive Questions

These questions explore the **concepts**, **assumptions**, **implications and consequences**, and **viewpoints/perspectives** in the chapter. They are relevant because they push you to think critically about the hidden beliefs behind the arguments, like human dominion and profit motives, and what real-world effects those ideas could have on nature and society.

1. What key concepts (stewardship, dominion mandate, property rights) does the chapter explain, and what assumptions does it make about how people should use the earth's resources without government control?
2. If we follow the chapter's ideas about free markets and less regulation, what implications and consequences (good and bad) might there be for pollution, energy use, or future generations?
3. How does the chapter present libertarian Christian viewpoints on climate change as something markets can fix, and what other perspectives (e.g., global government solutions or environmental alarmism) does it challenge or leave out?

Chapter 16

The American Revolution and the U.S. Constitution

General Understanding Questions

These questions help you think about the big picture of the chapter. They focus on the purpose (why the chapter was written), the problem to be solved (what issue it's addressing), the information provided (facts and details given), and the conclusions (main ideas or decisions reached).

1. What is the main purpose of this chapter on the American Revolution and the U.S. Constitution, and what big problems does it try to solve for people who mix libertarian ideas with Christian beliefs?
2. What key information does the chapter provide about the reasons for the Revolution, like complaints against the British king, and how the war was run, including things like taking private property?
3. What conclusions does the chapter reach about whether the Revolution and Constitution were truly libertarian, and what advice does it give on how to view the founders' good and bad choices?

Deep-Dive Questions

These questions help you dig deeper into the ideas. They focus on concepts (main ideas or terms), assumptions (things taken for granted), implications and consequences (what could happen as a result), and viewpoints and perspectives (different ways people see the issue).

1. What are the main concepts like the Non-Aggression Principle and just war theory in this chapter, and what assumptions does the author make about how they apply to the Revolution and the Bible?
2. If we accept the chapter's ideas about the Revolution's flaws, what implications and consequences might there be for how we think about modern governments, wars, and rights today?
3. How does the chapter show different viewpoints, such as from Christian leaders during the Revolution or abolitionists like Frederick Douglass, and what perspectives does it give on slavery and consent in the founding?

Chapter 17
Healthcare

General Understanding Questions

These questions are designed to help you quickly identify the chapter's **purpose** (why it was written), the **problem** it aims to solve (government interference in healthcare), the **key information** it provides, and the **main conclusions** it draws. They are relevant because they give you a clear, high-level summary of the document's core message on blending Christian values with libertarian ideas for better health access before you dive deeper.

1. What is the main purpose of this chapter on healthcare, and what problem does it try to solve by using Bible ideas and free market thinking to explain why government rules hurt more than help?
2. What information does the chapter provide about how government rules raise healthcare costs and limit choices, and what conclusions does it draw about how free markets could make things cheaper and better?
3. Based on examples like the Affordable Care Act, addiction treatment, or new tech like gene editing, what problems with government control does the chapter point out, and what conclusions does it offer about better ways to handle these through personal choice and charity?

Deep Dive Questions

These questions explore the **concepts**, **assumptions**, **implications and consequences**, and **viewpoints/perspectives** in the chapter. They are relevant because they push you to think critically about the hidden beliefs behind the arguments, like self-ownership and non-coercion, and what real-world effects those ideas could have on health, society, and faith.

1. What key concepts (free market healthcare, personal responsibility, informed consent) does the chapter explain, and what assumptions does it make about why people should control their own health without government force?
2. If we follow the chapter's ideas about less regulation and more market freedom, what implications and consequences (good and bad) might there be for poor people's access to care, medical innovation, or public health issues like diseases?
3. How does the chapter present libertarian Christian viewpoints on things like parental rights in medicine or ending the War on Drugs, and what other perspectives (e.g., government mandates or universal healthcare) does it challenge or leave out?

Chapter 18

Public Health and Pandemics

General Understanding Questions

These questions are designed to help you quickly identify the chapter's **purpose** (why it was written), the **problem** it aims to solve (government overreach in public health crises), the **key information** it provides, and the **main conclusions** it draws. They are relevant because they give you a clear, high-level summary of the document's core message on combining Christian values with libertarian ideas for handling pandemics before you dive deeper.

1. What is the main purpose of this chapter on public health and pandemics, and what problem does it try to solve by using quotes from C.S. Lewis and Bible ideas to explain why centralized government rules can hurt more than help?
2. What information does the chapter provide about how decentralized approaches like local groups and markets can handle health risks, and what conclusions does it draw about why they work better than big government mandates?
3. Based on examples like COVID-19 lockdowns and the Harm Principle, what problems with government actions does the chapter point out, and what conclusions does it offer about better ways to handle crises through personal choice and non-aggression?

Deep Dive Questions

These questions explore the **concepts**, **assumptions**, **implications and consequences**, and **viewpoints/perspectives** in the chapter. They are relevant because they push you to think critically about the hidden beliefs behind the arguments, like freedom over force and individual rights, and what real-world effects those ideas could have on health, society, and faith.

1. What key concepts (Non-Aggression Principle, personal responsibility, informed consent) does the chapter explain, and what assumptions does it make about why people should control their own health without government force?
2. If we follow the chapter's ideas about no lockdowns and more voluntary help, what implications and consequences (good and bad) might there be for vulnerable people, the economy, or trust in experts during a crisis?
3. How does the chapter present libertarian Christian viewpoints on public health as a matter of moral freedom and humility, and what other perspectives (e.g., strong government mandates or harm-based rules) does it challenge or leave out?

Chapter 19
The Culture Wars

General Understanding Questions

These questions help you think about the big picture of the chapter. They focus on the purpose (why the chapter was written), the problem to be solved (what issue it's addressing), the information provided (facts and details given), and the conclusions (main ideas or decisions reached).

1. What is the main purpose of this chapter on engaging the culture wars, and what big problem does it try to solve for Christians who want to mix faith with libertarian ideas like no force from the government?
2. What key information does the chapter give about culture wars, like fights over marriage, sexuality, and identity, and how it uses Bible verses and ideas like persuasion to explain them?
3. What conclusions does the chapter reach about using talk instead of laws to handle moral issues, and what advice does it give for dealing with things like gender education or transgender rules in a free society?

Deep-Dive Questions

These questions help you dig deeper into the ideas. They focus on concepts (main ideas or terms), assumptions (things taken for granted), implications and consequences (what could happen as a result), and viewpoints and perspectives (different ways people see the issue).

1. What are the main concepts like the Non-Aggression Principle and self-ownership in this chapter, and what assumptions does the author make about how Christians should use them in culture wars instead of government power?
2. If we accept the chapter's ideas about fixing culture through free speech and choice, what implications and consequences might there be for churches, families, and society, especially when dealing with sin or different beliefs?
3. How does the chapter show different viewpoints, such as from progressives, conservatives, and libertarian Christians on issues like sexuality or compassion, and what perspectives does it give on things like neutrality in public life or using the Bible for laws?

Chapter 20
Family & Education

General Understanding Questions

These questions help you think about the big picture of the chapter. They focus on the purpose (why the chapter was written), the problem to be solved (what issue it's addressing), the information provided (facts and details given), and the conclusions (main ideas or decisions reached).

1. What is the main purpose of this chapter on family and education, and what big problem does it try to solve for Christians who want to blend faith with libertarian ideas like limiting government power?
2. What key information does the chapter give about the family's role in society, like how it drives new ideas and markets, and how it uses Bible quotes and thinkers like Abraham Kuyper to explain family rights over state control?
3. What conclusions does the chapter reach about keeping the government out of family choices like medical care or schooling, and what advice does it give for handling issues like internet safety or divorce in a free society?

Deep-Dive Questions

These questions help you dig deeper into the ideas. They focus on concepts (main ideas or terms), assumptions (things taken for granted), implications and consequences (what could happen as a result), and viewpoints and perspectives (different ways people see the issue).

1. What are the main concepts like self-ownership and the Non-Aggression Principle in this chapter, and what assumptions does the author make about how they apply to parents, kids, and education instead of letting the government decide?
2. If we follow the chapter's ideas about families and schools without state rules, what implications and consequences might there be for kids' safety, learning quality, and society, especially in tough spots like health choices or cultural changes?
3. How does the chapter show different viewpoints, such as from libertarian Christians versus regular conservatives or progressives on things like marriage and no-fault divorce, and what perspectives does it give on using markets or communities for education and family support?

Chapter 21
Christian Nationalism

General Understanding Questions

These questions help you think about the big picture of the chapter. They focus on the purpose (why the chapter was written), the problem to be solved (what issue it's addressing), the information provided (facts and details given), and the conclusions (main ideas or decisions reached).

1. What is the main purpose of this chapter on Christian nationalism, and what big problem does it try to solve for Christians who want to blend faith with libertarian ideas like limiting government power?
2. What key information does the chapter give about what Christian nationalism is, like how its supporters use Bible verses to defend it, and how it talks about things like borders and morals?
3. What conclusions does the chapter reach about why Christian nationalism might not fit with Bible teachings or libertarian rules, and what advice does it give on how Christians should handle it instead?

Deep-Dive Questions

These questions help you dig deeper into the ideas. They focus on concepts (main ideas or terms), assumptions (things taken for granted), implications and consequences (what could happen as a result), and viewpoints and perspectives (different ways people see the issue).

1. What are the main concepts like natural law and the Non-Aggression Principle in this chapter, and what assumptions does the author make about how government should or shouldn't force Christian rules on people?
2. If we accept the chapter's ideas against using the government to push Christian values, what implications and consequences might there be for churches, personal faith, and society, especially if people mix politics with religion?
3. How does the chapter show different viewpoints, such as from Christian nationalists who want a strong Christian government versus libertarian Christians who prefer freedom and persuasion, and what perspectives does it give on how this affects groups like Catholics or Pentecostals?

Chapter 22

How do we get to a Free(r) Society?

General Understanding Questions

These questions help you think about the big picture of the chapter. They focus on the purpose (why the chapter was written), the problem to be solved (what issue it's addressing), the information provided (facts and details given), and the conclusions (main ideas or decisions reached).

1. What is the main purpose of this chapter on getting to a freer society, and what big problem does it try to solve for Christians who want to mix faith with libertarian ideas like less government control?
2. What key information does the chapter give about ways to promote liberty, like living your faith, being productive, and fighting anti-liberal ideas from the left and right, and how it uses Bible verses and thinkers like Étienne de La Boétie to explain them?
3. What conclusions does the chapter reach about using local actions, decentralization, and personal work to build freedom, and what advice does it give for handling risks like bad partnerships or staying true to your beliefs in a tough world?

Deep-Dive Questions

These questions help you dig deeper into the ideas. They focus on concepts (main ideas or terms), assumptions (things taken for granted), implications and consequences (what could happen as a result), and viewpoints and perspectives (different ways people see the issue).

1. What are the main concepts like non-aggression, decentralization, and vocation in this chapter, and what assumptions does the author make about how faith in God helps people live out liberty without using force?
2. If we accept the chapter's ideas about persuasion, secession, and building communities instead of big government changes, what implications and consequences might there be for daily life, churches, and society, especially if things go wrong like more division?
3. How does the chapter show different viewpoints, such as local actions versus national ones or partnering with other groups, and what perspectives does it give on balancing Christian duties with resisting bad rulers or working in a free market?

Subject Index

D

Proper Names Index

Scripture Index

Old Testament

JOSHUA

JUDGES

1 SAMUEL

2 SAMUEL

2 KINGS

1 CHRONICLES

EZRA

JOB

PSALMS

PROVERBS

ECCLESIASTES

ISAIAH

New Testament

MARK

LUKE

JOHN

ACTS

ROMANS

1 CORINTHIANS

2 CORINTHIANS

1 JOHN

REVELATION

Acknowledgements

Projects of this scope are not done without a strong network of support, and the Libertarian Christian Institute could not accomplish all that it does every day without the encouragement and support of our team members, readers, listeners, and donors. You are why we do what we do!

The first edition of this book could not have happened without the powerhouse editing team at Bellwether Communications, Elise Daniel, Jacqueline Isaacs, and Morgan Feddes Satre. Their careful work made ours much improved, and set the standard high for us as we embarked on expanding this edition. An extra shout out to Jacqueline Isaacs for connecting us with some of her colleagues to get a wider exposure.

To Gregory Baus, who sent us some helpful suggestions to the text (and caught a few errors!). To Gary Horn, who produced the original study guide, which was the foundation for what Alex Bernardo and Kerry Baldwin worked with to develop the Discussion Guide for this volume. To Erik Lindborg, who faithfully helped keep the original book project in check and on time! Your stabilizing force in our helped make this project a genuine success. To Chris Williams, who gave us important feedback during the writing process, and whose company, Podsworth Media, has helped the Christians for Liberty Network sound amazing!

To Mary Ruwart, whose book *Short Answers to the Tough Questions* inspired this work. Thank you for being a stalwart defender of individual liberty and encouraging us along the way with this project. To Larry Reed, whose personality and warmth leave as much an impression on those who know him as his rigorous and tireless defense of freedom does on everyone else. We are honored by your enthusiastic support for the work of LCI and for writing the Foreword to the 2020 edition of this book. To Doug

Bandow, our great friend and a beacon of light in the darkness that is Washington, D.C. Though we may be more than a little jealous whenever you share your latest travels with us, we also cannot help but be inspired by your curiosity for the world and your dedication to speaking the truth wherever it may lead. We are truly grateful for your Foreword to this 2026 edition.

To all our board members—both current and former—for walking with us along the journey and for being among our greatest advocates. To the late David Theroux, an early supporter of Norman's endeavors from the beginning with LibertarianChristians.com and into the LCI era as an advisory board member. We honor your memory and legacy for liberty.

The authors each wish to acknowledge important people in their lives.

From Norman

There are too many people to thank in these few words, but I'll give it a fair shot. I'm grateful to my wife, my parents, and my in-laws for always being encouraging of these efforts, in their own unique ways. My dad (Gary) deserves a special shout-out for reading an early draft of the book and offering so many helpful comments. I am immensely thankful for the supporters of LibertarianChristians.com and now LCI over the years. Without you guys, there's no reason to write a book. And finally, I am blessed by the team we put together to make this book happen. We turned an idea into reality, my friends, and I am thrilled to see where it takes us next.

From Doug

My gratitude begins with my co-authors and fellow LCI team. We would not be good libertarian colleagues if we never disagreed. The camaraderie and conflict alike have helped make this book better and have deepened my appreciation for each of you. A special thanks to Norman Horn, without whom this journey toward freedom would have been far less fun and rewarding.

I am also grateful for the many theological and libertarian influences that have shaped my thinking over the years. To those who taught me the way of nonviolence and how to read Scripture with a cruciform hermeneutic: Greg Boyd, N.T. Wright, Scot McKnight, Tim Keller, Brian Zahnd, Matthew Bates, and many others. To the libertarian thinkers who taught me to see beyond the false dichotomies of politics: Ron Paul, Jason Brennan, Bryan Caplan, Deirdre McCloskey, Bob Murphy, Tom Woods, Larry Reed, Andrew Napolitano, Steve Horwitz, Stephan Kinsella, Mike Maharrey, Kevin Vallier, Art Carden, Russ Roberts, and many more.

I am also thankful for my parents, who gave me room to question things (much to their frustration!). For my entire life, they have modeled intentional love and forgiveness.

Most importantly, my deepest thanks and love go to my wife, who has championed my pursuits, at times more than I have myself. My world is forever better with her, not only because she is my best friend and faithful partner, but also because she is a witty and intelligent thinker who sharpens my sometimes-sloppy reasoning in exactly the ways I need.

From Kerry

I'll begin by thanking The Libertarian Christian Institute for giving me the opportunity to write for them. To my parents, Dave and Nina Baldwin, I'm thankful for all of the support they've given me, especially in the last few years. To my kids, Aiden, Saoirse, and Deaglan, who've had the unfortunate task of distinguishing the difference between their playing on the computer for hours and my working on the computer for hours. I'm proud of them as they've persevered through difficult times. To Gregory, for being a dear and faithful friend, who helped me understand the works of Mises, Rothbard, and others particularly through a Reformed theological perspective. Finally, I give thanks to God for blessing me so much and giving me the freedom to do what I love with wonderful people. I can attest to the fact that God does "supply every need according to his riches in glory in Christ Jesus" (Phil 4:19). I pray the message of freedom will ring loudly once again and across the world and in the church, and I'm humbled by the opportunity to be one of many voices calling for it.

From Dick

My parents, Dick and Carolyn Clark, first told me about my sin, God's love, and the gift of salvation that Jesus Christ bought at Calvary. They taught me that this world is not our home, and that believers should never be afraid to stand on the solid foundation of God's word. I am forever indebted to Bob Murphy, who convinced me in 2001 that God's law is incompatible with statism. I am also grateful to many other tireless champions of liberty I first met in the Mises Institute orbit: Lew Rockwell, Jeff Tucker, John Sophocleus, Mark Thornton, Tom Woods, Walter Block, Robert Higgs, Guido Hulsmann, Joe Salerno, Roderick Long, Stephan Kinsella, Anthony Gregory, Manuel Lora, Robert Wicks, Daniel Coleman, Brian Martinez, and Gil Guillory. Finally, I must thank my beloved wife, Justina, who has been my indispensable framework, offering both encouragement and candid criticism when they were needed most.

From Jacob

To my wife Bria—your steadiness, faith, and grace toward my restless mind carried more of this than you know. I love you. To my pastor, Tim Dance, whose shepherding has quietly shaped how I read Scripture and think about the church's place in the world—more of this book reflects your influence than either of us might expect. To Dave Smith, who made taking liberty seriously feel like an obligation, and to Scott Horton, whose relentless commitment to peace is a model for what serious conviction looks like in practice.

To Stephen Rose and the AnarchoChristian community, who were among the first to show that libertarianism and Christian faithfulness could reinforce one another when handled with care for the text. To the team at the Libertarian Christian Institute—Norman, Cody, Doug, Greg, Kerry, Alex, and the rest. We have built a unique space where the exploration of faith and liberty are explored and cherished. And to every listener, reader, and interlocutor who pushed back, sharpened my arguments, or just kept showing up—this is yours too.

From Cody

I'm particularly thankful for the support of my talented colleagues at the Libertarian Christian Institute who have not only tolerated me, but have provided me a seat at their table. However, I truly couldn't do this work that I love without the longsuffering patience and encouragement of my dear heart, Raven. I also must thank the people who have spurred me forward to learn, write, and teach. Included in that list are teachers like Phillip Brown and Mark Bird, my family who doesn't always understand my work but are supportive anyway, leaders at my local church like Darryl Sumrall and Kevin Peyton who have trusted me to teach despite my offbeat sensibilities, and encouragers within the Brethren in Christ denomination like Bishop Lynn Thrush and Jonah Langenderfer. Finally, thank you to folks like Preston Sprinkle, Bob Murphy, Nick Gillespie, Derek Kreider, Chris Date, Nicholas Quient, and Craig Harguess who have shared their platform with me and given me an opportunity to get my unconventional ideas out into the wild.

About the Authors

Dr. Norman Horn is the founder and President of the Libertarian Christian Institute. He holds a Ph.D. in Chemical Engineering from the University of Texas at Austin and a Master of Arts in Theological Studies from the Austin Graduate School of Theology. He is the Director of Research in a healthcare technology company and resides in Missouri with his wife and three children. He has been a passionate defender of individual rights and libertarianism from a Christian perspective for over 20 years.

Doug Stuart is Content Director of the Libertarian Christian Institute and co-host of The Libertarian Christian Podcast. He holds an MDiv from Missio Seminary, and his writing and speaking focus on challenging the status quo. Doug operates a website design and video production company in Lancaster, Pennsylvania, where he currently lives with his wife, their three children.

Kerry Baldwin is an independent researcher and writer with a B.A. in Philosophy from Arizona State University. Her website is MereLiberty.com and she focuses on libertarian philosophy and reformed theology. She challenges readers to rethink prevailing paradigms in politics, theology, and culture. She is a confessionally Reformed Christian orthodox Presbyterian in the tradition of J. Gresham Machen (1881–1937), an outspoken libertarian and defender of Christian orthodoxy. Kerry holds libertarian anarchism to be properly grounded in Reformed Christian convictions, and finds an alternative to patriarchialism, feminism, egalitarianism, and complementarianism in a Reformed perspective. Kerry is a single, homeschooling mother of three. She enjoys outdoor activities in the Jemez mountains near her home, and stereotypically introverted hobbies such as puzzles and brain teasers.

Dick Clark is an attorney based in Lincoln, Nebraska. He is the author of five books and numerous articles and speeches. He currently works as a Committee Legal Counsel in the Nebraska Legislature and as an attorney in private practice focusing on firearms law. He has previously served as a policy advisor to Governor Dave Heineman of Nebraska and as research director at both the Platte Institute for Economic Research and Creighton University's Institute for Economic Inquiry. He holds a bachelor's degree from Auburn University and earned the degree of juris doctor from Suffolk University Law School. He is married to Justina—his second greatest blessing after salvation—and they are parents to three children. Dick serves as a Sunday School teacher and deacon at Southview Baptist Church in Lincoln.

Cody Cook is a writer and co-host of the Libertarian Christian Podcast. He holds a BA in biblical & theological studies and an MA in biblical studies from God's Bible School & College in Cincinnati, Ohio. He lives in South Lebanon, Ohio with his wife and three children where he teaches at his local church and has written articles for various publications, including Reason, Plough, FEE, and The Mises Institute. He is the author of a number of books, including *The Anarchist Anabaptist* (also available through the Libertarian Christian Institute), and is always available to discuss classic films or funk music over Korean food.

Jacob Winograd is a podcast host, writer, and content creator for the Libertarian Christian Institute, where he hosts the Biblical

Anarchy Podcast and LCI Greenroom. His professional background spans automotive repair as a transmission specialist, life insurance agent, and digital media and marketing. His writing and speaking focus on Reformed covenant theology, libertarian political philosophy, and the intersection of Christian ethics and anarchist theory. Jacob is an evangelical Christian with Reformed convictions in soteriology and covenant theology, and holds libertarian anarchism to be the natural outworking of a consistent biblical worldview. He has served in various roles in the Libertarian Party and is a co-founder of its Christian Caucus. In his free time he enjoys cooking, playing guitar, chess, and hiking with his family. Jacob lives in York, Pennsylvania with his wife Bria and their five children.

About the Libertarian Christian Institute

The Libertarian Christian Institute is a 501(c)(3) tax-exempt educational and religious nonprofit organization that promotes libertarianism from a Christian point of view. We are convinced that libertarianism is the most consistent expression of Christian political thought. LCI is ecumenical in nature, welcoming all those who confess the traditional creeds of the universal church.

LCI originally began as a small website, LibertarianChristians.com, started by Norman Horn in 2008 while he was a graduate student at the University of Texas at Austin. It quickly garnered a loyal following of Christian libertarians and other curious non-Christians, as its emphasis on sound theology and the concordance of libertarian theory with Christian ethics was not often heard in the libertarian sphere. LCI was incorporated as a nonprofit in 2015 to continue the mission of promoting individual liberty to Christians in a new way.

LCI's goals are to persuade our fellow Christians through online programs, publications, in-person conferences, and regional small group meetups, and to love our fellow libertarians as Jesus would have us do. Our online presence is unmatched in the libertarian community, with thousands of articles, book reviews, videos, podcasts, news reports, and much more. Our organization is regularly sought after for a Christian libertarian perspective on a variety of political and cultural topics.

As the Libertarian Christian Institute grows, we are actively seeking out donors who desire to see an organization such as this make a positive difference in the church and in the world today for liberty and for Christ. If you would like to participate in our mission to equip the church to make the Christian case for a free society, join us by visiting libertarianchristians.com/donate.

Our Mission: Equipping Christians to Spread the Message of Individual Liberty

The Libertarian Christian Institute exists to make the Christian case for a free society and provide the best content to proclaim that libertarianism is the most consistent expression of Christian political thought. We aim to persuade Christians that the political expression of our faith inclines us toward the principles of individual liberty and free markets.

Our Vision: That Christians Embrace the Principles of a Free Society

The Libertarian Christian Institute envisions a world where Christians around the world promote the values and principles of a free society as the most consistent expression of Christian political thought. We see a world where, instead of polarizing to the left or right, Christians demonstrate that individual liberty is a force for the common good. We aim to persuade Christians that the political expression of our faith inclines us toward the principles of individual liberty and free markets.

The Libertarian Christian Institute has five core values that we believe every Christian libertarian should feel confident affirming, even if those individuals express these values with their own nuance. Our aim is not to comprehensively spell out everything Christian libertarians must believe, but provide a central set of tenets that we can all start from, regardless of differences in denomination or theological inclinations.

LCI Core Values

We believe that every Christian libertarian should feel comfortable affirming our Core Values, even if they have their own nuance or "spin" on them. Our aim is not to comprehensively spell out what every Christian libertarian must believe, but provide a central set of tenets that we can all start from, regardless of differences in denomination or theological inclinations.

1. Christian Political Philosophy Should be Informed by a Holistic View of Scripture, Reason, and Historical Theology

A comprehensive view of the biblical narrative indicates that the Church's proclamation of Jesus' lordship is not a mere personal statement of allegiance; it is also an anti-imperial declaration that the way of peace comes through Christ's counter-cultural kingdom of love and service. Followers of Christ are called to be a prophetic voice against the powers of domination and violence. The State—the monopolized institution of force in society—is never to be confused with the Kingdom of God, and when the power of the state grows, the rightful influence of churches, families, and local communities is diminished.

2. A Free And Civil Society Depends Upon Respect For The Non-Aggression Principle

The ethics modeled by Christ and the early Church call us to change the world and build the Kingdom of God through service rather than force; through persuasion rather than coercion. The use of political force to compel ethical behavior does not change hearts and does not produce lasting social change. Christians must call for repentance from sin in humility and never with violence. As such, a consistently Christian ethic always embodies non-aggression.

3. Individual Liberty and the Common Good are not at Odds

As God is intrinsically relational within the Trinity, so also human beings are created to live in community. Sin has marred the communal relationships for which we were created by pitting individuals against God, against one another, and against the earth for which we are called to be wise stewards. Affirming the dignity, worth, and rights of the individual as an image-bearer of God is a first step toward restoring authentic, Christ-centered community among diverse individuals. Because society is composed of individuals, a healthy society requires healthy individuals. Through voluntary cooperation and respect for freedom, people can join together to trade, innovate, create, collaborate, share, and build a world that simultaneously respects the individual and betters our neighbor.

4. Social Institutions Matter for Human Flourishing

Humans are created to be social beings, and God's design is that we work together to develop institutions which promote human flourishing. Insofar as these institutions are voluntary, peaceful, and non-coercive, human beings possess the God-given capacity to solve the worst of problems in the best of ways. Social institutions founded upon mutual cooperation—such as marriage, family, church, organizations, and businesses—are vital for authentic humanity.

5. Christian Theology Affirms the Essential Tenets of Free Market Economics

Respect for private property, voluntary exchange, condemnation of theft, and the value of cooperation and service towards achieving common goals flow naturally from Christian thought and habit. This is what defines "capitalism" in the libertarian view. Wealth is a tool given by God, and all who possess such wealth are expected to utilize it for God's Kingdom and the good of our neighbor. Taxation and regulation tend to destroy wealth, discourage innovation, and centralize power, and therefore hamper our ability to fulfill the calling of God. Where free markets are allowed to flourish, human beings will prosper both materially and spiritually. Additionally, Christian ethics helps equip our economies for service toward God and neighbor.

Even if you don't call yourself a libertarian, if you share our affinity for these core values, we count you among our ranks. We hope that you will want to partner with us to help spread the message of liberty by making the Christian case for a free society. Help us keep the message alive and growing at libertarianchristians.com

Made in the USA
Coppell, TX
10 June 2026

79906205R00203